"[An] accessible and lively . . . primer on how wealth works in America." —*Bloomberg Businessweek*

"In *The Whiteness of Wealth,* [Dorothy A.] Brown brings the American tax code to life. Hands shape it and wield it like a shield in the defense of the most powerful among us. The tax code tells a story about American priorities. The news isn't good, Brown writes, but there's still time to change the future." —*New York*

"Brown . . . writes brilliantly and lucidly on systemic racism and injustice within the American tax system. [*The Whiteness of Wealth*] is an eye-opening, well-sourced and -argued account of tax law and economic policy at the intersection of racism and social history." —*Booklist* (starred review)

"An eye-opening look at race-based economic biases, with reasonable steps to undo them." —*Kirkus Reviews*

"An illuminating exploration of how U.S. tax policies exacerbate the Black-white wealth gap." —*Publishers Weekly*

"In this urgent account, Dorothy Brown incisively unpacks how racism is embedded in our nation's tax system, enhancing white wealth at the expense of Black Americans. *The Whiteness of Wealth* is important reading for those who want to understand how inequality is built into the bedrock of American society, and what a more equitable future might look like."
—Ibram X. Kendi, #1 *New York Times* bestselling author of *How to Be an Antiracist* and *Stamped from the Beginning*

"This book is a tour de force. With clarity and conviction, Dorothy Brown reveals how U.S. tax policy sustains and deepens the wealth gap between Black and white Americans. As I read *The Whiteness of Wealth,* I found myself shaking my head as I eagerly turned the pages and shouting 'damn' with each revelation. If we are finally to address the long history of racism in this country, we must grapple with the arguments of Brown's powerful book. This is a MUST read for these troubling times."

—Eddie S. Glaude Jr., *New York Times* bestselling author
of *Begin Again* and *Democracy in Black*

"For generations, centrist and conservative social architects have funneled their version of America's social contract through the U.S. tax code. It is a rare act of bipartisanship, which is precisely why it is ripe for perpetuating racial inequality. Dorothy Brown is one of the few scholars and public thinkers capable of exposing, in great detail, how the tax code is racist. That is precisely what she does with analytical precision in *The Whiteness of Wealth*. This enlightening book is a vital companion to *The New Jim Crow*, *The Color of Wealth*, and *Evicted*, for how it reimagines everything you thought you knew about U.S. social policy."

—Tressie McMillan Cottom, MacArthur Fellow
and author of *Thick: And Other Essays*

"Who knew reading about race and taxes could be so engaging? I couldn't put it down! From beginning to end, Dorothy Brown skillfully weaves her analysis of the racial bias in tax law with compelling personal stories of both Black and white taxpayers as well as policy recommendations for how to bring equity to our tax system. Highly recommended!"

—Beverly Daniel Tatum, PhD, *New York Times* bestselling author
of *Why Are All the Black Kids Sitting Together in the Cafeteria?*

"At once passionate and analytical, *The Whiteness of Wealth* is a bracing contribution to the history of policy racism that takes us to the heart of taxation's effects on patterns of economic distribution. The book's rich tour of provisions and loopholes in key enactments together with patterns of implementation and enforcement grounds the reparations debate by specifying intended and unintended harms and by proposing specific possibilities for redress."

—Ira Katznelson, author of
When Affirmative Action Was White

THE
WHITENESS
OF
WEALTH

How the Tax System Impoverishes Black
Americans—and How We Can Fix It

DOROTHY A. BROWN

CROWN
NEW YORK

2022 Crown Trade Paperback Edition

Copyright © 2021 by Dorothy A. Brown

All rights reserved.

Published in the United States by Crown, an imprint of Random House,
a division of Penguin Random House LLC, New York.

CROWN and the Crown colophon are registered trademarks of
Penguin Random House LLC.

Originally published in hardcover in the United States by Crown, an imprint of
Random House, a division of Penguin Random House LLC, New York, in 2021.

Library of Congress Cataloging-in-Publication Data
Names: Brown, Dorothy A., author.
Title: The whiteness of wealth / Dorothy A. Brown.
Description: New York : Crown, [2021] | Includes bibliographical
references and index.
Identifiers: LCCN 2020047390 (print) | LCCN 2020047391 (ebook) |
ISBN 9780525577331 (paperback) | ISBN 9780525577348 (ebook)
Subjects: LCSH: Taxation—Law and legislation—United States. |
Taxation—Moral and ethical aspects—United States. | African Americans—
Taxation. | African Americans—Economic conditions. | Racism—Economic
aspects—United States. | Tax incidence—United States. |
Fiscal policy—United States.
Classification: LCC KF6289 .B753 2021 (print) | LCC KF6289 (ebook) |
DDC 343.7304089—dc23
LC record available at https://lccn.loc.gov/2020047390
LC ebook record available at https://lccn.loc.gov/2020047391

Printed in the United States of America on acid-free paper

crownpublishing.com

1st Printing

Book design by Debbie Glasserman

FOR MISS DOTTIE . . . BECAUSE I OWE HER EVERYTHING

CONTENTS

THE
WHITENESS
OF
WEALTH

INTRODUCTION

I became a tax lawyer to get away from race.

I was born and raised in the South Bronx in New York City. My father, James, was a plumber who worked, without benefits, for a private company, because black men couldn't join the union that controlled the good public-sector jobs. My mother, Dottie, was a nurse and a seamstress who had left her job as a garment factory "floor girl" because she knew she could do better work than the white seamstresses who got all the opportunities. We lived in a three-family house at 1061 Morris Avenue, purchased with the help of a $6,000 loan from my father's white boss, and rented the upper and middle apartments to black tenants who became more like family. We didn't have a lot, but we had food on the table and clothes on our backs (handmade by my mother, of course), and my sister and I had a little bit of spending money. My parents had lived through the Jim Crow era and faced laws dictating what they could earn, what they could own, and where they could live, but they were determined that their children's generation would get educated and live on their own terms.

As a little girl, I believed that was a possibility.

Then, when I was around nine or ten years old, I left the house one day with my mother. I held her hand as we walked to the corner of 166th Street and waited for the light to change. A police car drove by, and as it passed I spotted a handcuffed black man in the backseat. Sitting beside him was a white officer, beating him. It was broad daylight.

I turned in horror to confirm that my mother was seeing this, too. In a low, emotionless voice, she said, "That happens sometimes."

My eyes returned to the car. The handcuffed man and I made eye contact. As the police car turned the corner, I held his gaze until I could no longer see him.

Normally my mother was no shrinking violet when it came to fighting racism. My sister and I would cringe whenever a white store manager chose to wait on a white customer before us; we knew what was about to happen, and it happened a lot.

"Excuse me!" my mother would say. "We were here first!" She would not use her inside voice, and she wouldn't budge from the head of the line. Standing her ground—that's Dottie Brown.

So when I saw that man in the back of the police car, my mother's reaction told me there was not a thing either one of us could do about it.

And that's how I became a tax lawyer. Because I learned early on that people might look at me and see black, but as far as tax law was concerned, the only color that mattered was green. I attended Fordham University and majored in accounting, then got my law degree from Georgetown and earned a master's in tax law from NYU. Tax law was about math, and I was sure I'd chosen a career where race had nothing to do with my work.

I have never been more wrong about anything in my life.

As I got older, things started looking up for my parents; when my sister and I were teenagers, my mother went back to work full-time as a licensed practical nurse, and my father, finally allowed in the union, got a job with the New York City Housing Authority. They were both earning a good living, with my father sometimes having a slight edge because of all the overtime he could make. On holidays, I'd ask him why he was so happy to head out to work on his day off. "Triple time!" he'd say, grinning as he walked out the door.

Imagine my surprise, years later, when I began preparing their tax returns and realized that "triple time" had actually cost my parents a bundle in taxes over the course of their life together.

After law school, I spent a couple of years working on Wall Street as an investment banker. My income was around $75,000—roughly equivalent to my parents' combined incomes—but when I compared our tax payments, I always came away thinking they were paying too much. It didn't make sense; what I had been taught about our progressive tax rate system was that the more money you make, the higher the tax rate that applies to your income. It is based on a concept called "ability to pay": If you have more, you should pay more. Each of my parents made half of what I did, so I should be paying much higher taxes than my parents. The numbers did not add up, and in my mind numbers never lied.

The puzzle gnawed at me throughout my career, until I became a tax law professor. As an investment banker working on municipal finance, I'd had many black colleagues, because we were working with cities that had black leadership and therefore hired black finance professionals. (Corporate investment banking is a much whiter—and much better-paying—field.) That changed when I joined a law firm and continued in the academy: I was the only black woman on the faculty at what was then called George Mason University School of Law (now Antonin Scalia Law School). It was a decade and two jobs later before I could count myself one of two. Race was a factor in my day-to-day life in a way that it had rarely been before.

George Mason was a tough environment for me as the lone black female law professor, made all the more difficult by the timing of my arrival in the summer of 1991. Another black female law professor at the University of Oklahoma College of Law, Anita Hill, was at the center of a national storm after accusing Clarence Thomas, a Supreme Court nominee, of sexual harassment. While I believed Anita, my only black colleague—a man—was working to support Thomas's confirmation as he testified before the Senate Judiciary Committee.[1]

As for my white colleagues, the kindest thing I could say was that they were clueless when it came to race. Less kind, but equally true, was that they treated me differently because I was black. One colleague—who would later use the N-word in class[2]—came to me out of the blue and asked me why all the black students sat together at lunch. I replied: *Why do all of the white students choose to sit with each other?* A different white male colleague took me to lunch at a private club in Washington, D.C. (you know, one of those private clubs with a prior history of discriminating against black Americans and women), and made a point of introducing me to our black female server—because, as he put it, he knew diversity was a concern of mine. Her name was Patty and she seemed as confused as I was about the encounter.

But it went beyond mere insensitivity. One year, I recall being the only faculty member who did not receive money to hire a research assistant. When I asked the associate dean in charge of funding how that happened, I was told that they had forgotten about me and that by the time they remembered, they had run out of money. As a result, I was expected to teach and produce scholarship just like my white male colleagues—but without the same resources and all while navigating a racially hostile environment.

Even worse, as a black woman, I had additional responsibilities—and unlike my father, I was not paid triple time. While my white colleagues could focus exclusively on their work, I met with black students who were also navigating the same hostile environment and with their white peers who were troubled by what they were observing. They leaned on me for guidance and I was more than sympathetic.

But where did I go for my own self-care?

I engaged with the kind of race-based scholarship my

white male colleagues could ignore because the academy supported and nurtured them. Although race scholarship wasn't critical to my tax law research, taking it in was a kind of comfort food for me, an act of self-preservation that acknowledged what I was experiencing was real.

One spring day, my comfort food was an article written by the late Jerome Culp, a mentor and particular inspiration to me. Jerome was fearless. A Duke law professor, and an extremely successful black man in a white academic world, he was not afraid to take on giants in his field or colleagues on his faculty, and he would *slay* them with his intellect and ferocity. He never failed to make me think about race in a different way.

As I read his article "Toward a Black Legal Scholarship: Race and Original Understandings," pieces of the puzzle started to fall in place for me. In it, Jerome argued that law professors, particularly black law professors, should engage in what he called "black legal scholarship" and examine which legal issues are specific to black America. He noted the ways in which the black perspective has been systemically eliminated from the legal record throughout American history, starting with the removal of a condemnation of slavery from the Declaration of Independence.[3] And near the end, he posed a question:

"To what extent have our tax laws been distorted now and historically by the question of slavery and continuing racism?"[4]

I'd known since that day on the corner of 166th Street and Morris Avenue how racism affected the administration of criminal justice. In school I learned how racism had affected where we lived, where we went to school, where we worked, and whom we could marry. But I had never before considered if racism affected how much we pay in taxes. I graduated from the premier tax program in the United States and never once did any of my professors suggest that race mattered when it came to tax law.

After I finished reading, I called Jerome. I told him that his article had inspired me to do something, and I made him a promise: I would figure out whether our tax laws had a disparate impact based on race. I had come full circle. I went into tax law to escape race and racism, but now I found myself searching through tax law to see how racism might have been there all along, waiting to be uncovered.

When I hung up and got to work, I realized how easy it was to make that promise but how hard it would be to keep it. The Internal Revenue Service (IRS) does not collect or publish tax statistics by race—a seemingly basic fact that somehow I had never noticed before. All sorts of other data exist: We know that less than 2 percent of all farmers nationwide are black Americans,[5] that 95 percent of visitors to our national parks are white Americans,[6] and that Native Americans (defined as American Indians/Native Alaskans in the study) had the highest motor vehicle fatality rate.[7] The federal government collects and publishes data on each of these topics. Yet we know nothing about taxpayers by race.

Determined to make good on my promise, I set out on a journey that would ultimately lead to my solving the mystery of my parents' tax returns. But because the data I needed about how much people of different races were paying in taxes wasn't available, I had to become a detective of sorts, looking for any scrap of information that might help me solve the puzzle. I looked at racial data that would make for good proxies, like household income data published by the U.S. Census Bureau. I dug into published research in other fields, like sociology, political science, and economics. I also learned how crucial history would be in understanding the story I was hoping to tell.

Once again, a single sentence would hold the key. I found it in *The Economic Status of Black Women: An Exploratory Investigation,* a 1990 staff report of the U.S. Commission on Civil Rights: On average married black women contribute 40 percent to household income compared with only 29 percent for white women.[8]

Simply put, all wives did not contribute to their households in the same way: Black women were likely to earn as much (or more) money as their husbands, while white women were likely to earn much less. This was certainly true in the case of my parents (whose income was more or less equal most years). But the joint tax return system, under which most married couples file their taxes together, offers the greatest benefits to households where one spouse contributes much less than the other to household income. That meant couples like my parents—my hardworking, home-owning, God-fearing parents, who wanted to earn a little bit more to enjoy their lives after raising two daughters—weren't getting those breaks. My parents' tax bill was so high because they were *married to each other*. Marriage—which many conservatives assure us is the road out of black poverty—is in fact making black couples *poorer*. And because the IRS does not publish statistics by race, we would never know.

It's long been understood that blacks and whites live in separate and unequal worlds that shape whom we marry, where we buy a home, whom we have as neighbors, and how we build a future for our children. Race affects where we go to college and how we pay for it. Race influences where we work and how much we are paid. What my research showed was that all of this *also* determines how much we pay in taxes. Taxpayers bring their racial identities to their tax returns. As in so many parts of American life, being black is more likely to hurt and being white is more likely to help.

The implications of this go far beyond the forms you file every April. In the long run, tax policy affects whether and how you'll be able to build wealth. If you're eligible for tax breaks, you either pay less in taxes throughout the year or receive a larger refund in the spring. If, like my parents, you're considered ineligible for a particular tax break, you never see that money. One missed tax break may not sound like much, but those dollars not given to Uncle Sam can be put into your bank account, invested in stocks or property, or used to build home equity through improvements or repairs every year. Think of that money as an annual pay raise—but if you do not get it, you cannot save it. Over time those dollars, or the lack of them, add up to increased or depleted wealth.

Needless to say, I didn't learn any of this in school.

What I did learn was the concept of "horizontal equity," which requires that taxpayers in similar circumstances should be taxed the same. As it's typically taught, horizontal equity looks at income as a marker of similar circumstances. For example, if two married couples, each with $100,000 of combined income, pay the same amount in taxes regardless of how much each spouse contributes, that satisfies the horizontal equity requirement.

When I looked at my parents' marriage, however, I began to realize that what I learned about horizontal equity was incorrect, or at least incomplete. Income and circumstances are not the same: A married couple with one working spouse, an investment banker, who makes $100,000 is not in the same circumstances as a nurse and a plumber who each earn $50,000. When viewed through a racial lens, we see that the latter situation is more likely for black taxpayers than white ones—and worse, the tax break goes to the single-earner couple, not the dual-earner couple. Our tax policy does all this in the name of horizontal equity, with no consideration that when you look beyond total income, the concept is just plain wrong!

That doesn't mean that the joint tax return was created as a way to punish hardworking black women and their husbands. Like most tax policies, it was the result of decisions made by many different actors, over many years. But when those actors—members of Congress, judges and clerks, lobbyists, and more—sit down to craft or modify tax law, they bring their conscious and unconscious biases to the table. And our most foundational tax laws were created at a time when racial bias wasn't just common—it was the norm and quite legal.

Our modern income tax system traces its roots to the Revenue Act of 1913, which instituted what's called a "progressive" income tax system: In theory, tax rates increase as income increases. The idea is that the wealthy—those with the greatest "ability to pay"—should carry more responsibility for funding government services than those who make less. The new federal income tax replaced a system of indirect taxes on imports and tariffs on tobacco and alcohol, which hit the poorest Americans the hardest because they paid the same tariff rates as the wealthy despite having less ability to pay.

The Revenue Act was passed by a Congress without a *single* black member and signed into law by President Woodrow Wilson, whose cabinet implemented (some historians say continued) racial segregation in the federal civil service. By the summer of 1913, Treasury Secretary William G. McAdoo, who oversaw the Bureau of Internal Revenue, the precursor to the Internal Revenue Service, had segregated toilets, lunchrooms, and working areas. In defending the Jim Crow practices, McAdoo said, "There has been an effort in the Department to remove the causes of complaint and irritation where white women have been forced unnecessarily to sit at desks with colored men."[9]

But while the department tasked with carrying out the new Revenue Act worked to diminish its black employees, it wasn't thinking of black Americans as taxpayers—a policy rooted in prejudice that nonetheless worked to black Americans' advantage. The system had been designed by whites (in Congress) to tax certain (working-class) white taxpayers less, and other (wealthy) white taxpayers more. Under the new law, only those who earned more than $3,000 as individuals, or $4,000 for a husband living with a stay-at-home spouse, were required to pay federal income tax. Between 1918 and 1932, this amounted to an average of 5.6 percent of Americans paying federal income tax each year.[10] In the late 1930s, the highest tax rate (for those with incomes greater than $5 million) applied to a single individual: John D. Rockefeller.

A generation or two removed from slavery, few black Americans had this kind of money, and the Great Depression only made their situation worse. In the 1930s, roughly 80 percent of black Americans were living in the South, and their unemployment rates were much higher than those of white Americans. Nearly 70 percent of Atlanta's black residents were unemployed in 1934—at least double the number of white Atlantans without a job.[11] One reason for this disparity is that during the Great Depression, when so many Americans were desperate for work, it was a regular practice for companies to replace black workers with white ones.[12] In 1936, more than half of all southern urban black families reported annual incomes of $750 or less, compared with 12 percent of white families. The median annual income for black families in Atlanta was only *one-third* that of white families in southern cities. While more than a quarter of white Americans earned more than $2,500, less than 2 percent of black Americans fell into that category.[13] Mired in poverty and unemployment, black Americans in general were beneficiaries of a policy that taxed only the wealthiest Americans. But that would soon change.

When the United States entered World War II in 1941, after the bombing of Pearl Harbor, Congress passed another Revenue Act to fund the war effort, almost doubling the number of Americans required to pay taxes.[14] Two new laws in 1943 further expanded the reach of the federal income tax system: First, Congress passed the Current Tax Payment Act, a bill requiring withholding, where taxes were taken out of employees' paychecks at the source. (There had been no need for such a widely applicable system until the vast majority of workers became liable for taxes.) Then, the Revenue Act of 1943 dropped exemptions to just $600 of income for single taxpayers and $1,200 for married taxpayers. In 1945, the median income for white families was just under $2,800, and for black families it was roughly $1,500.[15] Many black Americans, just like their white counterparts, became taxpayers for the first time as the taxpayer rolls exploded from seven million to more than forty-two million between 1940 and 1945.

After the war, the new taxation system stayed in place, creating an expanded income tax base. Federal revenue from individual income taxes increased exponentially: from $400 million in 1934 to almost $30 billion in 1954.[16] The flood of new revenue allowed the federal government to provide additional services. Returning service members could use GI benefits to attend college for free, and their families could become homeowners thanks to loans insured by the Federal Housing Administration (FHA). Between 1944 and 1971, federal spending for the GI Bill totaled more than $95 billion. But even as black Americans paid into the system, they were unable to reap its benefits.

"No other New Deal initiative had as great an impact on changing the country"[17] as the GI Bill, writes Ira Katznelson, Ruggles Professor of Political Science and History at Columbia University, in *When Affirmative Action Was White*. Katznelson's work explains how the GI Bill left the responsibility for implementing its homeownership, small-business, and education benefits up to state and local governments, many of which upheld the Jim Crow system. On the federal level, the FHA engaged in redlining of neighborhoods where black Americans lived, rendering homes there ineligible for low-interest-rate thirty-year FHA-insured loans. At the same time, legal and de facto discrimination prevented black Americans from buying homes elsewhere. Black veterans faced similar barriers at colleges and universities, few of which would enroll them. Black and white workers both paid the federal income taxes that generated the revenue to finance these benefits, but black Americans were prevented from receiving them. They could only watch from the sidelines as their money helped fund the creation of a robust middle class, one that was almost exclusively white. (This was hardly the first time black Americans were left out of a leap forward, either: When the federal government, through the Homestead Act of 1872, made it possible to buy land cheaply, black Americans were largely excluded.)

Note the "almost" in referring to the new mostly white middle class. Government assistance helped increase the white homeownership rate throughout the middle of the century, from 46 percent in 1940 to 57 percent in 1950 to 64 percent in 1960.[18] But even in the face of government opposition—it's estimated that black Americans received only 2 percent of all federally insured FHA loans issued between 1945 and 1959—black Americans also managed to increase their rate of homeownership from 23 percent in 1940 to 34 percent in 1950 to 38 percent in 1960. Individual black Americans have always found a way to navigate through a system not designed for our success.

Once I looked at the history of taxation in America, it became clear why so many tax policies have drastically different impacts on black and white families: They were created during a time when black families paid into the system without having the same legal rights to live, work, marry, vote, or receive an education as their white peers.

It was not until 1964 that the Civil Rights Act made it illegal to discriminate against black Americans in schools and in the workplace, and it took another year for the Voting Rights Act to guarantee black Americans the right to vote. The right for men and women to marry regardless of race wasn't the law of the land until the Supreme Court decided *Loving v. Virginia* in 1967. The following year, Congress made it illegal to discriminate against black Americans in providing housing opportunities. The law told black Americans that we could go to college, apply for jobs, get married, and buy homes without being denied access solely because of our race. That's a little more than fifty years to take advantage of the same rights that had been granted to white Americans for more than two centuries. The civil rights revolution moved the needle, but the struggle continues. Race-based voting disenfranchisement is alive and well today.[19] So is discrimination in housing and the job market. But perhaps the most glaring sign that our country has yet to achieve racial equality is the wealth gap.

As long as we have been measuring, white Americans have always had more wealth than black Americans. The black-white wealth gap couldn't even be discussed until December 6, 1865, when the Thirteenth Amendment was ratified. Before that, enslaved black Americans were legally deemed property in this country; white-owned companies were accumulating wealth through insurance policies written on enslaved blacks, and banks used them as collateral for loans. Slavery created wealth for more than just slaveholders, and the North profited along with the South. As "property" enslaved blacks could not get educated, could not get paid for their work. Property could not get married. Property could not own property. There can be no such thing as a black-white wealth gap when the only people the law counted as people were white.

Today, we can talk about the black-white wealth gap. But what we have to say isn't pretty. According to a Pew Research Center analysis in 2016, the median wealth of white households was $171,000 compared with $17,100 for black households and $20,600 for Latinx households. (Asians and other racial groups are not identified in the Survey of Consumer Finances database that was used for Pew's analysis.) White Americans have ten times the median wealth of black Americans and eight times that of Latinx Americans.

That does not mean that all white households have wealth or that no black or Latinx households have wealth. In fact, just under 16 percent of whites have zero or negative wealth, meaning they owe more than they own. But compare that with 37 percent of blacks and 33 percent of Latinx families who are in the same position.[20] White families are equally likely to have zero wealth as they are to be millionaires. Black families, on the other hand, are twenty times more likely to have zero or negative wealth than to be millionaires, and Latinx families are fourteen times more likely.

Despite these data, survey results show that most Americans—whites and blacks—overestimate economic racial equality, with the worst offenders being higher-income whites.[21] In other words, most Americans think the black-white wealth gap is small.

For white Americans it is easier to believe that things are

better than they really are, because it allows them to think there isn't much work left to be done, while still remaining ignorant of their privilege and how the system is rigged in their favor. For black Americans, it is easier to overestimate our progress because the alternative is to realize that even after doing everything right, we fall further and further behind.

Today, the black-white wealth gap only continues to grow. Between 1983 and 2016, median white family wealth increased by $1,000 annually compared with only a $66 increase for median Latinx wealth. Sadly, black families saw their wealth decrease by $83 annually.[22] Even college-educated black households saw their wealth decrease during a similar time period, from 1989 to 2013, as their white peers' wealth rose.[23] There is no end in sight.

Why is this gap so persistent? Why is it widening? Well, if you ask the political right, it's because black Americans do not make the right choices and do not work hard enough. According to the 2016 General Social Survey (GSS), a majority of white Republicans (55 percent) agreed with the statement that black Americans are worse off economically "because most just don't have the motivation or willpower to pull themselves up out of poverty," compared with 26 percent of white Democrats. Forty-two percent of white Republicans thought black Americans were lazier than white Americans, and 26 percent rated black Americans as less intelligent.[24] Just look at the election of President Barack Obama: The conservative commentator Bill Bennett said Obama's election meant there was no need to "take any excuses" from people who claimed "the deck was stacked" against black Americans succeeding.[25] The title of a 2018 *Newsweek* article about a meeting between President Trump and members of the Congressional Black Caucus summed up this attitude—and its inaccuracy: "Trump Thinks Only Black People Are on Welfare, but Really, White Americans Receive Most Benefits."[26]

The political left, which does admit to our racist history, doesn't do much better when it comes to understanding the situation. The left-wing narrative tends to center on blatant race discrimination by bad actors in the past: the FHA denying home loans to black Americans in the 1950s and '60s, or subprime lenders targeting black Americans during the Great Recession. This past discrimination has led to a disproportionate percentage of black Americans (21 percent) living in poverty, compared with white Americans (8 percent).[27] The economic gap has grown worse over time, the argument goes, simply because wealth begets more wealth, and black Americans are starting from behind.

But remember that GSS American Values Survey statistic I just gave you: 26 percent of white Democrats believe that black Americans are to blame for their relative poverty. And the same survey showed that almost one in four Democrats (24 percent) thought black Americans were lazier than white Americans. For black Americans, racism isn't just a part of our history. It's a part of our present.

The wealth gap isn't growing only because of the disproportionate percentage of black Americans in poverty. It's growing because whiteness has consistently and continually played a serious role in wealth building. Think a college education is an equalizer? Research shows that black households headed by a college graduate have less wealth ($23,400) than

me: my parents, James and Dottie Brown. I was right; they paid too much in taxes. But it wasn't because there are separate rate tables for black and white Americans. That would be against the law. Black taxpayers like my parents pay more because U.S. tax policies ignore the reality of societal differences based on race. The joint tax return exists because back in 1930, a wealthy white shipbuilder named Henry Seaborn convinced the Supreme Court to impute half of his taxable income to his stay-at-home wife, Charlotte, lowering his taxes. Congress gave all Americans access to the joint return in 1948. The policy rewarded people like the Seaborns, allowing a couple who could easily get by with one income to split it down the middle to avoid being taxed at the highest rate. But that same policy punished the Browns, who were striving to save and build a better future for themselves and their children and needed every penny of their two paychecks to do so. It is a pattern that has shaped the contour of being middle class and black, and it helps explain why black families have such a hard time maintaining middle-class status across decades and generations.

Unfortunately, even in the twenty-first century, that pattern remains, and black families who achieve financial stability are far more likely to lose it than their white peers, as reported in a 2015 study called "Five Bleak Facts on Black Opportunity."[30] A March 2018 intergenerational mobility study showed that black children had the most difficult time achieving upward mobility when compared with white, Latinx, and Asian children.[31] Black children of parents in the top income quintile are about as likely to fall to the bottom as they are to remain in the top. Compare that with white children of parents in the top income quintile, who are almost five times as likely to remain in the top as to fall to the bottom. Tax policy, by taking money out of the pockets of black parents while putting money into white pockets, can help explain why black children have a harder time remaining in the middle class as adults.

Solving the mystery of my parents' income taxes didn't lead me to a revolutionary discovery. Instead, it reinforced a truth I and most successful black Americans know: Our families found a way to work around a system designed to support white wealth building. Individual black Americans excel in spite of the roadblocks to building wealth; individual white Americans struggle in spite of their systemic advantages.

And anti-black racism doesn't exist only in the past of federal, state, or local governments; it is perpetuated every day by white Americans—many of whom consider themselves progressive. They are white parents selecting where to send their children to school. They are chief executive officers and board members of large private corporations who are comfortable with very few black Americans as executives or upwardly mobile employees, who do not commit real resources to the recruitment and retention of a diverse workforce or ensuring that equally credentialed black workers are as likely to receive the same opportunities and compensation as their white peers. They are white homeowners who choose to purchase houses in homogeneous white neighborhoods even though they would deny being uncomfortable living next door to "too many blacks." Until white Americans change their behavior, the black-white wealth gap will continue to expand.

The marriage penalty that started this journey for me is just one example of many tax policies that have a disparate impact by race. Not every policy will impact every black family negatively, and not every disparity can be fixed by adjusting the law—we can change the way married couples are taxed, for example, but we also need to look at why it often takes two black workers to match the salary of one white worker. Until anti-black racism is eliminated, tax reforms will need to factor in societal racism. Just as an annual tax refund, invested through the years, can add up to true wealth-building opportunity, many of our tax policies, over time and without race-conscious reforms, are pushing black families down and pulling white families up.

I can think of no better place to exemplify the struggle of the black middle class than Atlanta, Georgia, my home since 2007. Nicknamed "the Black Mecca of the South" and known as "the city too busy to hate," Atlanta is full of contradictions when it comes to racial equality for its black middle class.[32] Take Ivan Allen, Jr., the city's white mayor from 1962 to 1970, who had previously run for governor on a segregationist platform. During Allen's first term as mayor, a black graduate of Morehouse College moved into an all-white neighborhood in the southwest part of the city. Mayor Allen responded by signing legislation ordering barricades to be constructed across two of the city's streets,[33] in order to separate white from black neighborhoods.[34] Dubbed "the Berlin Wall" by protesters, the road remained blocked until a judge ruled the barriers unconstitutional the following year. Less than two years later, Allen[35] would cosponsor an integrated dinner celebrating the Reverend Martin Luther King, Jr.'s Nobel Peace Prize.

Atlanta is home to outstanding Historically Black Colleges and Universities (HBCUs), including Morehouse, and a significant black middle class with economic and political power. Yet the racism built into our tax policies still disadvantages blacks in a city that has been run by black mayors since 1974. Take Chris, a behavioral health clinician in Fulton County, who was months away from completing her doctorate at a for-profit university with an almost 80 percent[36] black enrollment when it abruptly shut down, eliminating the eight years of study she put in while working full-time and caring for her daughter. Or Ursula McCandless, a human resources manager at Cox Enterprises, who is financially supporting family members who could not overcome the obstacles of the past and present. (Many of the people you'll meet in this book are shouldering the same responsibility.) Even the most high-achieving black professionals face setbacks different from those encountered by their white peers; just consider John, a consultant and strategic planner with an advanced degree from one of the world's most competitive universities. He was forced to short-sell his first family home, in a black neighborhood, when he sought better public education for his children by moving to a street where his is the only black family.

While Atlanta has a unique history, the struggle of the black middle class here is representative of national trends.[37] Because of tax policy decisions made long ago, black married couples start off behind their white peers. When they purchase homes, they do not receive the home equity boost that their white peers get. Black Americans have more student loan debt to pay off. They work in lower-paying jobs than their qualifications would suggest, and they support extended family in ways foreign to most of their white peers. From one generation to the next, black wealth diminishes, evaporates, and is stolen by systemic racism. Meanwhile, white families continue to receive and accumulate wealth, scooping up tax cuts along the way.

The precarious position of so many black families becomes especially visible during moments of crisis. Nancy Flake Johnson, president of the Urban League of Greater Atlanta, said in an interview with NPR that the Great Recession that began in 2007 was devastating for all black Americans, even college graduates. "We've lost a third of the black middle class," she said, citing a recent Urban League study.[38] Nationwide, a report from Pew Research shows that the black-white racial wealth gap for middle-income families increased both during and after the crisis.[39] And in May 2020—months into the COVID-19 pandemic, with black Americans disproportionately impacted by poor health outcomes—*less than half* of black adults had a job. We can expect things will only get worse.

The way out demands work from whites, blacks, and the American public as a whole. White Americans have to come to terms with their privilege-based benefits, and black Americans have to accept how much the deck is stacked against us and take defensive actions. Only then can we hold our elected leaders accountable, forcing them to reckon with historical discrimination and identify tax policy decisions that every year take money out of black taxpayers' hands and put it into white taxpayers' pockets. With this information out in the open, the American public will be better equipped to demand tax reform that is racially just and equitable.

In the last chapter of the book, I propose some policies that might help us achieve this goal. These solutions—and the rest of this book—are aimed at reducing the wealth gap between black and white Americans in particular. Americans of Indigenous, Latinx, and Asian descent face wealth gaps of their own, and these, too, deserve study. But I've chosen to focus on the challenges facing black Americans for a few reasons. First, the black-white wealth gap is larger than the Latinx-white and Asian American–white wealth gaps.[40] (We do not have enough information to determine the depth of the Native American–white wealth gap.) Second, because the IRS doesn't publish tax statistics by race, we have to look elsewhere for proxies. The most relevant data that can be extracted from other sources concerns black and white families; it's simply where the most information is published.

Moreover, the focus on solutions designed to specifically reduce the black-white gap should also assist other groups. Racism in America is far more complicated than many think, and there is no one-size-fits-all approach for black Americans that will necessarily benefit all people of color (and as a seamstress's daughter, I know that one-size-fits-all never really does). I would encourage others to extend my work and consider the unique history of other racial and ethnic groups and their structural inequality issues.

Most important, creating opportunities to examine, subvert, and undo the racism in our tax laws is how I will keep my promise to Jerome Culp and to my parents, to do more with the opportunities they gave me.

At its core, *The Whiteness of Wealth* shows that the role tax policy plays in perpetuating the black-white wealth gap represents an ongoing failure to provide an equal opportunity to black Americans that neither the left nor the right truly understands. The conservatives are correct about one thing: The black-white wealth gap can be decreased if people make different decisions. But it is the decision-making by white Americans that is largely responsible for black outcomes today. The solution? Behavioral changes at every level. Black Americans need to be defensive players in an anti-black system unless or until it changes, choosing strategies in their educations, careers, and family lives that compensate for oppressive practices and policies. Meanwhile, white Americans need to recognize these anti-black practices and policies and actively work against them, even when doing so harms their pocketbooks. And all voters, black and white, need to be aware of the special interests, bad actors, and anti-black forces that shape our tax system. It will take sustained, systemic change, from the federal to the individual level, to upend the status quo.

ONE

MARRIED WHILE BLACK

ost Americans believe that getting married means paying lower taxes.[1] And one thing my parents could have used was a tax cut. When Mommy and Daddy got married in 1956, they didn't have money for a fancy wedding reception or a honeymoon; my mother made the potato salad they served to their guests, and they wouldn't take a vacation together until decades later. Money was so tight that after a couple of months of paying $25 per week for their own apartment, they moved into the spare room in my paternal grandmother's—Grandma Bertha's—apartment. (You can imagine how much fun that was for a couple of newlyweds.) And they stayed there after my sister and I were born, because they simply didn't have the resources to leave.

Like most couples, my parents started filing their tax returns jointly the year after they got married. When I was young they used a tax preparer, but later they happily handed over the responsibility to me. Even with all that education, I assumed that filing jointly was the best thing for my parents, since filing separately was likely to result in fewer tax breaks. Nearly 95 percent of all married couples file jointly, and those who don't typically choose to file separately to avoid liability for a spouse's potential tax problems.[2] (A well-known example is the late senator John McCain, and his wife, Cindy, who inherited ownership of the third-largest Anheuser-Busch distributor in the country.[3] Before they got married, they signed a prenuptial agreement that included a requirement that they would file separate tax returns.)[4]

Conventional wisdom assumes the tax subsidy for marriage benefits all married Americans equally, and doesn't give much consideration to its effects across race and income groups. When I saw that my parents' two incomes added up to a higher tax bill than had they remained single and filed individually, I started to question the conventional wisdom—and found that while in theory the provision should affect everyone equally, regardless of race, in practice it has a disproportionately detrimental impact on black couples. How a tax provision used by almost all married couples—the joint return—came to harm black families and their ability to build intergenerational wealth tells us much about American tax policy, its history, and its intentions.

Meet Henry and Charlotte Seaborn, the rich white society couple whose lawsuit led the Supreme Court to establish the joint tax return in 1948. Henry and Charlotte were married in

1902, before we even had a progressive income tax system. As noted in the introduction, when that system was enacted in 1913, taxpayers were required to file as individuals. That meant the same rate schedule applied whether you were married or single. There were different exemption amounts for individuals and married couples—$3,000 versus $4,000, on the grounds that it cost less to maintain one household for two people, than two separate households—which had the potential to provide a small tax cut when you got married. In 1913, however, only 1 percent of Americans had income high enough to have to pay taxes.[5] By 1930, exemption amounts had been lowered, requiring around 5 percent of Americans to file tax returns, including Henry and Charlotte, respectively the vice president of the Skinner & Eddy shipbuilding company and his socialite stay-at-home spouse.

According to court records, in 1927 Henry had taxable income of just under $38,500 (about $500,000 today, adjusted for inflation). More than half of that income came from investments. (That's a whole other piece of tax policy, but we'll get to that in chapter 5.) The lowest tax bracket, which applied to taxable income under $20,000 in 1913, had been lowered to $2,000 in 1917—which meant not only did Henry have to pay taxes, but he had to pay *a lot* in taxes. By 1927, the Seaborns were fed up. They decided to use their considerable resources to reduce their tax bills—and succeeded, with a little help from the United States Supreme Court. The Seaborns lived in Washington, a "community property" state, which gave Charlotte equal legal ownership of whatever income her husband received during their marriage. When they filed their taxes for 1927, Charlotte put half of Henry's income (and expenses) on her tax return, and Henry did the same. The married exemption was $3,500 that year, and the Seaborns each decided to take half of it—$1,750 each.

Here's how this worked, in practice—and for simplicity, let's count only Henry's wage income, not his investments. So Henry has income of $15,000, and Charlotte has none. If he'd obeyed the law, as a married taxpayer filing a joint return, he would subtract the personal exemption of $3,500 and have taxable income of $11,500. That would result in a $370 tax bill—roughly $5,400 in today's dollars.[6] His marginal tax rate was 6 percent—the highest rate his last dollars of income were taxed at.

Henry, however, chose not to obey the law, and allocated half his income to Charlotte for tax purposes. Each spouse thus reported net income of $7,500—and because there was no option for a person with no income, like Charlotte, to file a return, the Seaborns invented one, and deducted half of the married exemption from each income. That would put their taxable income at $5,750 each, with a resulting tax bill of $112.50 for each Seaborn.[7] Under this scenario, their highest marginal tax rate was only 3 percent.

Henry and Charlotte might have been charged with tax fraud, but their "ingenuity" was rewarded. When the IRS initially audited the Seaborns' tax returns and rejected them, arguing that all of the income (and expenses) should have been included on Henry's tax return because he was the sole wage earner and sole owner of the investments, Henry paid the extra taxes ($703.01, roughly $10,000 today) and then sued for a refund so that he could take his case to federal district court. With the help of Donworth, Todd & Holman (the precursor of Perkins Coie LLP, currently the largest law firm in the Pacific Northwest), the Seaborns won—first at the district court, and then, after another appeal from the IRS, at the Supreme Court. They were able to split Henry's income, using their wealth to get a permanent tax cut that would enable them to accumulate even more wealth.

In doing so, the Seaborns not only set a precedent for helping rich couples in community property states pay less tax but also made other wealthy Americans aware of the potential to change the laws in their favor. Initially, only couples in community property states, like Washington, could benefit from marital income splitting; in most states, income earned during the marriage belonged to the spouse who earned it.[8] Before *Poe v. Seaborn,* the 5 percenters who lived in separate property states had tried to find another way of reducing their tax burden, splitting their income by entering into contracts where the sole wage earner (the husband) transferred a half interest in his income and other property to his wife.[9] That case, too, had gone all the way to the Supreme Court; unlike in *Poe v. Seaborn,* the rich white married couple lost. The Supreme Court reasoned that in separate property states, "he who earns" the income is the one who will be taxed on it.[10]

The Supreme Court thus created a situation where married couples with identical income and expenses but who lived in different states would pay different federal income tax bills. However, this was a violation of the horizontal equity principle underpinning the progressive tax system—and still only the 5 percent wealthiest Americans were paying in. They were determined to make a change.

One approach was for husbands and wives to form family

partnerships and "split" their incomes equally. Family partnerships mimicked small businesses, such as two-person law
firms or retail stores; these are classified as "pass-through" en-
tities in which each individual partner pays taxes on their
share of the income. (The spousal approach ignored the fact
that no legitimate business partnership agreement would be
formed solely to award half of the income from the earner to
the nonearner.) When family partnerships weren't challenged
by the IRS, the couple got the same result as the Seaborns, and
a lower tax bill. When they were challenged, sometimes the
taxpayer won and sometimes they lost. This approach was
case by case, expensive, and unpredictable.

An alternative approach was directed toward state legisla-
tures. The goal was to get lawmakers to pass bills to convert
their states from separate property to community property. In
1939, Oklahoma, concerned about the exodus of its wealthy
oil barons to the neighboring community property state of
Texas, tried to create a community property "opt-in" law.[11]
Only those couples who wished to have community property
rules apply to them would be treated as if they were living in
a community property state. The Supreme Court held in 1944
that this opt-in approach was not a true community property
regime, hence no tax break for those spouses. The following
year, the Oklahoma legislature adopted a true community
property regime, which was upheld by the Supreme Court.
Now the Oklahoma 5 percenters could get a tax break just
like the Seaborns!

Oregon followed Oklahoma—with both an initial elective
version and then a mandatory one in 1947. As the post–World
War II tax rolls continued to expand, making more Americans

first-time taxpayers, others followed: Hawaii converted in 1945, followed in 1947 by Nebraska, Michigan, and Pennsylvania. Community property laws give legal rights to non-income-earning spouses during the marriage and in the event of a divorce. The National Woman's Party looked at community property as "a distinct advance for women." But not everyone was a fan. Specifically, men did not like giving up their legal rights in their own labor to their wives. And the popular press stoked the outrage with stories designed to evoke the horrors of a community property scheme. Here is an excerpt from a 1947 *Newsweek* story about the Pennsylvania community property law:

> The joy of many Pennsylvania husbands last week was curdled by a sober afterthought. A Green County judge had ruled that under the new law a coal miner who had deserted his wife must continue giving her half his earnings. . . . In most states, if a husband left his wife or if a wife went home to mother, the best she could hope for was a nominal support allowance. In any community-property state, the woman automatically came out with half the family bankroll.[12]

Needless to say, the idea of women getting "half the family bankroll" concerned members of Congress (all but eight of them men, and only two black members).[13] They enacted a solution that provided all the benefits of income splitting, but none of the legal protections afforded to stay-at-home spouses in community property regimes. Under the new law, all married couples (not just those in community property states) would be permitted to file a joint tax return based on an assumption that husbands and wives are effectively equal partners sharing income and expenses fifty-fifty. While community property laws actually *gave* each spouse an equal share, the joint return would merely *treat* spouses as if they were equal, with no underlying rights. (Had Congress not acted, it is highly likely that more states would have converted from separate property to community property regimes and afforded legal protection to stay-at-home spouses.)

As Congress was figuring out a tax cut that benefited most tax-paying white families, another important shift was taking place for American black families. When the Seaborns won their case in 1930, the silver lining for black families was that tax policy did not matter much to them in general. Remember, until World War II, only the richest Americans, who were almost exclusively white, paid taxes.

However, even before the tax rolls were expanded in the postwar era, it was clear that the marriage bonus was likely to disproportionately benefit white couples. Black wives, like my mother, have always worked outside the home more than white wives,[14] even after controlling for income.[15] In fact, even as income rises, the labor gap between white and black wives widens along with it—meaning that among the highest-earning couples, more black wives work and more white wives do not. (No matter how high the husband's income is, black wives are more likely to contribute significant amounts to household income than white wives.)[16]

TABLE 1.1. WIVES' LABOR FORCE PARTICIPATION BY RACE, 1880–2019[17]

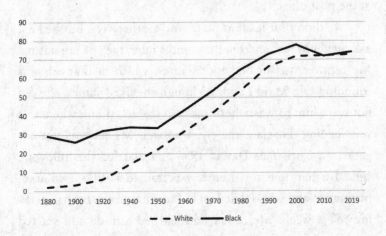

It was well established in the early twentieth century—and therefore predictable when *Poe v. Seaborn* was decided by the Supreme Court—that any system that gave tax cuts to single-wage-earner households like the Seaborns' would disadvantage black married couples.[18] But that didn't stop anyone from changing the law. By 1948, when the joint return was accessible to everyone, 85 percent of white families were in single-wage-earner households.[19] Four years later, in the fall of 1952, my parents met and set in motion decades of their paying more in taxes as a double-wage-earner household.

My mother, Dottie, was still working at a garment factory then, earning about $22 each week and paying room and board to live with her aunt on Union Avenue in the Bronx. One night, after she had already gone upstairs to bed, her cousin told her to get dressed, fix her hair, and come downstairs—because he had a fella he wanted her to meet.

That fella was my father, James, who worked with her cousin at the post office.

"We didn't hit it off at first," my mother says. But he kept asking about her, and finally, months later, they began dating. My mother was in her midtwenties, which in that era was rounding Old Maid Land. Although she liked James, she did not want him to waste her time—so she asked him where this was leading. He gave the right answer. My parents got engaged on Christmas Day in 1955 and married the following June. By that time, my mother was trained as a licensed practical nurse and worked at Jacobi Hospital in the Bronx, making $57 a week. My father had learned a trade and started working for a plumbing company. My parents' income was close together, although Mommy reminds me that she made a little more than Daddy.

Compare them to a couple—let's call them Henry and Charlotte—with a similar annual income earned by only one spouse. To keep it simple, let's say James and Dottie each earn $50,000; Henry earns $100,000, while Charlotte earns $0.

Let's assume for the sake of simplicity that the progressive tax system has only two rates and two brackets: one bracket for income up to $50,000, with a tax rate of 10 percent, and a second bracket for income greater than $50,000, with a tax rate of 50 percent.

Marriage doesn't affect James and Dottie's tax position; they'd each pay $5,000 ($50,000 × 10%), or together pay $10,000. Henry and Charlotte, however, have a strong financial incentive to get married. Unmarried Henry would pay a $30,000 tax bill (*$5,000* [10% of his first $50,000]; plus *$25,000* [50% of his second $50,000] for a total of *$5,000 + $25,000 =*

$30,000), leaving him with $70,000 after taxes. Thanks to the joint return, Married Henry pays only $10,000, leaving him and his wife $90,000 after taxes—a tax cut of $20,000.

Now, James and Dottie, too, have $90,000 after taxes. Under the principle of horizontal equity, all might seem well—the two couples have the same income and, accordingly, pay the same tax bill. But a single-wage-earner household is qualitatively different from a household where it takes two wage earners to get to the same income level (not to mention the very different jobs they hold; more on this in chapter 4). James and Dottie both work full-time to reach the income Henry earns by himself. Henry and Charlotte can divide up their labor so that he can spend long days getting ahead at work, and she can take care of the household (a common division of labor in very-high-earning families).

Our tax laws specifically ignore the value of the services that a nonworking spouse like Charlotte provides to her family. That income is called "imputed income" and escapes taxation. Charlotte may care for children or oversee a nanny, keep house or supervise a housekeeper, prepare meals, and run errands for her children and husband. All of it enables Henry to focus on his hypothetical six-figure job while Charlotte takes care of the home front. If she provided those services for a third party, it would be in exchange for wages, which would be taxable income. Because she provides them to her family, our tax laws treat her labor as a tax-free event.

James and Dottie, meanwhile, both have full-time jobs working outside of the home. They would have to hire outside help with *after-tax dollars* to get the equivalent of the services that Charlotte provides. If they chose to handle housework themselves, research shows that Dottie, as the working wife, would likely still perform a greater percentage of household labor than James.[20] But the amount of Dottie and James's imputed income will always be significantly less than Henry and Charlotte's because James and Dottie each have full-time jobs, while Charlotte's full-time job is working for her family. Given that there are only twenty-four hours in a day, James and Dottie simply have less time than Charlotte to spend on housework and family care. So even if we increased James and Dottie's household income by the value of their imputed labor, it would always be less than Charlotte's because she is contributing the equivalent of a full workday, while they are performing imputed labor in the hours before and after their other workday.

Even if tax law were to tax both families' imputed income, Henry and Charlotte's taxable income would be greater than James and Dottie's simply because one person is focused on home life full-time, while the others are working at least forty hours per week outside of the home. True horizontal equity would mean that James and Dottie's tax bill should never be equal to but always less than Henry and Charlotte's.

But those aren't the only advantages Henry and Charlotte receive. Henry, as a six-figure employee, is far more likely to also have health insurance, a retirement account, and other tax-free perks that come with his job (as we will see in chapter 4). Again, if our tax laws did not exempt those employer-provided benefits from being counted as wages, Henry and Charlotte's household income would be significantly greater than Dottie and James's and taxed accordingly—even assuming, unrealistically, that both couples were receiving identical employer-provided perks. (The value of an employer's percentage match on a retirement account associated with a $100,000 job is much greater than it would be for a $50,000 job.) In order to accommodate Henry and Charlotte and other couples like them, tax policy stretches the definition of "equal" so far as to break it.

It's not coincidental that, in this example, Henry and Charlotte are white and James and Dottie are black. There's plenty of evidence, statistical and anecdotal, that demonstrates how black men and women experience race discrimination in the labor market, and therefore require two salaries in order to have a middle-class standard of living. (There's also evidence that in practice, black married couples at all income levels are more egalitarian than white married couples when it comes to sharing power or making decisions.)[21] Our tax policies were built in total ignorance of—if not willful disregard for—black families' financial and social structures. The needs and interests of James and Dottie, and millions of families like theirs, were never part of this equation.

My parents both tried hard to get more lucrative jobs. When my mother left the garment factory to earn a better living, she tried to get hired as an insurance company clerk, but they told her she didn't pass the entrance exam.

"I knew I had passed," she says. "You know when you get the right answers. And a friend of mine, an Italian girl, told me, 'I'm not smart like you, Dorothy, and they told me I passed.' But there was a lot of that, back then."

She decided to become a nurse instead, a career that offered better opportunities but also required more training. Thankfully, even though the garment factory only employed her for nine months out of the year, my mother had managed to save some money that she was able to use to pay for nursing school. All but two of her nursing school classmates were black women, seeking one of the few professional careers open to them during that time.

My father, meanwhile, had to work as an assistant at a private plumbing company, because New York City's plumbers' union wouldn't admit black men until the mid-1960s.[22] Neither of my parents was earning at their peak salary potential, because the system just wouldn't allow it. And their two reduced salaries were critical to our survival.

A more equitable tax policy would not only cease to punish families who have two equal earners but allow our progressive tax system to operate more consistently with its origins in the idea that those with a greater ability to pay should shoulder a higher tax burden. A truly fair system would be one that ensures that James and Dottie pay less than Henry and Charlotte.

Privileged Americans have always had the power to mobilize for action when they feel that tax policy is mistreating them. Post-1948, the segment of the population who were unhappy with the tax cut received by wealthy couples like the Seaborns were those who were white, wealthy, and single. And they were fighting mad.

One such taxpayer, Dr. Donn R. Huf, wrote a letter of complaint that was included in the legislative history of the 1969 Tax Reform Act: "I, as a single person, . . . pay approximately $4,200 more per year than my [equal-income married business] partner . . . [and] my 15 percent higher tax bracket places me at a distinct disadvantage in investing my savings as compared to him. Consider what this can amount to over thirty years of productivity. . . . It is evident that this archaic method of taxation is only another form of discrimination that is perpetrated against a small group in this great country of ours. It is unfair, unjust and most of all unethical because these rules were formulated by those who were to benefit by them. If the unmarried had been truly represented, this could not have happened."[23]

Dr. Huf thought he was being discriminated against because he was not taxed the same way as a single-wage-earner husband with a stay-at-home wife. And there were a lot of Dr. Hufs out there. A different argument was made by Dorothy Shinder, president of Single Persons Tax Reform, a volunteer national service organization. Shinder argued that unmarried women were not spinsters by choice, but because World War II had deprived them of husbands—as had "the ever-increasing number of homosexuals."[24]

In practice, the singles' penalty could amount to taxpayers paying 40 percent more in taxes than a married couple with the same household income. Imagine Unmarried Henry Seaborn: white, wealthy, and powerful, only without a wife. Unmarried Henry would be taxed on his $100,000 of income and pay $30,000 in taxes, whereas Married Henry would pay $10,000 because half the income was considered his wife's and therefore taxed at a lower rate. Unmarried Henry viewed white, wealthy, and powerful single-wage-earner Married Henry as his "equal," and he and his bachelor cohort considered the singles' penalty unfair.

In response, Congress enacted the Tax Reform Act of 1969, which significantly reduced the penalty for unmarried taxpayers. The tax brackets were changed to cap the singles' penalty at 20 percent; no longer would single taxpayers pay 40 percent higher taxes than their married counterparts with equal household incomes. Dr. Huf got something, but not everything he wanted. As part of the deal, married couples like the Seaborns got a reduced marriage bonus and a smaller tax cut. Still, married couples with one stay-at-home spouse—by 1970, roughly 60 percent of married white women fell into this category—paid less in taxes than they would have if they'd remained single. The truly bad news was reserved for couples making roughly equivalent income—couples like my parents.

The legislation that made black married couples poorer was enacted by a Congress that included ten black members of the House and one black senator.[25] But there were no black members on the House Ways and Means Committee,[26] where tax legislation originates. There was no black Charlotte and Henry Seaborn, with the wealth and time to fight the laws that took money out of their pockets.

So as the system evolved, a mostly white male Congress introduced a "marriage penalty." When certain couples got married, not only would they not get a tax cut but their taxes would *increase* when compared with what they would have paid by remaining single. How this happens is hidden in plain sight in the rate structure.

Let's look at the tax rates from 1975, six years into tax reform: For a single wage earner with $45,000 of taxable income, black or white, her first $500 of taxable income was subject to a 14 percent tax, while her last $500 of income (income greater than $44,000) was taxed at 60 percent. Her marginal tax rate (the highest tax rate she is subject to) was 60 percent, the highest a single wage earner could be subjected to under the new law. (Yes, significantly higher than our current top marginal rate of 37 percent.)

A single wage earner making half that income—$22,500 (half of $45,000)—had a marginal tax rate of 40 percent. But if two singles each earning $22,500 got married—and statistically, if they were a black couple, kept earning two incomes—their last $1,000 of income (income greater than $44,000) was taxed at 50 percent, an *increase* of 10 percentage points from what they paid as unmarried individuals. A household with one wage earner making $45,000 a year and one earning no income—statistically speaking, most likely a white couple—had a marginal tax rate of 50 percent, too. But this represents a *decrease* of 10 percentage points from the single wage earner's marginal tax rate when unmarried. When the two $22,500 wage earners get married, their marginal tax rates increase from 40 to 50 percent, but when the $45,000 wage earner marries a nonworking spouse, his marginal tax rate decreases from 60 to 50 percent. That is how married white couples got a tax cut and married black couples paid higher taxes for equal household income.

Any couple with two working spouses in which one partner makes at least 20 percent of the family's total income will pay a marriage penalty. The more equal their contributions, the greater the penalty. Households where the lower-earning spouse contributes more than 20 percent of household income are marriage-penalty households, but they pay the smallest penalty. A household with a 30-70 split pays more and a household with a 50-50 split pays the highest penalty of all.

That was the solution to my mystery; that was why my parents paid so much in taxes. My father's overtime, which put his income close to my mother's, and of which he was so proud, caused them to pay a higher marginal tax rate than they would have had they never gotten married.

And although it's possible that no one in Congress was considering the effect on black families when the Tax Reform Act of 1969 was passed, a cynic could argue that they were certainly thinking about specific types of white married couples. The penalties enacted in the law protected the labor market advantage of white men by encouraging their competition—white women—to stay out of the paid workforce. It was simple: Marriage to and financial dependency on a working white man was rewarded with a tax cut. If you wanted to work as much as your husband, no tax cut for you. If you wanted to be equal in the home and outside of the home by financially contributing as much as he did, tax policy would punish you.

The majority of married couples[27] have always received a marriage bonus, and today roughly 95 percent of married couples file tax returns jointly.[28] But over time, as more white women joined the paid labor market and were hit with the marriage penalty, Congress began to make efforts to minimize it. My research based on the 1990 census, for example, showed that for households earning between $60,000 and $90,000, there were more white married couples where both partners worked and earned roughly the same income (putting them in the marriage penalty category) than there were couples where one spouse made no income (providing them the marriage bonus). In all other income ranges, white couples were still largely getting a bonus when they got married. But the trend was clear, and beginning in 2003, President George W. Bush signed into law tax cuts eliminating marriage penalties for married couples earning less than $56,800.

This reform came with a large caveat, however. The new law did not apply to taxpayers eligible for the earned income tax credit (EITC), which applies to low-income wage earners. (A tax credit is different from a deduction because it offsets tax liability rather than lowering taxable income.) Bush only slightly reduced the marriage penalty found in the EITC, which meant that those who needed it the most—hardworking, low-income Americans—got very little tax relief from being married. As a candidate in 2000, Bush had said, "What kind of a tax code is it that discourages marriage?" While in office, he instituted a Healthy Marriage Initiative, promoting marriage as a path to stability for low-income families.[29] Yet from a tax policy perspective, President Bush did very little to change things for low-income workers.

The reduction in the marriage penalty came with another price: an increase in the singles' penalty. Under the new system, an unmarried earner like Dr. Huf paid more, a middle-income married couple like James and Dottie paid the same as they would individually, and a married single wage earner like Henry Seaborn got a larger tax break. High-earning, dual-income married couples were hit the hardest of all.[30]

My father died in 1994, so my parents weren't able to benefit from the 2003 marriage-penalty relief. But other black married couples did (with the big exception of those who qualified for the earned income tax credit). They would benefit even more from the marriage-penalty relief offered in the 2017 Tax Cuts and Jobs Act. Treasury Department research had predicted that in 2016, a bare majority (51 percent) of married couples would receive a marriage bonus while 40 percent would pay a marriage penalty.[31] And it should come as no surprise that as more white married couples were subject to the marriage penalty, tax relief was right around the corner. The 2017 Tax Cuts and Jobs Act kept the marriage penalty for low-income taxpayers eligible for the EITC but temporarily eliminated it for almost all other households except those in the highest marginal tax bracket, 37 percent, which applies to very-high-income households (at least $500,000 for single taxpayers and $600,000 for married taxpayers).

But this round of marriage-penalty relief also came at a cost—an even *greater* marriage bonus. Mathematically speaking, that is the only way to provide marriage-penalty relief in a joint-return, progressive tax system. In order for dual-earning black married couples (outside of the lowest- and highest-income households) to not pay higher taxes when they get married, their white single-wage-earner "equal income" household peers would now pay even less. But remember, when it comes to income, two does not equal one.

Take Greg and Kristen Galloway, a black Atlanta couple whom I think of as the twenty-first-century version of my parents. Kristen and Greg have been married since 2015 and have one child, born the same year. They own a single-family home in Tucker, Georgia, about half an hour from downtown Atlanta, and both work full-time: Greg as the operations manager at the CNN Store, Kristen as an administrative assistant at the Goizueta Business School at Emory University. In 2019, Greg earned $58,389 working approximately a forty-hour week; Kristen earned $51,003.26, working about the same. Both have health benefits, a 401(k), and personal time off—but because Kristen's wages are 46 percent of household income, Greg and Kristen are the typical marriage-penalty couple. Due to the 2017 tax cuts, if they filed a joint return and took the standard deduction, their taxable income after deducting the standard deduction would be $84,992.26, with a tax bill, according to the IRS tax tables, of $10,412. If they simply lived together and filed individually, their combined tax bills would be roughly the same; marriage earns them a $70 bonus under the new law.

Now, contrast the Galloways with a couple consisting of one wage earner and one stay-at-home spouse—a pattern that, as we've seen, is significantly more common for white couples. If the wage earner makes the same as Kristen and Greg's combined income—$109,392.26—he and his wife will file a joint return, take the standard deduction, and also pay $10,412 in taxes. Horizontal equity requires this outcome.

However, if this (presumably) white couple were unmarried and living together, but still supported by one income, the single wage earner would pay taxes of $17,497. So a marriage between one high-earning spouse and one low-earning or nonearning spouse offers significant savings; in this case, around $7,000—one hundred times the amount Kristen and Greg get.

Meanwhile, Kristen and Greg rack up expenses that single-earning couples can avoid. They pay for daycare so they can both work; they own and pay for insurance for two cars so they can both commute to their jobs; and they take care of household needs after they come home in the evening, instead of having the flexibility to attend to them throughout the day. And both have student loan debt, though only Kristen has a degree. (As we'll see in chapter 3, having student debt without a degree is far more common for black families than white ones.) In other words, just as the Browns and the Seaborns earned their $90,000 under very different circumstances, a black dual-income couple and a white single-income couple may have the same taxable income—but they do not have the same ability to pay.

Even the most high-achieving black married couples can have a harder time building wealth than their white counterparts. A look at federal census records bears this out.[32]

I analyzed[33] 2010 Census Bureau data for same-race heterosexual couples as the best proxy for the overall population, since 90 percent of the married couples responding to the census identified as same-race couples, and at the time same-sex couples were unable to file jointly.[34] While some couples' marriage bonuses and penalties were reduced or eliminated due to changes in qualifying income or other tax provisions like the earned income tax credit and the child tax credit, the most consistent finding was that single-wage-earner couples are more likely to receive higher benefits (and tax credits) than coequal-wage-earner couples. Single-wage-earner couples (100-0 to 90-10 split) received the greatest marriage bonus, and coequal-wage-earner couples (60-40 to 50-50 split) received the highest marriage penalty.

TABLE 1.2. MARRIAGE-BONUS COMPARISON: WHITES AND BLACKS

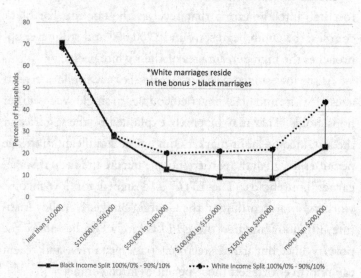

*White marriages reside in the bonus > black marriages

━■━ Black Income Split 100%/0% - 90%/10%   ● ● ● White Income Split 100%/0% - 90%/10%

Table 1.2 shows that single-wage-earner marriage-bonus households are more often white than black—even at higher income levels. Black couples never "earn" their way into marriage bonuses simply by making more money—in fact we see an even *wider* gap between black and white married couples at the highest income levels. In other words, when black and white Americans marry, they make different choices about spouses working in the paid labor market. (We'll examine the additional financial obligations that black families often carry—including support of other family members—in chapter 4.) It's predictable that any system that taxes dual-wage-earner households more will hit black married couples harder than their white counterparts.[35]

In the middle-income ranges, the percentage of white and black couples getting the marriage bonus decreases. However, once income hits $90,000, more white married couples begin to climb into the group that receives the tax cut. For black couples, the climb begins around $200,000 and still never approaches the high percentages of their white peers.

At the lowest income levels, we do see very similar percentages of white and black married couples in single-wage-earner households. That may be partly explained by the vagaries of the low-income labor market, and by the significant marriage penalties found in the earned income tax credit for dual-wage-earner households. The EITC is designed for low-income workers, and according to the Georgia Budget & Policy Institute, lifts four hundred thousand Georgia families above the poverty line. But it has steep marriage penalties, and recent tax reform efforts left those penalties largely intact.

Take a home healthcare worker in Atlanta with two children earning $19,000 a year. In 2020, she is eligible for an EITC of $5,920, which she can use to offset her tax bill. If her tax bill is smaller than $5,920, she gets refunded the difference.

Now let's say she meets a man with no children who earns $20,000. Because he's single and has no children, his salary is too high to qualify him for the EITC. If they want to get married, EITC rules require them to file a joint return—but when they do, it cuts her benefit to $2,626. If she were a high-earning home healthcare provider, with a salary of $30,000, the same circumstance would cut her EITC from $3,512 to zero. For families in this situation, losing 5 percent of their income is significant, and getting married should not be the choice that sends them into poverty. (Never mind that the EITC is incredibly complex, results in high rates of error, and those who claim it are twice as likely to be audited as high-income Americans.)

Next we compare white and black Americans in marriage-penalty households at all income levels.

TABLE 1.3. MARRIAGE-PENALTY COMPARISON: WHITES AND BLACKS

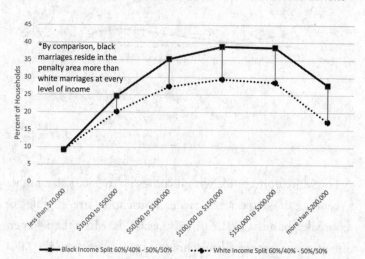

Table 1.3 shows how married black couples are more likely to be in the penalty zone than white married couples regardless of income. As income increases, black couples are still more likely to be in coequal households to a greater extent than their white peers because of black wives' significant earnings compared with their husbands'. High-income married black couples who are in the best position to save more, invest more, and build more wealth are instead paying Uncle Sam *more* for the privilege of being married.

Next we compare white married couples receiving tax cuts with those paying a penalty.

TABLE 1.4. COMPARISON OF WHITE MARRIAGE-BONUS (MB) AND

MARRIAGE-PENALTY (MP) HOUSEHOLDS

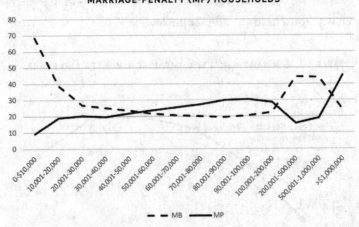

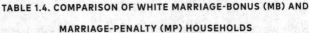

For white households with incomes up to $50,000, a higher percentage of single-wage-earner households are eligible for tax breaks than coequal-earner households. More than 40 percent of white married households earning between $200,001 and $1 million get tax cuts when they marry, while less than 20 percent pay a penalty. The overwhelming majority of that 40 percent are eligible for a marriage bonus because their marriages mirror a historical archetype of a single wage earner with a stay-at-home spouse that traces its roots back to tax policy decisions made in the first half of the twentieth century.

However, once household income exceeds $1 million, almost 25 percent are eligible for the marriage bonus, compared with 45 percent who pay a marriage penalty. Why? Because almost half of those couples are equal earners—like the anonymous couple featured in Refinery29's *Money Diaries* in 2017, who earned $1.2 million in salaries and bonuses. The diary, written by the wife, noted that she worked full-time as an "executive director" in "finance," and her husband worked full-time and earned a similar salary. The children were in full-day school programs, and both parents handled childcare in the evenings.[36] Think of them as rich white versions of my parents, experiencing marriage the way a dual-income family does.

For white married couples, this story is about both race and class. At the lowest household income levels, we see a significant percentage meeting the "ideal" archetype of a single-wage-earner household. The story is the same for upper-income couples. However, at the middle-income levels and extremely high-income levels, we see fewer white couples meeting the ideal of a single-wage-earner household, and paying a high price as a result.

Finally, table 1.5 compares the percentage of black married couples in marriage-bonus and marriage-penalty households.

TABLE 1.5. COMPARISON OF BLACK MARRIAGE-BONUS (MB) AND MARRIAGE-PENALTY (MP) HOUSEHOLDS

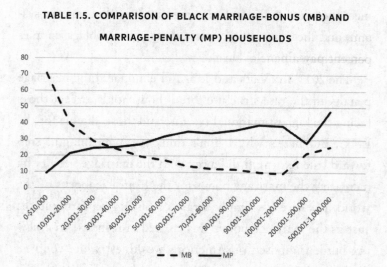

Some black households meet the single-wage-earner ideal, but a far greater percentage does not. The numbers are stark. Once household income rises above $60,000, there are more than twice as many black marriage-penalty households than marriage-bonus ones. Once household income exceeds $80,000, there are more than three times as many. At $100,000, it's four times as many. We never see this large a gap in white households.

Race plays a larger role than class here. Only at the lowest income levels are married blacks significantly more likely to be in the ideal single-wage-earner households. I have a hunch this is related to the instability of the labor market for low-wage workers—and especially for black men. (The single wage earner here is not necessarily the husband.) Once household income exceeds $30,000, black couples are always more likely to be found in coequal-wage-earner households *regardless of income*. Black households are far more likely to not meet the white "ideal" of marriage as defined in our tax system, and the joint return causes these married black couples considerable financial harm.

The 2017 Tax Cuts and Jobs Act eliminated the marriage penalty in the rate structure for all households, except those facing the highest marginal tax rate and those eligible for the EITC. But here's why I don't think it's a meaningful step toward true reform: It did away with the marriage penalty by increasing the marriage bonus for the Henry Seaborns of the world. I believe it's simply a case of history repeating itself: Just as the marriage bonus was created in response to a new tax burden imposed on America's wealthiest white couples, the increasing number of white married couples paying the marriage penalty was the impetus for the 2017 act's marriage-penalty relief. So once again, the wealthiest (and likely whitest) couples get a bonus. Meanwhile, history repeats itself for Kristen and Greg, too. Unlike my parents, they don't pay a penalty, but they also don't get the kind of tax savings that would allow them to put some money aside or invest in their retirement accounts or open a savings account for their son. (And frankly, any true tax policy reform would also address the decades of lost opportunities for older couples like my parents—but more on that later.) Also, you shouldn't feel too bad for the high-income white households who are still theoretically subject to the marriage penalty—a different loophole is in place to help them (more in chapter 5).

But the vast majority of black taxpayers are single like me—less than one-third of black adults are married compared with 54 percent of whites. By increasing the marriage bonus, the 2017 tax act created a huge singles' penalty. For example, in 2020, a married taxpayer with $50,000 of taxable income is subject to a marginal tax rate of 12 percent—their last dollar of income is taxed at 12 percent. A single taxpayer with $50,000 of household income is subject to a marginal tax rate of 22 percent. Ultimately, the 2017 Tax Cuts and Jobs Act did what tax policy has always done: prioritized shifts in recognition of white cultural norms at the expense of black cultural norms.

That's how our progressive tax system has put cash into the pockets of a majority of white married couples while *at the same time* taking money out of the pockets of most black married couples for the decades between 1969 and 2017. A study of black and white families over a twenty-five-year period between 1984 and 2009 showed that getting married increased white wealth by more than $75,000, but did nothing to increase black wealth.[37]

But the authors of the study made a common mistake—the same mistake that the political left often makes—citing black generational poverty as the reason blacks don't benefit from the wealth-building aspects of marriage. That explanation certainly holds some historical weight, but today, as my research shows, tax policy is key to understanding that equal income is not equal across racial lines: Two does not equal one. Tax policy decisions help make white married couples richer.

We also see why the conventional wisdom that marriage can lead to economic stability—espoused by conservatives but often supported by progressives, too—doesn't work for black couples. The Heritage Foundation has long argued for marriage as a solution to poverty and blamed low marriage rates particularly on black men who do not embrace marriage.[38] And the concept predates George W. Bush: Democrats and Republicans in Congress enacted welfare reform in 1996 (signed by President Bill Clinton) with funding provisions that allowed states to "encourage marriage." The idea of marriage as a panacea for poverty has been referred to as the "marriage cure."[39] The research here shows how mistaken conventional wisdom can be.

When my parents, James and Dottie, got married, they thought a lot about money and how to save it, right down to the homemade potato salad they served at their wedding reception. But they didn't think about their taxes as something that could help or hurt them. Most Americans go into marriage the same way, not factoring penalties or bonuses into their decisions (though a 2015 Tax Foundation report, which did not analyze results by race, suggested that those penalties and bonuses do ultimately affect how much each spouse works).[40] But marriage for most black Americans—especially low-income black Americans eligible for the EITC—is likely to result in a tax increase. For middle-class black Americans, marriage does not result in a tax cut, as it does for their white peers. Married black Americans are subject to the highest marginal tax rate and are less likely to get a tax cut like their white peers. Marriage pays off for most white Americans—but not most black Americans.

What is a better tax approach to marriage going forward? I will put aside until chapter 6 the question of how to compensate black families for the decades of potential savings that federal tax policy has taken from them. For now, I just want to push the reset button and consider the best way to treat marriage going forward. It's important to recognize that this tax policy was shaped by the needs of a very small, but very powerful, minority constituency: the Seaborns and the 5 percent of Americans who were paying taxes in the 1920s. Although the tax base has expanded, the policy continues to benefit one group—white married couples—at the expense of everyone else.

The better goal is marriage neutrality: Tax policy neither rewards nor punishes marriage, everyone files their own individual tax return, and marriage has little to no impact on your tax bill. For families who have been filing jointly for decades, this may seem like a big shift. But it's actually a return to the origins of our tax system, and puts us in line with the rest of the world: Today more than two-thirds of the countries in the Organization for Economic Cooperation and Development already tax married couples as individuals. The United States is an outlier. (Thank you Henry and Charlotte!) Canada, for example, has had a system of individual filing since 1917,[41] with certain tax benefits that apply solely to married couples and common-law partners, such as a tax credit for spousal or partner support. Their century's worth of experience could provide a model for moving forward.

When two people marry it is a personal decision. When a couple decides that one spouse will stay at home, they are making a second personal decision. And an established rule in our tax system is that your individual tax outcome should not be based on personal decisions. That's why the clothes we wear to work are generally not deductible. I like Celine handbags and Valentino shoes (Dottie Brown's daughter knows quality when I see it!), but I cannot take a deduction for them, because it wouldn't be fair to the person who likes shopping at Target—or the person who cannot afford to buy expensive things. If my tastes were tax-deductible, your deduction would be smaller than mine, and you would pay more in taxes than I do because I spend more money than you on designer clothes.

Marriage neutrality would require repealing the joint return provision and legislatively overturning *Poe v. Seaborn*. Now James and Dottie's individual taxes don't change when they marry, and neither do Charlotte and Henry's. If Henry pays more, it's because he's in a higher income bracket; his stay-at-home spouse has no taxable income and would not have to file a tax return. The single wage earners would be taxed on their income the way they were before they got married. The coequal wage earners would be taxed the same way they were when they were single—and they would pay less in taxes than their single-wage-earner counterparts. There would be no singles' penalty. Dr. Huf said it best in a follow-up letter to Congress: "There is no reason for a tax differential based on marital status. There should be one tax rate schedule to be used by the single, the married filing a joint or separate returns and the heads of households. Discrimination is fading from all facets of American life and I hope you seize this opportunity to place all Taxpayers on the same basis."[42]

Sounds simple.

Feminist scholars, like my Emory colleague Martha Albertson Fineman, Robert W. Woodruff Professor of Law, have long argued for a return to individual filing, noting that a marriage bonus or penalty subsidizes and privileges sexual affiliation in marriage (until relatively recently, legally defined as between a man and a woman) while ignoring other caretaking relationships, like that of parent and child.[43] Professor Fineman calls for the abolition of marriage as a legal category and the elimination of tax breaks tied to marriage—policy shifts she says are "totally consistent with repeal of the joint return." When tax policy privileges marital status by creating a joint return, it is excluding all of the other types of relationships that nurture and sustain us.

Yet nothing has happened. The biggest hurdle to repealing

the joint return remains the political one—which will not be easy to overcome, particularly since rich white married couples, like the Seaborns, will lobby Congress to retain their recently increased marriage bonuses.

But things are different today. Congress has many more black members, white women, and progressive allies. Today's electorate has many more black voters. The data prove that most black Americans do not benefit from joint filing status, in contrast to a bare majority of their white peers. We also have a growing population of single Americans—particularly unmarried women. In 2017, 45 percent of Americans over the age of eighteen were single and 53 percent were women.[44] We have more single people today than we have ever had in history. The singles' penalty will only be eliminated if the joint return is repealed.

However, for that to happen, the public needs to demand it—and for the public to demand repeal, they need to understand exactly how the same policy, so equitable on the surface, actually perpetuates inequality. When I told Kristen and Greg Galloway how marriage privileges the experience of a couple with their exact income, but only one working partner, Kristen said, "It almost leaves you speechless, it is so not fair."

Greg thought about the hours they put into their jobs every day, the childcare expenses that eat into their income, the advantages they'd have if one of them could afford to be a stay-at-home parent. I'll never forget the resignation in his voice when he asked me, "How can we ever get ahead?"

It's time to reexamine the idea that "most Americans" get a tax benefit through marriage, and be honest about what we find: "Most Americans" means most white Americans. The sooner we understand that, the sooner we'll have a productive answer to Greg's question. But if we allow these misperceptions to remain, the answer, for the Galloways and other young black couples like them, will be: "We can't."

TWO

BLACK HOUSE/WHITE MARKET

Before the Fair Housing Act was passed in 1968, black homeownership was mostly achieved through a mix of luck and strategy. Take my parents, James and Dottie, who bought a three-family home at 1061 Morris Avenue in the Bronx in 1964. At that time, only 38 percent of black Americans (compared with 64 percent of white Americans) were homeowners,[1] and the Fair Housing Act, which made race discrimination in housing illegal, was still four years away. So how did Daddy, a plumber, and Mommy, a licensed practical nurse, purchase a home? Luck and strategy.

Daddy (who, again, wasn't allowed to join the plumbers' union because he was black) worked for a man named Julius Gelman, and over the years helped him build up his business.

The Gelmans grew very fond of him, and one day, when he mentioned that he'd seen a house on Morris Avenue that he liked, Julius Gelman's mother decided to take action.

"She said, 'Yes, we need to get your children in a nice house with good schools and a backyard to play in,'" Mommy recalls. "I said, 'James, we don't have a pot or a window.' But I prayed, and I said, 'God, if it's for us, help us get it.'"

Between God and the Gelmans, they got it! The house on Morris Avenue was owned by Lorenzo May, a black real estate investor who owned many properties that Mr. Gelman did the plumbing for. (That was how my father first saw it.) Mr. May was ready to sell 1061 Morris Avenue because his wife didn't like it, and so the three men struck a deal. Mr. Gelman would loan my parents $6,000 for their down payment and take back a second mortgage. My parents would take over Mr. May's mortgage with Edison Bank for the balance, which was fifteen years and a principal amount of roughly $21,000. Mommy tells me Mr. Gelman's lawyer took care of all the paperwork. They stepped into Mr. May's shoes and got the terms *he* received. My parents weren't saddled with a 1950s version of a subprime mortgage. Their monthly mortgage payments were $180 to the bank and $100 to Mr. Gelman. We lived on the first floor, and our renters—strangers at first who later became "Aunt Mary" and "Uncle Sam," and "Aunt Margaret" and "Aunt Martha," to us—lived in the middle and upper apartments, paying us $120 and $130 in rent per month. The neighborhood was largely Jewish, with a synagogue on the corner and very good schools. And the first-floor apartment had a small backyard that my sister and I could play in. (Mr. Gelman's mother got her wish!) Without all of these people willing to work, pray, lend, and dream, my parents would have rented their whole life, just as their parents did.

My parents were put in a position to build wealth through homeownership because of exceptional circumstances. Most black Americans at the time could not tell the same story. In the middle of the last century, white homeownership was sped along by governmental tailwinds that increased the rate from less than half (45.7 percent) in 1940 to almost two-thirds (64 percent) by 1960. (Before the government provided subsidies through the Federal Housing Administration, most white Americans rented.) The black homeownership rate also increased during this time, from 22.8 percent to 38.4 percent, but black Americans largely did it without the subsidies enjoyed by whites, even as their taxpayer dollars helped pay for those subsidies.[2]

It's no longer a secret that the federal government systematically left black families out of the postwar homeownership programs that insured low-down-payment fixed-rate mortgages for whites and provided construction loans for homes and apartments that would be sold to and occupied by white Americans. In *The Color of Law: A Forgotten History of How Our Government Segregated America*, historian Richard Rothstein describes in great detail all the ways that black families were excluded and exploited by both the public and private sectors during a boom in white American homeownership.[3]

Two major bad actors of the period were the National Association of Real Estate Boards (NAREB, known today as the National Association of Realtors), a trade and regulation association with significant lobbying power,[4] and the Home

Owners' Loan Corporation, or HOLC, a government agency designed to help refinance mortgages after the Great Depression. Using guidelines from the Realtors Code of Ethics—which prohibited realtors from doing anything to "introduc[e] into a neighborhood . . . members of any race or nationality, or any individuals whose presence will clearly be detrimental to property values in that neighborhood"[5]—HOLC developed what it called Residential Security Maps designed to highlight safe locations for mortgages. Higher-income white neighborhoods were given an A rating and shaded green. All-black neighborhoods, regardless of income levels, got a D, the lowest rating, and were shaded red—or redlined. NAREB members were also required to accept the Realtors Code of Ethics.

In reality, there was no empirical data to support the belief that the mere presence of black Americans in a neighborhood caused homes to lose value.[6] When black Americans integrated a neighborhood, property values initially rose—black families were paying more for their homes than their new white neighbors had paid. The FHA admitted as much in a 1948 report.[7] This was primarily because prospective black purchasers were ripe for exploitation in the real estate market. Many predominantly white neighborhoods and new developments in areas deemed "safe" for mortgages were bound by covenants that prohibited sales to black homebuyers. Such covenants were legal (and upheld by the Supreme Court) until 1948; the FHA underwriting manual even provided a sample covenant to developers.[8] "If a neighborhood is to retain stability," the manual said, "it is necessary that properties shall continue to be occupied by the same social and racial classes."[9] That left limited choices for prospective black homeowners,

black families, the ways in which homeownership is subsidized through tax policy ignore the very real economic and social differences between black and white experiences.

"There's a carryover of the redlining and steering days, before the Fair Housing laws were passed, and the difference in property values almost tracks 100 percent with the demographics of the area," says Wayne Early, an Atlanta-based realtor and community economic activist. "As the percentage of black population increases, property values go down, and the rate of appreciation in values goes down. You can have two areas with the same median income, the same types of houses, even the same demand for those houses. And if one area has a much higher white population the prices are going to be two or three times what they are in the black area with a similar economic infrastructure."

This imbalance continues in our tax system, where two families can have similar homebuying experiences with very different results, depending on whether they're white or black. Putting aside the obstacles to entry for many black families (in chapter 5 we'll look at how generational wealth facilitates homeownership), there are two key components of tax policy that contribute to building white wealth and diminishing black wealth: mortgage interest deductions and how home sales are taxed.

Since our modern progressive income tax system was created with the Revenue Act of 1913, the government has always subsidized homeownership by offering tax subsidies for owning, but not for renting. Why? Because rent is a nondeductible "personal, living, or family" expense.[11] Remember in chapter 1, when we discussed how personal choices like my designer

Celine bag aren't deductible (but a personal choice like marriage is)? Well, the government will not give me a tax break if I rent an apartment in a fancy building with a doorman, but I do get a tax break if I *buy* an apartment in a fancy building with a doorman. The permitted deduction for mortgage interest is a huge exception to the general rule about personal choice.

Here's how that happened: When our tax system was created, few Americans paid taxes, and all interest was deductible—meaning you could subtract it from your reported income and potentially accumulate enough deductions to reduce your income into a lower tax bracket. There was a deduction for personal interest (think credit card or car loan) as well as business interest.

In 1944, as more Americans were taxed to fund the war effort, Congress adopted the standard deduction to simplify administering the income tax and save taxpayers the trouble of keeping receipts. So taxpayers had (and still have) a choice: Take the standard deduction and don't itemize, or itemize deductions if doing so will lower your tax bill even further.

The Tax Reform Act of 1986 changed everything by making most personal interest, including interest on credit card or student loan debt or automobile loans, nondeductible. However, the act carved out an exception for mortgage interest. As long as the combined mortgages are $750,000 or less, you can deduct the interest on the mortgages for up to two different homes. (Prior to 2018, the limit was $1 million.) You are also entitled to an *additional* mortgage interest deduction for up to $100,000 in home equity loans if the proceeds are used to improve a home, plus a tax deduction for the state-assessed real property taxes on your home—now capped at $10,000.[12]

A taxpayer can only reap these benefits by choosing to itemize deductions that, when combined, are greater than the standard deduction, which isn't the case for most people: A recent analysis of IRS statistics showed that only 22 percent of tax returns claimed deductions related to home mortgage interest.[13] The Center on Budget and Policy Priorities produced a report showing that 77 percent of the benefits of the mortgage interest deduction went to homeowners with incomes higher than $100,000, while almost half of homeowners with mortgages, who are mostly middle- and lower-income earners, did not receive any tax benefit.[14] Changes to the tax code in 2017 are likely to make this number even higher. The Tax Policy Center predicts that with the increase in the standard deduction and the cap on state and local taxes—which primarily limits deductions for high-income taxpayers in expensive real estate markets like New York and California, which just *happen* to lean Democrat—only 10 percent of Americans will itemize their deductions.[15]

None of the studies could provide a racial analysis because, of course, the IRS does not collect or publish statistics by race. However, a recent Tax Policy Center study looked at IRS statistics and matched them up with zip-code-level demographic data that serve as an effective proxy for race and income because of residential segregation.[16] The study found that the percentage of tax returns claiming a mortgage interest deduction increases with income. Those in the highest income level claimed the mortgage interest deduction at more than three times the rate of those in the lowest income level.

In the high-claiming zip codes, the population was 82 percent white and 5 percent black. In the low-claiming zip codes, the black population more than doubled, increasing to 13.4 percent. "The mortgage interest deduction is the largest tax expenditure for home ownership," the study concluded, "but its value is not distributed equally across the income distribution or localities. In particular, we find that roughly half of the aggregate mortgage interest deductions are claimed by twenty percent of zip codes; zip codes with high claiming rates tend to be disproportionately white, middle-aged, and married."

The conventional wisdom around the mortgage interest deduction (and its popularity among high-income, predominantly white taxpayers) has a lot in common with the conventional wisdom surrounding the marriage bonus: Both are widely seen as a sure way to save, but both benefit far fewer taxpayers than most people think. The financial journalist Roger Lowenstein describes the mortgage interest deduction as "an American folk legend: the government invented [it] to help people buy their own homes, and the level of homeownership has risen ever since."[17] Congressional legislative history also explicitly makes this connection.[18] In a speech to the National Association of Realtors in 1984, President Reagan promised, "In case there's still any doubt, I want you to know we will preserve that part of the American dream which the home mortgage interest deduction symbolizes."[19] Such language reinforced the idea that the tax break was a key ingredient of the American dream of homeownership, even though it was not an ingredient evenly distributed among black and white homeowners.

However, economists generally agree that the mortgage interest deduction does virtually nothing to encourage people to buy homes.[20] Instead, research suggests that it rewards a behavior that was probably going to occur anyway (again, like marriage). But it does change two associated behaviors. First, the tax deduction encourages homebuyers to purchase larger and more expensive homes, so they can maximize the deduction. That behavior creates a market response that increases home prices in general, making it more difficult for first-time homeowners to be able to afford to purchase. (If you're reading this and wondering who, exactly, does think the mortgage deduction is a good idea, the answer is realtors, developers, and their lobbying groups.)

The deduction and its impact on federal revenues are changing as a result of the 2017 Tax Cuts and Jobs Act; when I first began studying this in 2009, the estimated revenue loss created by the mortgage interest deduction, most often claimed in those "white, middle-aged, and married" zip codes, was projected to be $94.5 billion. In 2021, it's projected to be under $29.5 billion, and roughly just 10 percent of American taxpayers are now itemizing deductions instead of taking the standard deduction. Personal deductions, including the mortgage interest deduction, do not result in significant reductions to income like they used to.

Unfortunately, the increasingly irrelevant mortgage interest deduction doesn't work in black families' favor any more than repeal of the marriage penalty did. According to a Tax Policy Center analysis of 2017 and 2018 tax return data, the number of taxpayers taking the mortgage interest deduction decreased from 20 percent before the 2017 tax reform bill went into effect to 8 percent the following year. Of that 8 percent, more than half were in the top 1 percent of tax returns in the country.[21] Most black homeowners are not likely to be found in that population, or in the remaining group of taxpayers still itemizing. Once again, the shifts in the tax code are most likely to disproportionately benefit white Americans.

So while the mortgage interest deduction is what most people think of when they think of how the government subsidizes homeownership, its impact is in decline. But it's not the only subsidy the government offers homebuyers. A second, and more ominous, piece of our tax puzzle remains: how the government classifies gains and losses from home sales, and the different impact that classification has on black and white families. This policy also stems from the postwar era, when the majority of white Americans became homeowners. There were thousands of new taxpayers on the rolls—and thousands of laws legally discriminating against black Americans.

When you sell your home for more money than you paid for it, you receive income, and until 1951 that income was taxable. That year Congress enacted section 1034 of the Internal Revenue Code, which allowed homeowners to sell their residences without paying any tax on the gains, as long as they purchased a new home of equal or greater value. You might wonder why buying a more expensive home wasn't considered a matter of personal choice, like buying designer shoes. Just as funding the war required a change to the tax code, the rise of the postwar defense industry demanded more adjustment. As men and women followed defense industry jobs around the country, Congress sought to eliminate potential barriers to buying and selling homes.[22] The powerful real estate lobby, which only benefited from increased sales and purchases of more expensive homes, threw a lot of support behind this policy—which, you'll note, didn't help renters or downsizers. Calvin K. Snyder, the secretary of the Washington committee of the pro-redlining National Association of Real Estate Boards, explained:

> We believe that it is extremely important in this period of defense mobilization not to have provisions in the laws of the land that discourage or impair the mobility of working men and women. We believe that the existing provisions of the Internal Revenue Code—in their treatment of gains and losses from sales or exchanges of homes—do have this effect, because they penalize the people who have to move from one place to another in response to the demands of the mobilization program.[23]

Legally, the defense industry was supposed to include both black and white Americans; in 1941, President Roosevelt had signed Executive Order 8802, prohibiting racial discrimination in the government and the defense industry. But it rarely did in practice—in the ten weeks after the Executive Order became law, Boeing hired one thousand new employees each week, but none were black.[24] Eventually, the Executive Order did help increase the share of black Americans working in the defense industry from 3 percent to 8 percent, although the jobs were lower paying than those held by white employees.

(Marginal economic progress of some blacks in the workforce during this period may explain, in part, the increase in black homeownership rates.)

Nevertheless, when Mr. Snyder made his remarks before Congress, it was still legal to discriminate against black Americans in education, housing, public spaces, and many jobs. We did not have *Brown v. Board of Education,* the Civil Rights Act of 1964, the Voting Rights Act of 1965, or the Fair Housing Act of 1968. The workers who needed to sell their homes and follow defense industry jobs—the workers who were being hired and would benefit from this new tax loophole— were mainly white and able to build more wealth as a result of this new policy.

That change set the stage for a series of amendments and exclusions that would transform the way homeownership affected wealth for the rest of the twentieth century. In 1964, the same year the Civil Rights Act passed, section 121 of the Internal Revenue Code was passed,[25] allowing taxpayers aged sixty-five and up to receive $20,000 in tax-free gain from the sale of their homes regardless of whether or not they purchased a new, more expensive home.[26] (At the time, the median home value was approximately $12,000.)[27] Congress's rationale was that offering a tax break only for upsizing placed a financial burden on the elderly, who might be downsizing and in need of money for retirement.[28] Again, white homeowners were by far the greatest beneficiaries of the new rule. In 1960, almost 71 percent of white Americans between the ages of sixty-five and seventy-four owned homes.[29]

Section 121 was amended several times over the next couple of decades. The age was lowered to fifty-five, the exclusion raised to $125,000. Then, at the 1996 Democratic National Convention, President Bill Clinton changed the game. As he accepted his party's nomination, he promised: "Tonight I propose a new tax cut for homeownership that says to every middle income working family in this country, if you sell your home, you will not have to pay a capital gains tax on it ever, not ever."[30]

The law was passed in 1997,[31] eliminating the age restriction and increasing the exclusion again, to $500,000 for a married couple and $250,000 for a single person. This structure remains in place today: If you sell your house at a gain, you get to keep up to half a million dollars tax-free.

Meanwhile, the tax treatment for home-sale losses has never changed, bound by Congress's restrictive definitions on personal versus business or investment income and deductions. Income is considered income "from whatever source derived" and taxed (or not) accordingly, but losses are only deductible if they are connected to trade or business property or assets held for the production of income—like stock.[32] Personal assets—like your personal residence—are not eligible for loss deductions, so if you sell your home at a loss, no deduction for you.[33]

That doesn't seem like a policy that would have a profoundly disparate racial impact—until you ask someone like John, an Atlanta taxpayer, parent, and nonprofit consultant, about his experience buying and selling a home. A graduate of the Massachusetts Institute of Technology and Emory University, he's lived in Atlanta for more than twenty years, and bought his first family home on Feldwood Road, in the predominantly black area of College Park.

"Growing up, I always lived in a black neighborhood," he says. "And although my wife is Japanese, and we are a mixed-race family, I wanted our boys to grow up in a black neighborhood because I knew they would come to see themselves as black men. I wanted them to be in the village of black community life, and to understand the cadences and relationships that are built there."

John and his family started out living in College Park, a neighborhood that's almost 88 percent black. Unfortunately, they encountered a problem endemic to public school systems across the country: The anti-black housing market, which has led to such profound racial and economic segregation in American cities, perpetuates racial and economic inequities in the surrounding schools. As an article in *The Atlantic* put it: "These factors have left most African American and Hispanic students marooned in schools where economic struggle is the rule and financial stability—and all the social and educational benefits that flow from that—is very much the exception."[34]

Worried about the local public school's poor ratings, John and his wife enrolled their first son in private school. But when their second son was born, they wanted to move into a stronger public school district to avoid paying two private school tuitions. They made a choice that many families, white and black, do: They left behind a starter home in a neighborhood with low-performing schools and purchased a new home in a neighborhood with higher-performing public schools. (It's worth noting that these choices, too, tend to be inflected by race: Research shows that advantaged white parents "appear to determine school quality by how many other White, advantaged parents send their child to a school, without doing the legwork to determine what schools in a district are actually high-quality and a good fit for their child.")[35]

To get their children into a highly rated public school system, John and his wife bought a house in Candler Park, whose population is 88 percent white and less than 5 percent black, and decided to rent out their house in College Park. And that's when they discovered that owning a home in a black neighborhood was a losing proposition.

After a series of disappointing renters who didn't take good care of the house, John and his wife decided to sell the Feldwood Road property. But life kept getting in their way. The Great Recession reduced buying rates across the country. Plus, their two mortgages, one for each property, left them without extra income to fix up the house for potential buyers. When John went through a job transition and had a few months of unemployment, he became concerned about defaulting on their loan, and reached out to the bank that held their mortgage to see if he could negotiate a new payment schedule.

"I was probably about three months away from finding gainful employment, and I said, 'I'd like to do something that would allow me to make a bridge to be able to continue paying both mortgages,'" he says. "And they said they couldn't do anything until I'd missed three payments, which didn't make sense to me. But that's what we had to do. We stopped payment on the house in College Park, and after three months they agreed to talk to me and we negotiated a short sale."

A short sale typically means the bank agrees to let the borrower sell the property for its fair market value, which is less than the amount owed on the mortgage. In return, the bank does not come after the homeowner for the difference. John bought the Feldwood Road property for $204,000 in 2004, and sold it for $60,000 in 2014. He took no deduction on the loss, of course, and had a three-year flag on his credit report, preventing him and his wife from making any other significant purchases before the mortgage default cleared.

While both properties experienced assessed value fluctuations in the past decade, at its lowest assessed value, the Candler Park Drive home was worth $31,000 more than the Feldwood Road home; the gap widened to $254,000 in 2017, and as of 2019, the assessed value was twice that of the Feldwood Road property.

"There are no other black people that live on my street," John says. And as a member of a mixed-race family, he finds that local businesses have a hard time recognizing that he, as a black man, is part of the same group that includes his wife and children. "It's always, 'Table for one?' or 'Table for three?' when there are four of us standing there," he says. "But the appreciation of the house has been phenomenal. In terms of long-term value, I would absolutely choose this neighborhood again."

John's experiences highlight a key difference in how homeownership affects whites and blacks: When blacks become homeowners, we get less wealth largely due to the personal choices of *white* homebuyers. Numerous studies show when too many of your neighbors are black, your home will not appreciate the way it would if you lived in an all-white neighborhood, and you may lose money when you sell, just as John did on his Feldwood Road property.[36] When your neighbors are virtually all white, you are most likely to make tax-free money when you sell your home—again, just as John probably would, based on the rising value of his Candler Park home.

Ironically, this is a shift that took place after it became illegal to discriminate against black homebuyers. Remember, when the FHA explicitly endorsed and promoted all-white neighborhoods, black families actually paid more for their homes because they had so few options to choose from; the prices they paid increased surrounding property values. After the passage of the Fair Housing Act, supply could no longer be legally restricted, and more neighborhoods became available to black buyers. However, with explicit discrimination prohibited, another insidious factor remained: white preferences and fears, stoked by realtors and developers who wanted to drive out white homeowners and buy up their properties. When black families moved in, developers warned white families their property values would fall—and then, when they left and sold their homes at a loss, they did.

Those federal policies that boosted white homeownership at black expense still haunt us today because white Americans, the majority of all homebuyers, are still not interested in buying in racially diverse neighborhoods. Studies show that the average black homeowner lives in a neighborhood that is 51 percent black, while the average white homeowner lives in a neighborhood that is 80 percent white.[37] And when that shifts, research shows, property values start falling when black presence in the neighborhood exceeds 10 percent. The values fall even further as black presence increases.[38] Research shows that black Americans are the most "disfavored" of racial and ethnic groups; similar property devaluation has not been found for Latinx or Asian American homeowners.[39] White

American preferences create what I have called an "appreciation gap" that depresses the market value of homes in diverse
or all-black neighborhoods, while increasing the value of
homes in all-white neighborhoods.[40]

This is why homeownership is not a straightforward
wealth builder for black families: because the only guaranteed
return on their investment is to buy in a community where
they will be a small and vulnerable minority. A recent study of
fifteen cities between 2012 and 2017 showed that the black
Americans in the study had higher estimated appreciation (38
percent versus 30 percent) than their white counterparts because "the majority of Black buyers . . . purchased homes in
neighborhoods that are not majority Black."[41] Instead, they
chose neighborhoods where the percentage of black residents
ranged from 7 percent to 34 percent.

It's *possible* for a black homeowner to live in a white neighborhood with no personal or social repercussions, but many
will probably identify with John, accepting small slights and
indignities for the sake of the investment. Others may experience more overt discrimination, like Nnenna Agoucha. In
2018, the radiologist was coming home from work when a
white man parked his SUV in front of the gates to her residence to prevent her from entering. He reportedly told police
that although he didn't live there, he owned property nearby
and was trying to prevent theft.[42] Buckhead, the Atlanta neighborhood where this took place, is almost 80 percent white and
just under 10 percent black.

And then there's the worst-case scenario for a black homeowner in a white community. Here is how Dr. Agoucha puts it:
"When this altercation was going on, what went through my

mind was this [white] guy could do absolutely anything to me. He could shoot me dead on the spot because he was trying to protect the neighborhood and the property, and people would make up stories later."

There can also be unanticipated financial challenges for black families moving into majority-white spaces, as another black Atlanta couple learned recently. The Hancocks bought their house on Walker Avenue SE after participating in a homeownership program through Focused Community Strategies (FCS), an Atlanta nonprofit that specializes in revitalizing struggling neighborhoods by investing in mixed-income housing and small-business creation. The family had previously lived in public housing in Nashville, and this was their first opportunity to own a home.

"When I lived in an apartment, that's all I used to say: 'One day, I'm going to have me a house,'" Mary Hancock says. "Especially when we got married, and one month your rent is this much, and then you go back and 'No, we changed the rent, you're making a little bit more money.' I was like, you know what? I'm going to get out of here. I'm going to get me a house."

Working with FCS's homeownership program, Mary and her husband took classes in budgeting, saved up their down payment and obtained a mortgage, and moved into their home—a four-bedroom one-bath that they converted into a three-bedroom two-bath to accommodate their children—in 2008.

"We was in our forties, and most people that lived on the street was a lot older. And we were black, and most of them white," she recalls. "And they used to come down and walk down the side of my house, watching us. It was like they was keeping an eye on us—you know, are they going to be a rowdy bunch, or whatever?"

Part of FCS's stated mission is building strong neighborhoods; it offers both owning and renting options for mixed-income families, and asks people who qualify for some of its homeownership programs to commit to investing time into the surrounding community.[43] That should be a good thing, when it comes to black homeownership—and in fact, the value of the Hancocks' home has increased.

However, as the value rose, their Fulton County property tax bill doubled from 2017 to 2018. At the same time, their home insurance company terminated their policy in the fall of 2018, because, Ms. Hancock says, they couldn't afford to replace the roof. Now she and her husband, respectively a janitor and a line cook, are being told that their house is too run-down to insure, but at the same time worth twice as much as they bought it for.

"It's pretty much because of the neighborhood," she says, which, according to census data by zip code, has seen its white population climb and black population decrease between 2010 and 2017. "People are moving in and they are building bigger houses. The house next to mine, it was a two-story at first, but then they also added on to the back."

Though the Hancocks are from a very different socioeconomic background than John and his wife, both couples have experienced the vagaries of a real estate market driven by the preferences and priorities of white homebuyers. The situation begs the question: Do these preferences reflect a rational fear of falling property values, or are they simply racist? And the answer is: What difference does it make? The impact is the same: Black homeowners and their neighbors get financially hurt because of decisions white homeowners make. When neighborhoods remain predominantly black, the housing stock has lower value, and the schools are more likely to be underfunded and underperforming, as John and his family found; when neighborhoods go through a gentrification process, white families move in, and as the housing increases in value, black low- and middle-income homeowners like the Hancocks face skyrocketing tax bills. Either way, black Americans lose.

Research by the Institute on Assets and Social Policy (IASP) at the Heller School for Social Policy and Management at Brandeis University followed a group of American families over a twenty-five-year period (1984–2009) and showed that the single largest contributor to the racial wealth gap was homeownership.[44] The homeownership rate for white families in the study was almost 30 percentage points higher than the homeownership rate for black families. Home equity, too, was greater for whites than blacks. These numbers mirror national statistics: 73 percent of white Americans are homeowners, compared with only 44 percent of black Americans. A different study of home sales to low- and moderate-income households between 2000 and 2010—a period that includes the Great Recession—showed that white families gained or lost money depending on when they purchased, but black families consistently lost money, regardless of timing.[45] Homebuying is statistically more likely to lead to a nondeductible loss if you are black than if you are white.

Much of the current research attributes the racial homeownership gap to historical governmental discrimination and discrimination in the mortgage lending industry, both of which are indeed real problems. White Americans have benefited from what the IASP study calls "residential segregation by government design," as well as more generations of family wealth building, which often reduces borrowing for down payments. And while mortgage discrimination may be illegal, it remains alive and well today. Twenty-seven percent of black applicants and 19 percent of Latinx applicants were denied mortgages in 2015, compared with 11 percent of white and Asian American applicants.[46] Research also showed that in 2006, at the height of the real estate boom, black families making more than $200,000 of income per year on average were more likely to get a subprime mortgage than white families with less than $30,000 of income.[47] (A subprime mortgage, which has a higher interest rate, is generally offered to borrowers considered too high-risk to qualify for a conventional mortgage, but a borrower with $200,000 of income would not normally be considered riskier than a borrower with only $30,000 of income.) White Americans are far less likely (26 percent) than black (53 percent) and Latinx (47 percent) Americans to have subprime mortgages.[48] And even though higher interest rates may mean higher mortgage interest deductions, those come at the expense of building equity, as the higher interest payments mean homebuyers are reducing their principal very slowly—if at all.

There is a third factor, however, that those on the political left have failed to acknowledge: The real estate market is anti-black because most white homebuyers engage in anti-black behavior. As Rothstein describes in *The Color of Law,* for decades white real estate speculators engaged in "block busting"—selling or renting houses to a few black families at above-market prices, then hiring other black families to push baby carriages, knock on doors, and drive around the block to frighten white homebuyers into selling at reduced prices, and then turning around and selling those same homes to black Americans at excessive markups. But if that kind of behavior is in the past, what explains today's "appreciation gap" or the direct correlation between black families moving in and property values falling?

White Americans—present-day, twenty-first-century white Americans—simply do not want to live next to too many blacks, even when they can get everything they want in a racially diverse neighborhood. It is specifically the presence of black people, not other racial or ethnic minorities, that brings out white Americans' concerns. In one study, subjects were shown videos of different but actual neighborhoods with actors playing residents—all-white, all-black, and 60 percent white/40 percent black—and asked which they preferred.[49] The videos controlled for social class, which meant amenities in the white neighborhoods were like the amenities in the other neighborhoods. White Americans still preferred the all-white neighborhoods. Black Americans, on the other hand, least preferred the all-white neighborhoods, and viewed the all-black and racially diverse neighborhoods similarly and preferred them.

This is why solutions like the ones proposed by the 2020 Democratic presidential candidates missed the mark. They each had plans to increase black homeownership rates, including providing down payment assistance or allowing homesteading as a path to homeownership for those living in neighborhoods with high vacancy rates for a period of years. But even Senator Elizabeth Warren, who tied down payment assistance to home purchases in historically redlined neighborhoods, ignored present-day racism by white homeowners.[50] Neither she nor any of her fellow hopefuls addressed current-day racism and the catch-22 black homeowners face.

Ultimately, homeownership in America is a bad deal for most black Americans. Choosing the home that gives you the best shot at financial success means choosing to be a racial outlier, with all the slights and insults associated with that. And if you choose what John calls "the village of black community life," it is more likely to be a financial failure. White Americans are (and have always been) more likely to be homeowners, and their homes appreciate (with tax-free gain) because the neighborhoods they live in are attractive to other white American homebuyers. When black Americans, who face increased obstacles in becoming homeowners in the first place, do buy, the market disadvantages the neighborhoods they live in. Their homes do not appreciate the way that white people's homes do, so if they do sell for a gain, their gain is significantly less and they are more likely to sell their homes at a nondeductible loss. Once again, it's a matter of personal choice—who you want your neighbors to be—but tax policies reward most white taxpayers' personal choices and punish those made by black ones.

The solution isn't for black Americans to avoid homeownership completely and stay in the (nondeductible) rental market forever, however. The path to black homeownership is filled with complications and setbacks, yet it can still yield important rewards. The net worth of black homeowners is significantly greater than that of renters,[51] specifically because of the equity found in their homes. While home equity makes up only 38 percent of net worth for white Americans, for black Americans, it's 66 percent.[52] So how can we make home-ownership more equitable and profitable for black Americans?

I argue for neutrality as one potential reform goal, as I did for marriage. Just as getting married is a personal choice that should not change your tax liability, neither should your taxes be affected by whether you choose to buy or rent your home. In other words, either mortgage interest (and real property taxes) and rent should both be deductible, or neither should be—and gains on the sale of a home should be subject to the progressive tax system like the sale of any other property would be.

Personally, I fall on the nondeductible side for a few reasons. First, allowing a rent deduction would likely enrich only landlords, who would increase rents to take advantage of the new tax break. And given that renters are disproportionately low-income, a deduction won't help those who simply take the standard deduction, or are already too poor to pay federal income taxes.[53]

Second, when it comes to subsidies for homeownership, as with the joint return, the United States is already an outlier. Most of our counterparts in the Organization for Economic Cooperation and Development provide significantly fewer tax benefits for homeowners, and those benefits are often limited to first-time homebuyers, as well as means-tested or capped based on home price.[54] Contrary to the fears of the real estate industry, this doesn't appear to dissuade people from wanting to buy a home. Canada, for example, has a similar homeownership rate, but it does not allow a tax break for mortgage interest.[55]

The real estate lobby is powerful, however, and here's how they will likely argue against neutrality: Any repeal of the mortgage interest deduction will have consequences for current home values. The price of the mortgage interest deduction is believed to be factored into the price of homes by anywhere from 1 percent to 13 percent;[56] such a repeal, the lobby would argue, will reduce the value of homes by a comparable amount. (The National Association of Realtors estimates a 10 percent decline, while the Council of Economic Advisers says the impact is likely to be merely "modest.")[57] History has shown us that stoking fear in white homeowners is a powerful tool, and one that the real estate industry has used freely.

That said, black homeowners, too, will lose value in their homes if the mortgage interest deduction goes away. Given that black home equity represents roughly two-thirds of black wealth, this is a concern I take very seriously. (It's also worth saying that I'm a homeowner myself, so I know I am advocating for a reform that will hurt me financially.)

Nevertheless, in war there are casualties, and our current tax system is nothing less than a war on the financial stability of most black Americans. And at the end of the day, most black Americans remain renters, though a Pew Research Center study shows a growing number of renters of all races since

2006.[58] And just as we saw the marriage penalty repealed when it hit white Americans hard, I might predict a similar outcome here. If we want tax reform that will help black Americans, we have to talk about leveling the playing field when it comes to renters and homeowners.

The real estate lobby is quite effective at getting what it wants from Congress. After all, the only personal interest that survived the Tax Reform Act of 1986 was the deduction for mortgage interest. But here is where history can help us: The real estate lobby's open complicity in the discrimination against prospective black homeowners should go a long way toward muting them. We have to keep reminding the real estate lobby of the things that happened to black people at their hands, to make them less formidable opponents this time around.

The real estate lobby also proved vulnerable recently when it lost a round with the temporary 2017 Tax Cuts and Jobs Act, which is scheduled to expire on December 31, 2025. That legislation increased the standard deduction—which means fewer taxpayers will bother to itemize their mortgage interest deduction and just take the standard deduction instead. It also reduced the amount of mortgages you could have outstanding and still qualify for the mortgage interest deduction from $1 million to $750,000. And it limited the interest deduction for home equity loans, by requiring that the proceeds of the loan be used for home improvement. (The law used to allow you to take out a home equity loan for up to $100,000 and deduct the interest regardless of how you used the proceeds.)

After all of these changes, there was no public outcry, despite what the real estate lobby had predicted. Indeed, as *The New York Times* reported, the response was so minimal that some in Washington are proposing getting rid of the deduction altogether.[59] Score one for the economists and tax policy experts, who've been advocating for this all along!

However, let's assume inertia wins. My next best option, after a full repeal of federal tax subsidies for homeowners, would be to reserve those subsidies for homeowners living in the neighborhoods that suffer under the system.

I propose we revise all homeownership subsidies to target them directly to those living in neighborhoods that are undervalued because of the race of their occupants. Those neighborhoods deserve government tax subsidies, because the government's original discrimination against black Americans gave rise to the current discrimination perpetuated by private white homebuyers. Since 10 percent seems to be the magic number of black homeowners that makes a neighborhood lose value, homeowners living in neighborhoods with more than 10 percent black homeowners would be eligible for all current tax subsidies. Won't that lead to gentrification? Well, a tax break could help offset rising property taxes, and keep black homeowners in place; and as we've seen, when black homeowners remain, neighborhoods are much less attractive to many white homeowners.

This isn't likely to be upheld by the Supreme Court, however. Why? When it comes to allowing race-based remedies, the Supreme Court requires evidence of discriminatory intent as well as discriminatory impact. It wouldn't matter that the government caused the problem by discriminating against the very racial group that would benefit from this new tax subsidy, as long as the federal government can claim that it didn't *intend* these tax policies to be discriminatory.

Put more simply, as Charles Dickens wrote in *Oliver Twist,* "the law is a ass."

What *would* be allowed is to tie all homeownership subsidies to neighborhoods and neighborhood wealth. If you compare neighborhood median wealth to citywide median wealth, you could legally create subsidies that exclusively go to homebuyers in neighborhoods below the citywide median. As part of a neighborhood-based subsidy policy, we could also tie in deductions for home-sale losses in these neighborhoods. Wealth, as we will see in chapter 6, is a typical metric for limiting access to government benefits, so this fix would be unlikely to face serious constitutional challenges.[60]

The racial wealth gap means that my proposal will likely apply to the majority of black homeowners who live in racially diverse neighborhoods, as well as to the residents of some all-white neighborhoods in poorer rural areas. From my perspective, that makes the neighborhood-based subsidy a less than ideal solution, but it's potentially the most politically and legally viable.

In addition, as noted above, I'd partner these subsidies with one new tax break, allowing losses on the sale of homes to be fully deductible—just as investors are allowed to deduct their losses if their stock portfolio takes a hit in a given year. (Wonder why we privilege stock gains and losses? We'll dig into that in chapter 5.)

The symbolism attached to the mortgage deduction and other tax subsidies for homeownership is powerful, as is the message that homeownership is an unqualified good for all. I think of my mother, and her prayer that they'd get the house on Morris Avenue, and Mary Hancock's refrain, from her subsidized rental apartment in Nashville: "One day, I'm going to have me a house."

In truth, homeownership in America is rigged and has been from the beginning. Most white homeowners win, and all but a few black homeowners lose. Forget the Fair Housing Act, forget redlining, forget the illegal but still active practice of mortgage discrimination. Today's federal government creates and perpetuates pro-white policies in the form of tax subsidies for homeownership that are perfectly lawful. Tax subsidies for homeownership are little more than the twenty-first-century version of redlining, and they must be repealed.

Look at the families in this chapter who've managed to buy and keep their homes. The Browns pursued their dream with significant financial help from a white family—and the luck of having very good tenants. John and his wife suffered a huge setback, and ultimately chose to be a minority in their neighborhood for the sake of financial security and the promise of a better future for their children. And Mary Hancock and her husband got the house she wanted, with help from a community organization, and still found themselves vulnerable to real estate trends driven by white buyers. Yet each of them has been fortunate in a way that most black Americans are not. Black exceptionalism, not an equitable system, underlies the success of those in the black community who manage to wrestle some degree of wealth from homeownership.

The question remains: Is it worth it? Should black Americans try to grab this piece of the American dream—or should we understand that it will never work for us in the same way it works for white homeowners? The answer to both questions is yes—but a qualified yes. Black homeowners need to be especially careful to protect themselves in a white-dominated market. (Chapter 6 details steps that white homeowners should take to make the market more equitable and accessible to black families.)

But as we've seen with the declining mortgage interest deduction, a single policy change isn't enough to shift the fortunes of black families. Luck and strategy paved the way for black homeownership in generations past, and unfortunately, they're still a requirement for the type of black homeownership that leads to wealth building. To dismantle the system means fully acknowledging the racist past that shaped today's real estate market—but it also requires each of us, black and white, to confront the market's racist present.

THREE

THE GREAT UN-EQUALIZER

Je'lon Alexander, a graduate of Morehouse College, was at the school's commencement the day black billionaire Robert F. Smith announced his plan to pay off all the student debt for the class of 2019. It was a sunny, humid Atlanta day in May—the temperature peaked close to ninety—and he and some of his friends were messaging back and forth in a group chat. When Smith made his pledge, Je'lon says, he was so overheated and distracted he practically missed it.

"I had a delayed reaction," he says. "My friends were texting me, and one of them said that Robert F. Smith is paying off student loans. Social media started blowing up."

That day, and for several after, Je'lon had the same conversation all over greater Atlanta—on campus, at Target, at the drugstore: *What's going on at Morehouse? Are you part of that class?*

And he'd explain that no, he wasn't. He graduated in 2018, one year before, finishing with almost $55,000 in student loan debt.

Mr. Smith's pledge offered an extraordinary boost to the graduating class at the legendary all-male Historically Black College and University, or HBCU. One student, who'd estimated twenty-five years of student loan payments ahead, told the Associated Press he was excited not to have to live on peanut butter and jelly sandwiches to save money. Dr. David A. Thomas, the president of Morehouse, said that Smith's generosity represented "a liberation gift" that would open up new opportunities for the men to pursue their passions.[1]

But what Robert Smith did for the Morehouse Men in the class of 2019 also highlights those like Je'lon who were left behind. Je'lon, who is pursuing a master's in African American history at Georgia State University, and plans to get his PhD, is not the only member of his family with significant loan debt: Both of his parents have advanced degrees and close to $400,000 in accumulated debt from them.

The Alexanders, unfortunately, aren't outliers. Research shows that the average black college graduate carries $7,400 more student loan debt than their average white classmate, and that number only increases over time.[2] Four years after graduation, black Americans owe an average of $52,726 in student debt compared with $28,006 for white college graduates. And the gap exists across income levels—a University of Wisconsin study showed that while in general, the children of richer parents borrow less money for college, "as black parental wealth increases, we do not see black student loan debt decreasing."[3]

The drastic disparity in student loan debt, like most components of the wealth gap, doesn't exist in isolation: The obstacles to wealth building black families have historically experienced, and continue to experience, all contribute to why black students take on more student loans than their white peers and take longer to pay them back. But the way black students experience college gives the lie to another beloved American folk legend: that higher education (like homeownership) is the ticket to a financially secure future.

The truth, once again, is that the legend works best for white families. Higher education has long been believed to be the key to getting ahead in America. President Barack Obama described it as the "secret sauce" of Americans' economic success.[4] But college does not pay off for black graduates the way it does for white graduates. While a four-year college degree translates to a higher salary regardless of race, for most black college students the picture is more complicated. In fact, for the average black family, a twenty-first-century college education only creates greater imbalance in the racial wealth gap: In 1989, college-educated white households had roughly five times greater wealth than their black peers. That gap had tripled by 2013.[5]

There are four key ways black and white Americans experience college differently: which institutions they attend; how they pay for them; whether they graduate; and how much debt they have afterward. Each of these, often invisibly, is shaped by a piece of tax policy that almost always advantages the white American college experience. From the tax exemption for nonprofit institutions, which perpetuates the wealth and success of highly selective, predominantly white private colleges, to the deduction for student loan interest, which offers very limited benefit to those who self-finance their education, most tax policies offer greater rewards to white students and fewer benefits for black students.

To understand the link between tax policy and higher education, it's helpful to think of the whole secondary-education industry as a pyramid. At the top, you'll find the most selective four-year colleges, both public (meaning state-supported, like the University of California system) and private (meaning self-funded through tuition and gifts). These are all nonprofit institutions receiving associated tax breaks. They also all have a predominantly white student population and admit the fewest applicants.

At the bottom, you'll find for-profit schools. They receive no tax breaks, relying almost exclusively on tuition to cover operating costs. They admit virtually all applicants and have the highest percentage of black students. But as we'll see, without the tax breaks nonprofits receive, for-profits have to operate like businesses. And when businesses focus on the bottom line, their customers—in this case, a predominantly black student population—fall prey to profit-maximizing decisions.

Everything else, from community colleges (ranked higher than for-profits for their low cost and affordability) to HBCUs like Morehouse, is somewhere in between.[6] If college is a purchase, it would appear that choosing a selective, well-resourced, predominantly white institution at the top of the pyramid will yield the best return on investment for most black students—just like buying a home in a homogeneous white neighborhood.

As shown in the table below, selective colleges yield the best outcomes for black students, with a graduation rate of 70 percent. The majority of black Americans (60 percent) who begin college do not graduate compared with the minority of their white peers (40 percent), but at selective institutions both the majority of white and black students who attend graduate.[7]

TABLE 3.1. GRADUATION RATES FOR FOUR-YEAR COLLEGES

Type of Institution	Black	White
Selective	70.2%	80.5%
Private, not-for-profit	45%	69%
Public	41%	62%
For-profit	20%	37%

Why the disparities? Resources. The most selective colleges far outspend the others: on average, $92,000 per student compared with $12,000 spent by less selective colleges.[8] That doesn't translate to simple math, however: Tuition may be high at the most selective colleges, but it doesn't necessarily decrease as per-student expenditures do. The missing link when it comes to resources in higher education is college endowments—and, of course, the tax policies surrounding them that keep selective, predominantly white institutions (PWIs) wealthy.

A college's endowment is the sum total of donations and income the college invests for its long-term future. It is like an enormous rainy-day fund, only a small portion of which goes toward educational activities and scholarships. The rest is invested to ensure the continued viability of the institution. (During the COVID-19 pandemic—a rainy-day event if ever there was one—wealthy institutions did not withdraw available funds from their endowments. They imposed salary and hiring freezes instead, along with student fee increases and layoffs.)

If a college is spending $92,000 per student, you might ask, why does it have so much left to invest? Here, again, we see how one tax break combines with another to yield huge returns. Nonprofit institutions—which, you'll remember, include both public and private four-year colleges—enjoy tax breaks in the form of federal income tax exemption, and typically state and local income and property tax exemptions, too. Universities often own significant real estate, which makes this exemption extremely valuable. In New Haven, Connecticut, for example, an estimated 60 percent of city property was tax-exempt in 2020; of that 60 percent, Yale University, a top-of-the-pyramid school, owned 40 percent of the exempt property. It's a benefit with far-reaching effects across all of higher education, and it's probably the least-discussed benefit out there. (A Congressional Research Service analysis of tax benefits for higher education never mentions it.)[9]

But it's not even the biggest tax break they get. Private nonprofit colleges and universities—which include every school in the Ivy League, along with others such as Stanford, Northwestern, Duke, and Emory—don't pay taxes on their endowment income. If you or I have a savings or investment account that increases every year, we have to report the interest income and pay taxes on it, but nonprofit colleges and universities don't.[10] Put another way: By saving enough money to cover costs with plenty left over, thanks in part to the income and property tax exemptions, the wealthiest nonprofit colleges and universities avoid paying taxes on that excess, enabling them to save even more.

Better outcomes, better resources—why wouldn't all black college students simply choose selective institutions? Because these same institutions disproportionately admit white students, leaving black students attending under-resourced colleges and falling financially further behind.

Nonwhite college enrollment at all institutions—public and private, two-year and four-year—has increased over the past twenty years, from 30 percent in 1996 to 47 percent in 2016. If you separate out the data on two- and four-year institutions, however, white representation is much higher—63 percent at nonprofit four-year colleges in 2016, according to a Pew Research study.[11] White students are five times more likely to go to a selective university than black students. The pattern holds *even when controlling for income;* in fact, the gap grows as income grows. Higher-income white Americans are four times more likely to attend selective schools than higher-income black Americans, when at the lowest income levels whites are two to three times as likely to attend selective schools as blacks. At every income level a statistically significant higher percentage of white students attend selective universities than blacks.[12] According to a *New York Times* analysis, even as colleges have begun admitting more nonwhite applicants overall, the percentage of black students at the nation's top colleges is roughly the same today as it was thirty-five years ago.[13]

Just as purchasing a home in a white neighborhood can require significant financial and emotional investment for a black family, attending a predominantly white elite institution can present financial and emotional obstacles for black students. Cost is a factor: The most selective institutions are expensive, with the University of Chicago topping the 2019 list at $80,000 for a year of tuition, fees, and housing.[14] Just because the "sticker price" is $80,000 does not mean every student pays that price. Some pay less (or get it at a "discount") because their college awarded them scholarships or financial aid grants. But tuition doesn't tell the whole story: Even a student with a generous financial aid package can lack money for textbooks, housing, and food. Anthony Abraham Jack, an assistant professor at the Harvard Graduate School of Education and author of *The Privileged Poor,* successfully petitioned Harvard to keep its dining halls open during spring break after a low-income student told him that the closed dining halls meant "famine" to students like her.[15]

When black students do attend the most selective institutions, they are a distinct minority: The 2016 Pew Research analysis found that on average, at very selective four-year schools, the student body was only 9 percent black compared with 56 percent white, 14 percent Latinx, 16 percent Asian, and 5 percent who identified in some other way. When a student is one of a few black people their peers encounter every day (or, in some cases, the only black person), it often means performing what I call "racism triage": Facing a broad range of aggressions from peers and superiors, but lacking the capacity to respond to each and every one, you reserve your energies for only the worst.

Racism triage became a part of my life early on, when my mother discovered that both my sister and I were being mistreated by white teachers at our elementary school. My first-grade teacher, unhappy that my grades were the best in the class, told my mother that she'd hoped she'd be there when I "fell off my high horse." My sister's fourth-grade teacher, meanwhile, deliberately lowered her grades so that a black student wouldn't have the best scores in the class. (She bragged about her deception to a white friend, who then tipped off my mother—Miss Dottie was an involved and well-liked parent at the school.) While both incidents were harmful, Mommy said she was willing to put up with my teacher because I was "getting 100s with her racism." My sister, on the other hand, was having her test results falsified, and that my mother couldn't tolerate. She took action, removing us from the school with the racist teachers, and using my grandmother's address to enroll us in another one. (Today my mother's lie about our home address might result in her being charged with a crime.)[16]

By the time high-achieving black students get to college, it's very likely they'll have performed a lot of racism triage, which leads many to seek out institutions where they can stop. As one 2013 graduate of Spelman College puts it: "I wanted to go somewhere where I wasn't going to be 'the smart black girl.' I just wanted to be Racheal."

A musician and an international studies major, Racheal attended a performing arts high school, where she got excellent grades. She'd always planned to go to college, she says, but at some point during high school, she began to think about what it would mean to attend an elite school as a black student.

"You start to see patterns—you get into the honor courses,

and you're the only one. You get accepted into honor socie-
ties, and you're the only one," she says. "It wasn't something
that someone explicitly said. It was like, the writing's on the
wall."

Racheal chose Spelman, another outstanding HBCU in Atlanta, specifically to spare herself the experience of being "the
smart black girl." Black students at predominantly white institutions often aren't as lucky, and face tokenism, microag-
gressions, and outright disbelief that they belong. In a 2014
photo essay called "I, Too, Am Harvard," black Harvard students posed with texts that reflected some aspect of their college experience; one student held a sign that read "You're
Lucky to Be Black . . . So Easy to Get into College!" and at-
tributed the remark to a former friend.[17]

The institutions themselves perpetuate the problem, too,
by not considering the ways they deprive black or low-income
students of the same college experience as their white peers.
Take the work-study model, for example; why make a lower-
income student's attendance at the university contingent on
their employment there? Or consider on-campus job recruitment: Are colleges ensuring that the companies who recruit
have fair hiring practices, or are they providing opportunities
for white students at the expense of black students? Even the
question of who works for the university affects black and
white students differently: In 2018, a black student at Smith
College, an exclusive women's college in Massachusetts, was
eating lunch in a dormitory when the police arrived; an employee had called them, saying that the student "seemed out
of place."[18]

And because black enrollment at predominantly white institutions has not increased significantly over time, today's black students often find themselves fighting last century's civil rights battles over representation and fair treatment. At Emory University, where I teach, the undergraduate student population is just 8 percent black; a former student activist pointed out that a 2015 list of demands for a more equitable campus was depressingly similar to a list from 1969.

"All of these things historically have been asked for time and time again, and time and time again, the University has somehow pushed it to the side," former residence hall director and graduate Troizel Carr told the student newspaper. "Fifty years ago, students that looked like me were asking the same questions . . . and to this day, we still have not gotten the same things. And that's frustrating."[19] Among the unmet demands, forty-six years apart, were increases in black faculty and administrators, and counseling services geared toward the experiences of black students in predominantly white environments.

If the most selective and best-resourced colleges and universities (which receive the greatest tax breaks) aren't welcoming and accessible for black students, what does that leave? The broad pool of less selective four-year colleges, where black graduation rates decline regardless of income. Research shows that "six years after first enrolling in college, even higher-income black and Hispanic students are far less likely to have earned a bachelor's degree than their higher-income white peers (18 and 24 percentage points less, respectively)."[20]

To understand the reasons behind this discrepancy, we need to go from the top of the education pyramid to the bottom, where for-profit colleges lie. While students at for-profits are eligible for federal financial aid, that's essentially the only opportunity they have in common with students at nonprofits. For-profit institutions do not award scholarships because their goal is to increase returns for their shareholders, just like any other for-profit corporation. For-profits are focused on the bottom line and far more subject to the ups and downs of the economy—and only one in five black students who attends a for-profit college graduates. Eighty percent leave with significant debt and no degree.[21]

The abrupt closure of Argosy University in 2019 provides some insight into how this occurs. For years, Argosy was a chain of for-profit colleges operating around the United States, with 17,600 students enrolled across campuses in twelve states, including one in Atlanta. (Morehouse and Spelman, by contrast, have roughly 2,200 students each.) "We used to say that Argosy was the largest HBCU," says Chris, a behavioral health clinician in the juvenile court system who spent eight years at Argosy Atlanta—a program with 78 percent black enrollment—working toward her doctor of psychology degree. A single mother who helps care for her aging parents, Chris had previously earned a master's degree at Argosy, and felt the experience was a perfect fit for her lifestyle.

"My blood boils when I hear people say, 'For-profit schools, it's a joke,'" she says. "The professors, most of them were from really rigorous schools giving other adults, adults that were not traditional learners, working adults, a stellar education. We're going on weekends and evenings, and we're working, and we're getting our education and we're coming out into the industry with the knowledge."

Argosy's trouble began in 2017, when its parent group, Education Management Corporation (owned by several private equity groups, including Goldman Sachs), sold the chain of institutions to a new parent company, Dream Center Foundation, an offshoot of a California-based Pentecostal missionary group.[22] The new parent company, DCF, had never run educational institutions before, but said its goal was to transform all of the parent group's holdings into nonprofit colleges; in addition to all Argosy campuses, this included all campuses of The Art Institutes. (Several years earlier, the new CEO had tried and failed to convert another for-profit college into a nonprofit.)[23]

In hindsight, Chris says, she saw signs of disruption as soon as 2018. "Classes weren't meeting," she says. "It used to be the halls were teeming with people—then, all of a sudden, you started wondering how come stuff was messed up." Then, her aid was abruptly reduced, from $20,000 to $7,000, with no explanation. It didn't make sense, she said, but she assumed it was happening only to her.

In early 2019, she was beginning her dissertation when Argosy University abruptly announced that it was shuttering all its campuses—in some cases, within days. The plans to convert to a nonprofit had failed, and DCF entered receivership.

"They literally locked all the doors," she says.

The closure left Chris and thousands of other students with a no-win choice: retain their debt from Argosy and try to transfer some of their credits to another for-profit college, or discharge the debt and lose all the credit hours completed. After weeks of deliberation, Chris decided to discharge her debt—at this point close to $140,000, plus interest—and lose the work she'd done. Other for-profit schools recruited her, she says, but few accredited programs would accept all of her transferred credits—which would mean repeating and paying a second time for some courses, requiring additional loans on top of the $140,000 she owed for Argosy. Ultimately, she chose not to complete her doctorate, deciding that discharging her loans would offer greater value than any potential increased earnings from the degree.

"No one can take the knowledge that I have away," she says. But, unfortunately, the labor market values the degree alone (as we will see in the next chapter). According to Pay-Scale, the average salary for the holder of a doctorate in psychology is $78,000.[24] At the job she held when Argosy closed, Chris's salary was around $56,000.

Choosing a for-profit institution has inherently greater risks than choosing a nonprofit. But it's misguided to simply say that black Americans should make different choices. In her eloquent examination of for-profit schools, *Lower Ed*, Dr. Tressie McMillan Cottom, a sociology professor at the University of North Carolina at Chapel Hill, argues that nonprofit institutions, particularly selective ones, fetishize education without actually making space for people, like Chris, who require a more flexible or affordable system.

"Lower Ed can exist precisely because elite Higher Ed does," Dr. McMillan Cottom writes. "The latter legitimizes the education gospel while the former absorbs all manner of vulnerable groups who believe in it: single mothers, downsized workers, veterans, people of color, and people transitioning from welfare to work."[25]

Students at for-profit colleges are likely to be increasingly vulnerable in the years ahead, particularly since the 2019 repeal of an Obama-era policy requiring for-profit colleges to prove that their graduates could find gainful employment.[26] And even those who make it through statistically earn less than their peers in similar programs in the public sector. According to a Brookings Institution study, "public sector students outperform for-profit students on nearly every measure, suggesting that the overwhelming majority of for-profit students would be better off attending a public institution. But what if attending a public community college is not an option? Our results suggest that many for-profit students would be better off not attending college at all."[27]

So far, we've looked at how and why a small percentage of black Americans have the best outcomes at the top of the higher-education pyramid, while a significantly higher percentage experience the worst outcomes at for-profit institutions at the bottom. What about HBCUs—which offer some of the reputation and resources of elite institutions, while providing a majority-black experience?

At HBCUs black students don't have to be in the minority, an experience that many say has been critical to their well-being and personal development. Racheal, who longed to get away from being labeled "the smart black girl," had the college experience she'd hoped for at Spelman.

"There were girls who looked like me who were majoring in political science!" she says. "I'd never met somebody that looked like me who wanted to do political science."

Je'lon, the 2018 Morehouse graduate, says he simply felt more at ease at a majority-black college. "Black students who go to PWIs are often alone. They feel like a number; there's no sense of safe space," he says. "At an HBCU, you're able to have that safe space. You're able to grow and be around other black students who come from different walks of life."

Interestingly, even in environments that are designed explicitly to uplift and support black college students, graduation rates don't match those at elite institutions.[28] HBCUs, which include both private and public colleges, have overall graduation rates of 38 percent. However, that statistic doesn't tell the full story. Research shows that when you compare HBCUs and predominantly white institutions with a similar percentage of low-income students, HBCU graduation rates are higher—38 percent for HBCUs versus 32 percent for comparable PWIs.[29] Institutional resource disparity plays a significant role, too: just look at graduation rates and endowment levels. In Atlanta, Emory (predominantly white and ranked "most competitive" by *Barron's Profiles of American Colleges*) has a 93 percent graduation rate for black students; in 2019, its endowment was close to $7 billion. Spelman (considered "very competitive") has a 75 percent graduation rate and an endowment of $389 million. Morehouse (not ranked by *Barron's*) has a 54 percent graduation rate and an endowment of $145 million. Endowments, you'll remember, earn tax-free investment income, providing more funds for a better-resourced campus. HBCUs quite simply do more with less.

In addition, HBCUs are top-notch when it comes to economic mobility: Though they enroll a far greater percentage of low-income students than PWIs, more students experience upward mobility. Two-thirds of low-income students at HBCUs end up in at least the middle class, and nearly 70 percent of all HBCU students do the same. At Emory, in contrast, a 2017 report noted that only 13 percent of students moved up two or more income quintiles, and only 1.8 percent moved from the bottom to the top.[30]

Both Racheal and Je'lon, however, incurred significant debt to attend their respective HBCUs. Racheal graduated with approximately $65,000 in debt and, unable to afford the $500 monthly principal payment on her loans, chose to live in public housing after graduating so she could pay off the $160 monthly interest. Je'lon received a $15,000 annual tuition scholarship, took out loans, and received some financial assistance from his parents, who deferred their own loans and ultimately took jobs on opposite sides of the country to maximize their earning while he was in school.

"It can be frustrating to think about the fact that you have these student loans to pay off and it's going to take the rest of your life to pay them off," he says. "But just being at Morehouse College really changed my life."

Both Je'lon and Racheal have plans to pay off their debt—he received an undergraduate fellowship that will forgive some of his loans if he enrolls in a PhD program, and she plans to continue with stringent budgeting. However, their family circumstances reflect an unfortunate side effect of black educational achievement: Blacks attending college are more likely not only to take out student loans but also to take out larger student loans than white college students. Why? Because debt is the key mechanism of financing a college education for black students.[31]

White college students are far more likely to have their college education paid for by parents or grandparents, a form of what in tax law we call "family financial transfers." In a study that tracked college-educated households over a twenty-four-year period, researchers found that white heads of household were far more likely to have both received money for college from their own parents, and to have provided college funding to their children. Sixty percent of white heads of households reported that their parent paid for college, and 64 percent of white households reported that they had helped pay for their children's education, contributing on average close to $73,500. By contrast, only 37 percent of black heads of households reported that their parent had helped pay for college, and 34 percent reported that they had helped pay for their children's education. These parents also contributed less—just over $16,000 on average.[32] As a result, black graduates end up owing more than their white peers, a disparity that only increases over time.

Surprisingly, the trend holds even for black students from wealthy households, whose parents are unable to protect their children from debt the way the parents of their white peers do. Research shows that even at the top end of the wealth spectrum, black students have higher student loans than their white peers (an average of $4,643 versus $3,835), and black parents are more likely to take out greater loans to assist them ($3,303 versus $1,903). Dr. Fenaba R. Addo, Lorna Jorgenson Wendt Associate Professor in Money, Relationships, and Equality at the University of Wisconsin–Madison, has found that students with wealthier parents have less debt in general, but that changes when the data are disaggregated by race.

"As black parental wealth increases, we do not see black

student loan debt decreasing," she writes. "At the higher wealth ends, student loan debt is higher for blacks than whites."[33]

Why aren't wealthy black families contributing more? A common explanation for racial disparities in education, from the elementary to the college level, targets black parents as the culprits. This isn't just a right-wing talking point either; two 2020 Democratic presidential candidates, former New York City mayor Michael Bloomberg and former South Bend, Indiana, mayor Pete Buttigieg, explained achievement gaps in their cities by saying that black families lacked the experience to understand the value of an education.[34]

But the idea that black families simply don't see the value of education—that they contribute less to college tuition because they don't see education as a priority, and my parents, or Je'lon's, are outliers for being so dedicated to their children's education—is entirely incorrect.[35] In fact, the research reveals the opposite: A recent Pew Research survey showed that more than half of a group of black and Latinx parents surveyed (62 percent and 52 percent, respectively) said getting a college degree for their children was extremely important; among white parents, only 34 percent said the same.[36]

Controlling for socioeconomic factors, such as income, education level, and household type, black families are also more likely to make what researchers call "significant non-monetary" investments in their children's future education.[37] These can include anything from engaging their children in conversations about schoolwork at an early age to exposing them to cultural resources like museums. My mother often took me and my sister to New York's many museums (including my favorite, the American Museum of Natural History) and also made the major "nonmonetary investment" of pulling us out of the elementary school where we were targeted by racist teachers, and using my grandmother's address to enroll us in a better one. At that new elementary school, I met the teacher who selected me to sit for the entrance exam for one of the city's best public high schools—Hunter College High School—which prepared me for anything the selective college I attended, Fordham University, had in store for me. My parents' nonmonetary investments changed my life. (If you're asking where my father was in all this, his smartest nonmonetary investment was to let Miss Dottie handle the decisions about our education!)

Those are clear indications that black parents are indeed at least as committed to the education of their children as are white parents—if not more so. The Pew study also showed the importance of parental financial support in eliminating the college graduation gap. Without financial support, only 11.2 percent of black children complete college, compared with 25 percent of white children. However, with financial support, the percentages of whites (68 percent) and blacks (66 percent) who complete college are comparable.

Why, then, is college debt so much more prevalent among all black families? I believe that loan-deferral programs, designed to lighten the load for those with student loans, are actually making things worse for them in the long run. In theory, deferral programs make it easier for students with significant debt to pursue advanced degrees; in practice, however, as interest accumulates, borrowers end up with a balance higher than the original principal. Consider how black college graduates are more likely to enroll in graduate school compared with their white peers (47 percent versus 38 percent) and more likely to have graduate school debt (40 percent versus 22 percent).[38] A graduate degree should position them for better earnings that will reduce their student loan debt. (We'll look at the ways the labor market undermines this assumption, and restricts black mobility, in chapter 4.) However, if they have outstanding student loans from their undergraduate degrees (statistically likely) and need to defer those payments while in graduate school, both the outstanding loans plus any unpaid interest will accumulate, increasing the principal balance over time. As a result, the interest on their undergraduate debt is deferred and graduate school debt adds even more.

Income-based repayment, which black college graduates use nearly twice as much as their white counterparts, also plays a role.[39] Income-based repayment reduces the amount borrowers are legally obligated to pay, based on their income. But, as with graduate school deferrals, the unpaid balance accumulates interest and increases the overall outstanding debt. Both of these programs were created with the best of intentions, but both are leading to ever-increasing black student debt.

Je'lon and his mother, Veronica, are using both of these plans to address their loan debt; he is deferring his loans while he pursues his graduate degrees, and she uses income-based repayment for hers. Veronica is a former special education teacher now working for the Norfolk Naval Shipyard in Virginia. She has a bachelor's degree in organizational study and a master's in special education. She deferred her loans to help Je'lon pay for his education at Morehouse; with interest, she estimates she now owes $270,000, which she's paying off using income-based repayment at a monthly rate of $170. Even so, she says she'd do it again—she was the first in her family to attend college, and the value of the degree is worth the steep price she's paying.

"Education is not a wealthy line of work," she says. "You get a lot of your reward from reaching students and changing their lives. It was a passion of mine, and that's why I pursued it."

The federal government does have some provisions for loan forgiveness that might apply to someone like Veronica. If she'd worked as a special ed teacher in a public school for ten years, she might qualify for Public Service Loan Forgiveness (PSLF), which would discharge her remaining loan balance tax-free. At least, that's the idea. In practice, 99 percent of applications for Public Service Loan Forgiveness were rejected in the program's first year, which spanned from May 2018 to May 2019;[40] this year, that number has crept down slightly—to a little over 97 percent.[41] Assuming Veronica doesn't qualify for PSLF, she may be able to get the balance of her loan forgiven after twenty or twenty-five years of on-time payments under her income-based plan—but since the amount of the forgiven debt will be treated as income, she'll be hit with a potentially massive tax bill.[42] Taking into account Veronica's periods of deferral and the tax consequences of "forgiveness," there's a good chance she'll be paying her loans forever.

The failure of deferral and income-based repayment programs, we see, is significant. But it doesn't address why black students borrow so much in the first place. That answer lies in what we learned in the last chapter: Higher-income black parents have less home equity, and other assets, than their white peers. Remember how the white families in the twenty-four-year study both received money from their parents and gave it to their children more frequently and in larger amounts than black families? Home equity, and the various opportunities it provides for wealth building, is less available to black families. That's true both historically, which accounts for the lack of funds received from parents, and in the present day, which explains the lack of funds provided for children. Some of these heads of households were in college in the mid- to late 1970s, meaning when they were growing up, housing discrimination was not only common but legal. Today, as we saw in the last chapter, black and white Americans still buy homes in different neighborhoods and receive unequal returns, and consistent growth in home equity (meaning you can sell for a profit or receive more on a home equity loan) still comes from living in a predominantly white neighborhood.

Another part of the explanation for increased borrowing by black students is that even wealthy black parents have fewer liquid financial assets like stocks that can be sold to pay for college. (Wealthy black Americans hold their wealth differently from their white peers, something I will discuss more in chapter 5.) Both of these differences make it harder for black parents, even the small percentage of them with significant wealth, to protect their children from graduating with student debt.

This is where tax policy comes into play again, rewarding white choices and punishing black ones at both individual and institutional levels. What Robert Smith did for those Morehouse Men, however great, cannot fix the systemic nature of the problem: With statistically less family wealth, black Americans are more likely to attend colleges whose smaller endowments inhibit them from awarding scholarships at the same level as elite, mostly predominantly white institutions. This leads black students to take on more debt to finance their education. White students, in contrast, are more likely to both attend universities with substantial endowments and have family members who contribute to their educations. Both of these paths have tax policies associated with them, and once again those policies make things better for white Americans and worse for black Americans.

Back when very few Americans, and almost exclusively the wealthy, attended college, their families received significant tax breaks that continue today. If the bank of Mom and Dad (or Grandma and Grandpa) is paying for you to attend college, that money is treated as a tax-free gift to you for federal income tax purposes, provided it's sent directly to the educational institution.[43] Let's pretend that I attend Emory and have a grandparent who can afford to cover the $55,998 for tuition and fees Emory charged for the 2020–21 academic year. (My paternal grandmother, Bertha, was a domestic worker, and my maternal great-grandfather was born enslaved in South Carolina in 1862, so this isn't a particularly likely scenario, but stay with me.) If Grandma Bertha were to give me the money as a gift, it would be tax-free for her only to the extent of $15,000; she would need to account (for gift tax purposes) for the other $40,998. But if she could write a $55,998 tuition check directly to Emory University, the entire amount would be tax-free and there would be no need to further account for it.[44] (Under current law, this is largely an academic distinction. Even if Grandma Bertha did give the money directly to me, requiring her to account for it on her taxes, it's unlikely she'd actually reach the threshold required for gifts to be taxed. Tax-free family transfers will be discussed in more detail in chapter 5.)

As college became more accessible with the passing of the GI Bill after World War II, the tax treatment of scholarships became more important. Recall, however, that black veterans were still subject to Jim Crow laws. Those laws prevented them from taking advantage of government benefits to become homeowners. When it came to accessing benefits for college, something similar took place: Black veterans were denied entry to historically white universities and had to choose from a limited number of HBCUs, where officials at the Veterans Administration (today the Department of Veterans Affairs) often steered them toward vocational training instead of college.[45]

In the early days of the income tax, the IRS took the position that receipt of a scholarship in exchange for education was an exchange of services, which made scholarships taxable income. Congress, however, disagreed. In 1954, the same year that *Brown v. Board of Education* was decided, it established a tax exclusion for scholarships.[46] Those milestones, plus the creation of Pell Grants for low-income families as part of the Higher Education Act of 1965, led to significant gains in college attendance rates.[47] The number of white men, white women, and black women attending college had nearly doubled by 1970; the number of black men tripled.

The Pell Grant program represents one of the few scholarship exclusion advantages that black students disproportionately benefit from: Pell Grants are awarded by income, and roughly 70 percent of black college students receive them compared with 34 percent of whites.[48] In 1975, a Pell Grant covered 79 percent of the average costs of tuition, fees, room, and board at a public four-year college.[49]

The next major shift in education tax policy took place in 1986, when the deduction for all personal interest—except mortgage interest—was repealed, and student loan interest was no longer deductible. At the same time, federal tuition subsidies were being branded as an unfair burden to taxpayers who did not attend college. The Reagan administration's Office of Management and Budget director, David Stockman, testifying before Congress in 1981, referred to federal subsidies for higher education like Pell Grants and guaranteed student loans as "entitlements that we created in the 1970s" and "excessive";[50] shortly after the 1986 Tax Reform Act became law, Bill Bennett, the secretary of education, wrote in a *New York Times* op-ed: "On average, college graduates earn $640,000 more over their lifetimes than nongraduates do. It is simply not fair to ask taxpayers, many of whom do not go to college, to pay more than their fair share of the tuition burden."[51]

A decade later, when college costs had grown and the maximum Pell Grants were not keeping pace, two more changes took place. In 1996, 529 plans that provide favorable tax treatment for certain college savings accounts were approved by Congress. Money deposited into the account by parents or other family members is from after-tax dollars, and the investment income is not taxed as the account grows. In addition, any withdrawals for tuition, books, and room and board are treated as tax-free intrafamily gifts. To participate, of course, a family must have extra income to set aside, and as of 2012, only about 3 percent of Americans were saving for college using a tax-preferred account, according to the Government Accountability Office.[52] Of those, 84 percent were white and 5 percent were black. A Federal Reserve study showed that the average black family's balance was $27,068, while the average white family's balance was $40,786.[53]

A year later, Congress shifted its position again, and student loan interest became an allowable deduction.[54] A white dental student named Jennifer Long testified before the Senate Committee on Finance, advocating for the change. She told committee members that she would owe $90,000 upon graduation, which she would pay in installments of $1,100 per month. She estimated that she would pay $7,500 in interest in her first year of repayment. (She also called out the hypocrisy of the Republicans' line of attack on student borrowers, given that the mortgage interest deduction had survived the 1986 reforms despite primarily benefiting the wealthy.)

"I could only afford to attend dental school with loans, and for many other students and parents, loans are the only way to finance their higher education," she said in her testimony. "Oddly, the Tax Code allows for individuals to deduct for a second house, but not for a first education."[55]

Congress agreed to change the tax code, but with a catch: As it still stands today, the maximum interest deduction is $2,500, and you cannot take any deduction if your income is above $85,000 for an individual, or $170,000 for a married couple. Jennifer Long did not get the Seaborn treatment. Even if she'd met the income requirements, a tax break that capped the interest deduction at $2,500 was not going to do much good for someone like her with an annual interest payment of $7,500.

It doesn't do much good for a lot of black college graduates either. Take the research mentioned earlier in the chapter that shows black college graduates, four years out, have $53,000 in student loans, while whites have $28,000. Assume a 6 percent interest rate, a ten-year term, and income that does not disqualify you for the deduction.

With $28,000 of debt, at that rate and term, the white college graduate will pay a total of $310.86 per month. Of that, roughly $135 will be interest each month during the first year, for a total of $1,622.67 in interest the first year. Because $1,622.67 is less than the $2,500 cap, all interest will be deducted. So in the first year, the white graduate will be eligible to deduct *all* of their student loan interest, and each year thereafter, the interest paid will decrease, as the principal decreases.

With $53,000 of debt, at the same rate and term, the black college graduate will pay $588.41 per month. Of that, roughly $260 will be interest each month during the first year, for a total of $3,071.48 in interest. Because the interest deduction is capped at $2,500, the black student cannot deduct the excess. Like the white graduate, the black graduate will see a decrease in the interest each year, and will eventually be able to deduct all of it when it falls under $2,500—but they'll have to wait a while before that happens. (By my calculations, this hypothetical graduate's loan interest would be fully deductible in years 3 through 10.)

White Americans are less likely than blacks to finance their college expenses through student loans, but more likely to benefit from the student loan tax subsidy when they do. And black Americans are far more likely to finance their college education with debt, but less likely than whites to be eligible to deduct *all* of their interest payments on their debt—especially if they're lucky enough to get a job that pays reasonably well.

It can get even worse: If two black college graduates get married, they're statistically likely to enter the marriage with significant loan debt. As single taxpayers, they can each deduct up to $2,500 of student loan interest. But if they are married and file a joint return, the maximum amount of student loan interest they can deduct between the two of them remains $2,500.[56] And the deduction decreases as income increases—if you earned more than $85,000 as a single person in 2020, you were ineligible. Compare this with the mortgage interest deduction, which, as we've seen, has no restrictions based on marital status or income.

There are both historical and contemporary reasons that black student debt remains a drag on wealth building, but hidden in plain sight is a tax system that rewards those who can pay for college outright, and those people are mostly white. This results in black families carrying more student debt than their white peers, which, as we saw when comparing the debt loads and interest payments of the average black graduate and average white graduate, has a snowball effect on the black-white wealth gap.[57] And that example was the best-case scenario, in which a black graduate's principal and interest are reduced over time. If a graduate is limited to income-based repayment or defers, the interest accumulates and is added to the principal, making repayment even more out of reach. Dr. Jason Houle, associate professor of sociology at Dartmouth College (along with his co-author, Dr. Addo), researched student debt and race and found that student loan debt accounts for "about 10 percent" of the racial wealth gap when a college graduate is twenty-five years old; by age thirty or thirty-five, it explains 25 percent of the wealth gap.

The apparent solution, according to many progressive politicians, is to forgive all federal student loan debt. Blanket student loan forgiveness would disproportionately benefit black college students—both dropouts and graduates—and I support it, with some conditions. I'd want to make sure the forgiveness itself was tax-free, and not treated as taxable income, and to extend the same relief to debt taken out by parents to finance their children's education—which is what ultimately happened for the Morehouse Men and their families—because that, too, would disproportionately benefit black parents.

However, loan forgiveness is unlikely to actually level the playing field. For example, 30 percent of people with incomes over $114,000—a group that is predominantly white—carry student loan debt; loan forgiveness for them would still largely benefit white wealth building.[58] And most student loan forgiveness plans do not include Direct PLUS loans, higher-interest loans taken out by parents that are common among black families.[59] Canceling all student loan debt, while helping many black families, will not reduce the black-white wealth gap; the only way to do that would be to cancel *only* black

student loan debt, and it's unlikely any debt-canceling proposal based on race will be upheld as constitutional.

Targeted debt relief will do more to reduce the racial
wealth gap than blanket debt relief, but here, too, obstacles
remain. A white family with low income is likely to still have
greater wealth than a black family with a similar income, so
targeting debt relief based on household income may exclude
some high-income blacks with significant student loan debt
and include low-income whites who still have greater wealth
than the average black family. (Remember, even if your family
pays for your college education and gives you a down payment
on a house, you can still technically be low-income.) For that
reason, my preference would be to target relief based on
wealth and not income.

As for tax reform, to keep this problem from replicating,
my first step would be to increase Pell Grants; rising tuitions
have made them far less effective than they were designed to
be. In 2020–21, the maximum grant was $6,345, which covers
less than 30 percent of the average tuition and fees at a public
four-year college; when the program was first put into place,
Pell Grants covered nearly 80 percent of these costs.[60] Raising
the maximum Pell Grant so that it covers more of tuition,
room and board, and course materials would both increase
the percentage of blacks who *graduate* and help more blacks
to graduate debt-free. On an institutional level, Pell Grants
should be restricted to those schools that have high graduation rates for black students. Currently, the highest graduation
rates among Pell Grant recipients are at private not-for-profit
colleges and universities;[61] the lowest graduation rates are at
for-profit colleges.

This would, of course, be expensive. How do we pay for it? Well, first, remember the huge tax breaks that not-for-profit colleges receive in the form of exemptions—the most selective colleges and universities are, by and large, sitting on a lot of tax-exempt money. As admissions expert Jon Boeckenstedt told *The New York Times Magazine* in 2019, "Some of the most selective colleges have so much money that they could easily admit freshman classes made up entirely of academically excellent Pell-eligible students and charge them nothing at all. . . . But not only do those and other selective colleges not take that step; they generally do the opposite, year after year. As a group, they admit fewer Pell-eligible students than almost any other institutions."[62]

Based on this premise—that selective colleges can afford to fix this, but choose not to—I propose an income tax levied on the institutions at the very top of the higher-ed pyramid, with endowments greater than $750 million. For decades, largely white administrators at selective universities have chosen to maintain the status quo (only sometimes tinkering around the edges). At the very least, we can make them pay for the right they've held, explicitly or implicitly, to maintain overwhelmingly white student bodies. Yes, the Supreme Court, with its burden of proof for racial discrimination, constrains what universities can do specifically for black students. However, they are not without options for more aggressive recruiting policies when it comes to low-income students or Pell Grant recipients. (And for perspective, in fiscal year 2017, 120 schools had endowments of at least $800 million; the highest-endowed HBCU, Howard University, had less than $700 million in its endowment.)[63]

Sunlight must be cast on the revenue losses caused by the endowment exemptions, and the other tax breaks colleges and universities receive, such as exemptions from property taxes. (The Treasury, oddly, projects revenue losses for education tax breaks claimed by individuals but not institutions; estimates show that the endowment exemption alone results in $13 billion lost annually, and I suspect that number is low.) Such exemptions enable selective colleges to hoard resources, taking them away from their surrounding communities—and for many of the most selective colleges at the top of the pyramid, these communities often include largely black or brown neighborhoods with underfunded K–12 schools (underfunded, of course, because their neighbors, the colleges, do not pay property taxes).

However, even with these arguments, taxing extremely wealthy, selective institutions will not be easy, because as we've seen, the wealthy have significant influence over tax policy. My reforms would get pushback and be difficult to enact. Once the 2017 Tax Cuts and Jobs Act went into effect, and Stanford University, with its almost $30 billion endowment as of February 2020, was found to owe $43 million, it pushed back with the force of a thousand furies (or the academic equivalent). Stanford said the tax was going to hurt students by forcing the university to reduce financial aid. Next it vowed to work on repealing the tax or lessening its impact. Wealthy not-for-profits facing a tax increase, like wealthy individuals, will fight against it and leverage their considerable resources in the process. An easier change would be to increase the amount of interest that is deductible for student loan debt. If mortgage interest is allowed for up to $750,000 of debt, then we can certainly afford an unlimited deduction for student loan interest.

When it comes to higher education and tax reform, however, the real solutions lie at the institutional level. Current tax subsidies for education generally do nothing to disrupt the current system, which makes it hard for blacks to gain access to the schools that provide the best return on investment. For-profits prey on the vulnerable without transparency, and selective colleges and universities—which have made little progress in several decades on increasing black enrollments in spite of their superior graduation rates for black students who matriculate—benefit from a federally subsidized system that must be radically changed.

The late Supreme Court justice Louis Brandeis said "sunlight is said to be the best of disinfectants," and such exposure, at a minimum, should be a tax-exemption requirement for nonprofit colleges and universities. Colleges must publish annually, on their websites, debt loads and scholarship information by race, as well as by family income and wealth. Recent research discussed in *The New York Times* offered a look at how some colleges (notably the City University of New York, where 24 percent of the student body is black) effectively bring lower-income students into higher-income classes, but was focused on economic and not racial diversity.[64] When the research leaves race out of the conversation, we ignore the struggles and challenges faced by the black middle class, which then contributes to the view that solving class issues will resolve most black problems. We need detailed information about both race and income if we are serious about making college an engine of growth for all.

Exposing this information should also result in some introspection, by colleges, about how they incorporate black students into campus life. We've already seen how the well-being of black students often simply isn't a priority—just look at the Emory protests in 1969 and in 2015. But the introspection needs to go beyond hiring black faculty and administrators, to look at whether black and white students have the same opportunities to benefit from the social and preprofessional connections built at college. I lived at home during college because I did not want to go into debt for room and board, and I have no regrets—in fact, I was spoiled rotten by my mother's cooking and laundry service. Because I didn't make friends with my classmates outside of the classroom, I wasn't able to build the social connections that could have helped me with a future job or promotion. As we've seen, socializing with wealthy white students will probably come with its own form of racism triage, but that doesn't mean institutions should restrict black students' opportunities. At the end of the day it should be the black students' choice, and the institution should empower that.

Similarly, not-for-profit colleges and universities (both public and private) need to do a better job of accommodating nontraditional students who have been steered toward for-profit colleges. Perhaps one upside of COVID-19 has been the increased use of online courses by selective institutions (and higher education more broadly), which may allow for better outreach to those vulnerable to the for-profit industry going forward. Students like Chris, and the hundreds of others who missed out on their degrees when Argosy University closed, deserve the opportunity to achieve better outcomes.

College degrees generally translate into higher income, but those who do not graduate—the majority of black college students—leave without degrees and saddled with debt. Among those who attend for-profit colleges, an even greater majority do not graduate. Since the Great Recession, 95 percent of jobs filled went to applicants with at least some college.[65] The wage premium has risen significantly for a college degree.[66] So I understand the drive of black Americans to pursue higher education. Degrees, however, do not fix racial income or wealth inequality. White Americans without a four-year college degree earn less than blacks with a college degree, but they still have more than twice the family net worth.[67] Black households headed by a college graduate have less wealth than white households *headed by a high school dropout*.[68] College, like marriage and homeownership, is only one part of the black wealth story. The next chapter—both in this book and in a black graduate's life—involves taking that debt-laden college degree into the labor market.

FOUR

THE BEST JOBS

Racheal, the Spelman College graduate we met in the last chapter, has never been afraid of hard work. At age seven, she offered to walk her neighbors' trash to the shared dumpster for a dollar per bag and spent the profits at the ice cream truck. Throughout high school she worked in retail and telemarketing, saving diligently for college. As an undergraduate, eager to get experience and discover new interests, she worked hard to secure internships at well-known corporations. One, at a major consumer goods manufacturer, seemed to offer the opportunity to work on a marketing campaign about black women's health and beauty products; another, at an information technology company, offered training in a fast-growing field.

Unfortunately, Racheal's entry into the corporate labor market wasn't all she'd hoped for. At the information technology company, Racheal found herself isolated in a predominantly white office located in a predominantly white town. At the consumer goods manufacturer, she asked to be included on the project about black women and was told there was no room on the majority-white team. Her boss—a white woman—frequently disparaged Racheal's education at a performing arts high school, telling her, "I know you like to sing and dance. You're not really the science type."

"I thought, 'Maybe corporate America just isn't for me,'" Racheal recalls. "So that's when I decided to look into the nonprofit route."

Building on a connection she'd made at a student leadership conference in college, she applied for and got a job with an Atlanta nonprofit that focused on diversifying the field of environmental conservation. The organization had black leadership and a majority-black staff—a welcome change. But the salary was so low that Racheal qualified to live in public housing, and she didn't have health insurance until she'd been at the company for two years. She was determined to keep paying off her student loans and establish her own retirement savings account, but her efforts left very little for other expenses. Healthcare became a treat, instead of a given.

"They didn't provide vision or dental, so whenever I did have to go to the dentist, it was coming straight out of pocket—and the dentist was not cheap," Racheal says. "For Christmas, or my birthday, my mom was always like, 'What do you want?' I'd say, 'If you could just pay for me to go to the dentist I would call it even.'"

For many black workers like Racheal, entering an anti-black labor market is rife with challenges. Whether the discrimination is overt—like Racheal's supervisor suggesting she liked to "sing and dance"—or harder to prove, most black workers will struggle, over the course of their careers, to gain employment and succeed in it. The unemployment rate for black college graduates is higher now than it was fifty years ago.[1] Black graduates of elite colleges have to send out an average of eight applications to receive an interview, while white graduates send six.[2] Chris, the Argosy University student, attended Xavier University, an HBCU, for her undergraduate degree and says the career advice she received there was explicitly about how to create résumés that could beat the sorting algorithms on recruiting websites, then prepare for job interviews enough to overcome the stigma of being an identifiably black candidate. "It was talked about: Some people just don't want to hire from HBCUs," she says. "There was a lot of, 'You need to do your homework and prepare.'"

Once a black graduate is employed, things don't necessarily improve: Black workers consistently receive less compensation and have their performance judged by different standards.[3] At the highest graduate and professional levels, black workers over a lifetime earn close to a million dollars less than their white peers.[4]

That's because when it comes to employee compensation, salary is only part of the picture—approximately two-thirds, according to a recent study by the Institute on Assets and Social Policy. One-third of employee compensation comes in the form of benefits like health insurance and a retirement account, which come with significant tax advantages for both the employer and the employee. Employees are able to contribute a portion of their income to a retirement account, paying taxes on the money only when they retire, while employers can deduct both employee salaries and payments made to the trusts that hold the retirement funds, resulting in less reported taxable income and therefore lower taxes.[5] Health insurance premiums are deducted by employers as well as excluded from reported income by employees.[6] Those two perks are significant because retirement accounts enable wealth building, while good health insurance can prevent wealth depletion.

For those employees with access to the tax-subsidized perks, participating is a win-win. Unfortunately, as in so many other areas, a seemingly straightforward tax break leaves out most black employees. The occupational segregation that defines the labor market works both within companies and across industries. So not only do qualified black workers often earn less than their white peers—giving them less income to put into a retirement account—but they are less likely to have access to a retirement account or health benefits at all. Occupational segregation constrains black wealth building by creating "white" jobs and "black" jobs, and tax policy does not treat those jobs the same way.

Like so many of today's implicitly racist systems, this is rooted in America's explicitly racist past. In the labor market, full access to government subsidies has often been preconditioned on being white. (Think back to previous chapters: Who could get an FHA-insured mortgage? Which returning World War II veterans could access college benefits?) Wage discrimination was explicit and legal in the early twentieth century. The Fair Labor Standards Act of 1938 (FLSA), which included minimum-wage provisions, excluded farm laborers and domestic workers specifically because those were majority-black occupations—according to the 1930 census, 65 percent of all black workers were in one of the two fields.[7] Several members of Congress objected to creating equal wage standards for black and white workers as the bill was being debated, but Florida congressman James Mark Wilcox's explanation was most plain: "There has always been a difference in the wage scale of white and colored labor. . . . We may rest assured, therefore, that when we turn over to a federal bureau or board the power to fix wages, it will prescribe the same wage for the Negro that it prescribes for the white man. Now, such a plan might work in some sections of the United States but those of us who know the true situation know that it just will not work in the South. You cannot put the Negro and the white man on the same basis and get away with it."[8]

The lack of wage protections meant that black workers were simply not considered when retirement plans became more common among American workers during World War II. Those retirement plans had become tied to employment as "an unintended byproduct of its wartime efforts to standardize tax policies and regulate wages," writes the sociologist Beth Stevens.[9] In 1942, two acts of Congress—the Revenue Act and the Stabilization Act—incentivized employers to create pensions and offer other benefits. Pensions, which are typically sponsored by an employer or union, allow both workers and companies to set a portion of their earnings into a retirement account. Workers avoid paying taxes on the contribution, or on any interest earned on the account, which is typically invested. There are two different types of employment-based

retirement accounts: defined benefit plans and defined contribution plans. Defined benefit plans, more commonly referred
to as pensions, are generally found in union-represented work-
places. A defined benefit plan guarantees a payout at retirement, regardless of how much is invested. It's low-risk for
employees and puts the burden of the payout on the employer—
which is why employers don't like them, and in recent decades
have shifted toward defined contribution plans. Defined contribution plans like 401(k) accounts, which are now the most
common kind of employment-based retirement plan, depend
on worker contributions, sometimes with employer-matched
funds. They also don't guarantee income; if, at retirement, a
worker's account balance is $1,000, that's the sum total of the
worker's retirement benefit. In both cases, any money set aside
by the employer to provide that payout is treated as tax-free to
the employee, though the employee does pay taxes on money
when it is withdrawn at retirement or when the retiree turns
seventy-two.

Retirement accounts allow people to have income once
they stop working—without them, many more Americans
would spend their final decades in poverty—but don't think
they were created out of care and concern for older workers.
The Revenue Act of 1942 incentivized companies to create
pensions by levying a huge tax (between 80 percent and 90
percent) on excess profits—defined as corporate profits that
were greater than they'd been prior to the war.[10] Companies
could avoid the tax by placing some profits into pension
trusts, and then deducting those amounts from their overall
profits.

At the same time, Congress enacted the Stabilization Act

of 1942, which created wage controls limiting raises, but excluded benefits such as health insurance and pensions from those controls.[11] The Revenue Act forced employers to find new ways to compete for the best workers (who in their minds were white), and tax-free benefits were a way to attract them. Two key provisions of the Revenue Act led more employers to provide more benefits: One required pension plans to cover at least 70 percent of employees in order for the employer to receive tax breaks; and a second stated that the calculation of benefits could not be skewed in favor of high-income workers. Employers can't, for example, agree to a 1 percent 401(k) contribution for wages up to $50,000 and then an additional 15 percent contribution for the excess over $50,000, because it would benefit higher-compensated employees. So as the percentage of Americans subject to tax increased, these tax-free benefits moved down the income scale from higher-income to lower- and middle-class white working taxpayers. Between 1941 and 1945, contributions to pension trusts went from $171 million to $857 million, and by the end of World War II, health insurance coverage tripled and pension coverage increased by a third.[12]

Black workers, however, simply weren't part of the new wave of employment incentives and protections. By deliberately leaving majority-black occupations out of the Fair Labor Standards Act, Congress ensured that black workers would have to work for whatever wages an employer wanted to provide—and forget about raises or pensions. Employers were permitted to pay black workers less, keep them out of jobs that could be filled by white workers, and exclude them from insurance and benefit plans, all with the legal backing of the federal government.

Take my father, for example: Daddy was a plumber who worked for many years for a small private company. Though his boss, Mr. Gelman, was very generous (you may recall he helped my parents buy their house), like most small employers he did not offer health insurance or a retirement plan. For years, my parents worked and raised a family paying for our healthcare with after-tax dollars, and like Racheal, we were very lucky to avoid serious illness. My parents couldn't afford to pay for dentist visits for all four of us, so Miss Dottie took only me and my sister.

There were better jobs out there for a skilled plumber, and the best of them were in the public sector, which offered tax-free health insurance and a defined benefit plan. From 1950 to 1970 the proportion of the workforce with some type of health insurance through their jobs went from roughly 50 percent to 80 percent.[13] Almost 50 percent of workers in the private sector had retirement plans, more than twice the percentage in 1950. But my father was not one of those employees.

To get a job in the coveted public sector, you had to belong to the union. In fact, the existence of the union was part of the reason the job was so coveted; the expansion in benefits like pension and health insurance in the postwar years was due in large part to collective bargaining. But the union was famous for creating obstacles that prevented nonwhite workers from joining. In 1964, there were only sixteen black plumbers in the union, out of a total of 4,100. When the city forced a contractor to hire four nonwhite plumbers on a huge project in the Bronx that year, the union plumbers walked off the job.[14]

When the Civil Rights Act was passed later that year, the unions were forced to integrate, and in the mid-1970s my father got a job with the New York City Housing Authority. My father died in 1994, and the pension he earned, thanks to the union, continues to support my mother. But he worked for twenty years before he had access to the same wealth-building benefits as the city's white plumbers.

Thanks to the Civil Rights Act, today's employers aren't permitted to openly offer higher wages and better benefits plans to white employees. But the explicit discrimination of the FLSA laid the groundwork for the implicit discrimination that is alive and well in the labor market today, excluding black Americans from jobs that offer health insurance and retirement accounts. If we think of retirement accounts as a pyramid (the way we did with higher education), then the best, those at the top, are defined benefit plans, followed by employer-matching defined contribution accounts. At the bottom are IRAs: They're available to anyone with earned income, but employees are responsible for funding them and paying any fees associated with them. Over the last few decades, the percentage of employees covered by defined contribution as opposed to defined benefit plans has significantly increased—from 41 percent in 1985 to 61.3 percent in 2010, according to my research.[15]

When it comes to who gets what kind of retirement account, the racial divide is stark. The Bureau of Labor Statistics classifies jobs outside of service, sales, transportation, and construction as "professional and related occupations"; this broad category includes everything from architect to zoologist, but what these jobs have in common is that they're the most likely to come with tax-free perks.[16] Almost two-thirds (66.4 percent) of employers in those professional industries sponsor retirement accounts, and their workforce is 80 percent white and 9.4 percent black.

In contrast, in the service occupations, which includes custodians or restaurant staff, and where retirement sponsorship rates are only around 34 percent, black Americans make up 16.8 percent of the workforce. If we narrow the focus, black overrepresentation and white underrepresentation increase. Dr. Tatjana Meschede, associate director of the IASP and senior scientist at the Heller School for Social Policy and Management, described in her co-authored research: "Historical legacy and contemporary employment practices concentrate Black and Latino working people disproportionately in jobs and industries stripped of or lacking in benefits that connect work to wealth and better livelihoods."[17]

The healthcare industry, for example, is one of the fastest-growing fields in the country today, projected to add about 1.9 million new jobs by 2028. The median annual wage for practitioners and technical employees (such as doctors, nurses, and dental hygienists) is more than one and a half times higher than the median wage for all occupations, but the median annual wage for workers in health support fields, like health aides and assistants, is below that median.[18]

Guess which are the "white" jobs and which are the "black" jobs—the ones where the pay is better or worse than the median?

Meschede and her colleagues found that while black workers made up 16 percent of the healthcare labor force, they are more than three times as likely to work as lower-paid health aides than their white counterparts. And even when black and white healthcare workers earned comparable salaries, there were huge discrepancies in their overall wealth, which Meschede's report attributes to the lack of access to "asset-building benefits"—the health insurance and retirement benefits that make up one-third of total employee compensation. Black health aides earning $23,100 in income had median wealth of $900; white health aides earning $23,600 had median wealth of $5,300. Among registered nurses, black and white nurses reporting comparable incomes near $55,000 reported median wealth of $20,000 and $93,500, respectively.

A common argument, when it comes to both care and compensation in the health field, focuses on education and training. It's true that home health aides and anesthesiologists don't require the same levels of training and certification to do their jobs, and becoming a physician requires significant financial investment. However, the healthcare field isn't an outlier when it comes to these racial wealth discrepancies; it's the standard. Meschede and her colleagues found that the discrepancies exist across industries, regardless of education or specialization, including in highly paid fields like technology and finance. Not only were blacks and Latinos underrepresented in STEM fields, Meschede found, "for Black employees, pay is also significantly lower than Whites in finance and STEM with the same degrees. While incomes increase for all in more highly compensated sectors, the gains from entering a higher-paying field are not shared equally."[19]

And it's important to remember that income is not the same as wealth, and increases in income alone will not compensate for lack of benefits. Researchers found that median wealth would go up substantially for black workers in all fields if they had equal coverage rates for employer-based healthcare and pensions: a 25 percent increase if health access were equalized, and a 53 percent increase if pension rates were equalized.

Unfortunately, in the twenty-first-century economy, the wealth building associated with benefits is even less accessible than it used to be. Increasingly, corporations avoid hiring full-time direct workers, and instead hire long- or short-term sub-contractors. It's a win for the corporation, which gets the labor without having to provide the guaranteed salary or benefits that full-time employees receive. However, the practice is creating a new form of occupational segregation, where white workers are more likely to have direct jobs, and nonwhite workers are more likely to have contract jobs. A 2016 report on subcontracting and diversity in Silicon Valley revealed that while black and Latino workers made up 10 percent of direct-hire employees, they constituted 26 percent of white-collar contract hires and 58 percent of blue-collar contract hires. "Contract workers often do not have access to the generous health, parental leave, child care, employee shuttles, and other benefits that tech companies offer their core employees," the report noted.[20]

They also miss out on bonuses like profit sharing—a policy that Atlanta-based Delta Air Lines Inc. has used as a big public relations boost. In February 2020, the airline announced a $1.6 billion profit-sharing bonus of roughly two months' pay for its employees. "For years, I would get beaten up by Wall Street," CEO Ed Bastian said at an event at the Cobb Chamber of Commerce in Atlanta. "They thought the profits were theirs, and 'Why are you giving the profits away to the employees?' Wall Street has actually come full circle, and they realize that Delta is the most awarded airline in the world because of its employees."[21]

However, Bastian didn't mention the ninety thousand contract workers—who push Delta passengers in wheelchairs, operate Delta connection regional flights, and at some airports check in customers and handle their baggage—who, because they were not direct employees, didn't get a share of the profits.[22]

Occupational segregation has existed for as long as there have been occupations, and studies across the board point to it—whether calling it out blatantly as "hiring discrimination" or referring to it more obliquely as "unconscious bias"—as a major factor in the black-white wealth gap. It's not coincidental that black workers are primarily the low-paid aides in healthcare or the subcontractors without benefits in the tech world. Breaking into the lucrative and white-dominated professional fields can be a difficult and fraught process for the average black worker—even before he or she starts working.

Racism in the labor market begins with something as simple as a name. In a 2004 study, researchers crafted résumés with a white-sounding name and a black-sounding name, and sent them out in response to employment ads. Job applicants with white-sounding names needed to send out about ten résumés to get an invitation to interview, while job applicants with black-sounding names needed to send about fifteen résumés (50 percent more); the resulting paper was called "Are Emily and Greg More Employable Than Lakisha and Jamal?"[23]

Colleges—which, we've seen, already play a major role in

black wealth outcomes—are culpable when it comes to the labor market as well. The elite schools invite recruiters from top companies to campus, positioning their students to get competitive salary and benefit packages right after graduating. But the on-campus recruiting system doesn't work in black students' favor. Associate Professor Lauren Rivera of the Kellogg School of Management at Northwestern University studied how elite investment banks, management consulting companies, and law firms recruit, and found a consistent bias toward "white, upper-middle-class culture."[24] Instead of judging candidates on traditionally analyzed labor market signals such as grades, standardized test scores, prior employer prestige, or prior work experience, recruiters emphasized extracurricular activities and prioritized those that involved significant financial investment.[25] As a white male banker said about a candidate whose résumé expressed interest in community service: "I would ask him about the volunteering. . . . Does he drive around with his mom with Meals on Wheels, or did he go to Costa Rica and build houses with Habitat for Humanity?"[26]

The prize for giving the right answer? The ridiculously high salaries and tax-free benefit packages that are only available for those students who have the time and money to be able to pursue the "right" extracurricular activities. A college student like me, who worked to keep my debt load down, and had no idea that grades weren't the only thing that mattered, could never do that.

We've seen, already, that black graduates of the most elite colleges (places like Harvard, Stanford, and Duke) had to send out an average of eight applications to receive an interview, while white graduates had to send out six. The same study showed that as the institutions grew less selective, the discrepancy increased: When the study looked at public colleges (including the University of Massachusetts Amherst; the University of California, Riverside; and the University of North Carolina at Greensboro), white graduates sent out nine applications before getting an interview, and black graduates sent out fifteen. (Connecting the dots between selectivity and tuition rates, that means white students can afford to attend a cheaper, less selective college and receive about the same opportunities as a black student who goes to a more expensive, highly selective college.) And when black applicants received responses from employers, they weren't asked to interview for the jobs they applied for; instead, they were steered toward jobs with lower starting salaries by an average of $3,000. The black-white income gap is the lowest right after graduation, so we should expect that $3,000 differential to grow over time due to racial differences in salary increases and bonuses.

When black professionals do get higher-paying positions, they encounter the same racism that informs the recruitment and interview processes. In a study performed by Nextions, a Chicago-based diversity consulting firm, identical legal memoranda were sent to sixty law firm partners who were asked to evaluate them. There was only one difference: One group was told that a white man wrote the memos, and the other was told that a black man wrote them. The partners consistently rated the memo lower when they believed that the author was black; they were also more likely to point out spelling, grammar, and technical errors when they were "grading" the black memo.[27]

All of this adds up to fewer opportunities, lower salaries, and restricted access to tax-free benefits that keep the black-white wealth gap alive and growing.[28]

Occupational segregation also refutes one of the fundamental assumptions behind the joint return discussed in chapter 1—horizontal equity. Horizontal equity treats two households with the same income as equal and requires that they pay the same amount in taxes. I've demonstrated that a household where one partner earns $70,000 and the other stays home is very different from a household where both partners earn $35,000 each. However, occupational segregation reveals that a black household where each partner earns $35,000 is also different from a white household with the same income distribution. Black workers and white workers earning the same salary are rarely true peers, because of the different ways black and white workers are hired and compensated. A black worker and a white worker may each earn $35,000, for example, but the black worker is statistically more likely to be a contract employee, which means they're missing out on the additional one-third of compensation that comes through retirement benefits and health insurance. Or, if both are full-time employees with the same salary and benefits packages, the black worker is likely to be better educated and more qualified than the white worker earning the same amount—but because the black worker was hired into a lower-level, lower-paying position, it's taken them more time to advance and earn the same salary the white worker receives. It is not comparing apples to apples. Built into the idea of horizontal equity is the idea that the labor market is race neutral. Nothing could be further from the truth.

Nevertheless, the lucky full-time employee who does receive health and pension benefits is theoretically well positioned to avoid wealth depletion and begin wealth accumulation. The best type of retirement account, the defined benefit plan my father had, is increasingly a relic of the past. (Remember, it guarantees a retirement payout regardless of the amount contributed, which means the employer takes on the risk of how the funds are invested, putting the financial burden on them rather than on the employee.) The most common type of retirement plan available today is the defined contribution plan, most commonly referred to as a 401(k): If your employer sponsors one and you decide to participate, you agree that a certain portion of your salary will be placed, tax-free, into your retirement account. If you are lucky enough to have an employer match, then your employer will pay additional funds up to a certain amount. However, defined contribution plans only guarantee that an employee will have whatever money remains in the account at retirement based on the *employee's* investment decisions. If the employee makes what turns out to be poor investment choices, or is just unlucky, then they will have little to no retirement funds. And while employers often match contributions, the burden of funding the plan remains on employees. If the employees don't contribute, the employers don't match.

In 2013, 51.3 percent of American workers had access to a retirement plan sponsored by their employer or union. Of that group, only 40.8 percent participated.[29] What this means is that the majority of Americans—black and white—are facing retirement without an employer-provided cushion. But the future is particularly bleak for black employees. In every field and at every salary level, black workers are less likely than their white counterparts to participate in an employer-sponsored retirement plan. When they do participate, they have lower account balances—even when they are in the same salary range as their white peers. Why? If black workers can beat the odds and get a salaried job with benefits, why wouldn't they have the same retirement outcomes as their white colleagues?

The shifting corporate landscape, in which companies increasingly look for ways to hire without benefits, or to offer a benefit plan that costs them less, is one factor. Another is the shrinking of the public sector. Overall, half of white workers (50.8 percent) and less than half of black workers (42.4 percent) have a retirement account provided by their employer or union. But those numbers look very different if we break them out according to whether the employer is private or public. In the public sector, 77 percent of white workers and 67 percent of black workers participate in a retirement plan. Many of them enjoy defined benefit plans like my father's, which guarantee a certain amount of income in retirement. Chris, the behavioral health counselor and former Argosy student, has worked in both the public and private sectors and has a defined contribution retirement plan. Her mother, who worked in the public sector as an office administrator for Fulton County, had a defined benefit plan, and is now the only one of her friends able to retire. This generational shift isn't unusual—while most government jobs still offer defined benefit plans, cuts to federal agency budgets have made those jobs harder to obtain. The federal government is at its lowest levels of employment as a percentage of total workers since 1952, and state and local governments since the mid- to late 1960s.[30]

That leaves the private sector, where the majority of both

black and white college graduates begin their careers. While government employees can generally count on having access to a retirement plan, the same isn't true for their private-sector peers. In the private sector, 56.2 percent of white workers and 50.2 percent of black workers have access to a retirement plan through their employer.[31] Perhaps even more striking is that of those employees with access to a retirement plan, 45.8 percent of white employees and only 36.6 percent of black employees participate. And when you examine participation rates, account balances, and withdrawals through a black-and-white lens, the magnitude of the wealth gap grows increasingly clear.

Participation rates alone reveal the power individual companies have in decreasing—or maintaining—the black-white wealth gap among their employees. An Ariel/Aon Hewitt study in 2012 analyzed the records of 2.4 million employees who work for sixty of the largest U.S. employers from a variety of industries (including some not-for-profit employers) and found that while retirement account balances do vary by race, participation rates corresponded to company practice rather than income.[32] At companies with automatic enrollment, where workers are enrolled in company retirement plans by default, black and white participation was comparable, at 82 percent versus 85 percent, respectively; the gap was larger, 64 percent participation for black workers compared with 77 percent for white workers, at companies without automatic enrollment. Among low-salaried workers subject to automatic enrollment, the gap was virtually nonexistent.

Still, we should expect to see better results for the subgroup of black employees included in the study, since they work for some of the largest companies in the country, which tend to provide the greatest benefits and higher wages. If these companies offer the best benefit packages, and also use best practices like automatic enrollment, why don't participation rates and retirement account balances of black workers match those of white workers? At every income level, the balances of white workers' retirement accounts outstrip those of black workers' accounts: Even at the lowest household income levels, the balances of accounts held by whites are almost double the balances of accounts held by blacks. While the gap narrows as income grows, even at the highest household income levels, the balances of white workers' accounts were almost one and a half times higher than the balances of black workers' accounts.

Conservatives might argue that this is all a matter of priorities—that black Americans aren't saving for retirement because they're too busy spending their money on the wrong things, like expensive sneakers or fancy cars. But the truth is that when it comes to "clothing, jewelry, personal care, entertainment, eating out, and other non-essential spending," as one report noted, "findings show that black consumers in fact spend the same or much less than whites, at all income levels."[33] In comparable income groups, the average white household spends 1.3 times more than the average black household.[34] So if it's not overspending that leaves black workers with less money to invest in their retirement, what accounts for these discrepancies?

The answer, once again, can be found in the tax code, which favors white family structures and the opportunities that go with them. Black families are far more likely than white families to accumulate what researchers call "negative social capital"—a social structure that depletes black wealth and restricts mobility and growth potential. Many black women and men in corporate America stretch their salaries to support extended family members who haven't had the same wealth-building opportunities; by helping their parents, siblings, or grandparents, each of them reduces their ability to provide for themselves or their children.[35] And they are doing it with after-tax dollars in a tax system that disadvantages most black families.

Racheal, even while living in public housing to pay down her student loans, sent money home to her grandmother. Chris, the Argosy graduate, lives with her parents and contributes to their household expenses. John, the homeowner in chapter 2 who moved to a white neighborhood with a better school system, also sends money to his parents and worries about how to account for it on his sons' college financial aid applications.

"That's sort of an invisible care—I don't deduct it from my taxes," he says. "Which means that as my sons are applying to these elite schools, and they do their tuition calculation, they see more income than that really is. I'm afraid it's going to be beyond our means to be able to pay for it, honestly, and keep everybody that we're supporting intact."

Now assume you get a high-paying job, with the same salary and benefits enjoyed by your white peers. If you have a family member who was denied access to wealth-building perks because of their race, you are more likely to provide some financial support for them—meaning you won't be able to build wealth as easily as your white peers.[36]

And while there are certain tax breaks that come with having children—parents qualify for child tax credits and an increase in earned income tax credits—as John noted, payments to parents or anyone who doesn't legally qualify as a dependent are not deductible because, as discussed in chapter 2, they are considered personal, family, and living expenses. The tax code subsidizes certain familial relationships, but not all.

Racheal, Chris, and John are not unique among black college graduates, who are more likely to provide financial support to their parents, while white college graduates are more likely to receive financial support *from* their parents, which they can use to buy a home or pay for their education while their black counterparts continue renting or take out student loans.[37] Add this to the fact that black workers are less likely to get a marriage-based tax cut and more likely to pay the singles' penalty, and that if they've sold a home the chances are higher that they sold it at a nondeductible loss. Then add in the fact that they may have high student loan debt and may be unable to deduct all of their interest. Black workers simply have to make their dollars go further than their white peers do.

These financial constraints don't just leave black families with less disposable income; they leave them unable to make significant contributions to their retirement accounts—so even if an employer matches their contribution, they may not be able to maximize the benefit. They also mean that when black employees do have retirement accounts, they are more likely to make what's called a "hardship withdrawal"—taking money out of the account before they retire in order to pay a bill or deal with some other pressing financial need. Hardship withdrawals are taxed aggressively—and in my opinion, paternalistically and unfairly.

When you put money into your retirement account, tax policy allows it to remain there, untaxed, until you retire, make an early withdrawal, or turn seventy-two. But if you take an early withdrawal (prior to turning fifty-nine and a half), the penalties are steep—not only is the withdrawal included in your taxable income, but the government also levies an additional 10 percent income tax penalty.[38] The penalty is designed as a deterrent, to discourage withdrawals. But early retirement account withdrawals are generally a last resort. If employees could get the money elsewhere—through a loan or a gift from family, or from savings—they would not be withdrawing it from their retirement accounts. So it's not surprising that black employees, who have fewer of these kinds of resources to draw on, are significantly more likely to take hardship withdrawals.

Ursula McCandless, a human resources manager at Atlanta's Cox Enterprises, who we first met in the introduction, has an MBA, earns about $175,000 annually, and contributes regularly to her 401(k) plan. Her lifetime wealth-building potential should be excellent, from a tax perspective, but the reality of her life as a black worker reduces her opportunities: Ursula supports other family members and has withdrawn from her retirement account to pay off credit card debt. She's not alone; black workers are five times more likely to make hardship withdrawals than their white peers (8.8 percent versus 1.7 percent).[39] Even my mother, who was incredibly careful with her finances, took money from her 401(k) a few times: once to help me pay for law school expenses, and again for home repairs.

As table 4.1 shows, withdrawals vary by race and income, with black workers withdrawing at significantly higher rates than white workers *regardless of income*.[40]

TABLE 4.1. HARDSHIP WITHDRAWALS BY SALARY LEVEL

Salary	Black	White
Up to $30,000	6.3 percent	1.2 percent
$30K–$59,999	11.9	2.6
$60,000–$89,999	7.1	1.4
$90,000–$119,999	4.1	.7
$120,000 and over	2.4	.4

At the highest income levels the black withdrawal percentage is six times the white withdrawal percentage; at the lowest, it is five times as high, demonstrating that either lower-income white workers do not have financial pressures equal to those of their black peers, or they have access to funds other than their retirement accounts.

Black women are driving this phenomenon: 9 percent of black women compared with 6 percent of black men have taken hardship withdrawals. Gender differences are significant between black and white workers: Just as we saw in chapter 1, the marriage penalty is higher for black couples because black wives are more likely to contribute a significant portion of the household income than white wives, and that plays a major role in the wealth gap over time. Black women actually dominate the black labor market, making up 53 percent of the black labor force in 2018.[41] The roles are reversed for white workers—where men make up 54.3 percent of the labor force.[42] But black women are also compensated less than white men, white women, and black men, and face their own unique forms of discrimination in the workplace. (California, for example, became the first state, in 2019, to pass a bill prohibiting workplace discrimination against black women's hairstyles. When Ursula heard about the bill, she says, it was an unwelcome reminder of how dire the circumstances can be for black women in the workplace. "Imagine that a law had to be passed for you to be able to wear your hair in its natural state," she says.) If the labor market is so openly prejudiced against black women—and they, in turn, are the predominant workers in the black labor market—it's no wonder that their financial circumstances force them to make early withdrawals.

There is one alternative to a costly withdrawal: a loan from the retirement account. The proceeds from a 401(k) loan are tax-free, because you are obligated to repay them, and because they do not constitute income, they don't come with the 10 percent penalty. The problem is that the default rate is high: 80 percent for blacks, and 71 percent for whites. Employees default on loans if they quit their job (or are fired) and do not pay off the loans within sixty days. At that point, the loan is converted to a withdrawal and the employee is hit with the penalty.

There are, I admit, two factors besides employment, salary, and family obligations that can account for lower black participation levels in retirement accounts: inertia and financial anxiety. I know, because I experienced both myself.

Thanks to my parents' saving and sacrifice, I was able to attend college, law school, and then NYU, where I got a master's degree in tax law. I was able to secure good-paying jobs with tax-free perks. In 2002, I was working at the Washington and Lee University School of Law, part of a small private liberal arts university that employed just over 2,500 people. Like other large employers, they gave their employees access to a retirement account. If I remember correctly, if I contributed up to 3 percent of my salary, they would contribute an additional 3 percent. (At small firms, the cost of setting up such a system is often prohibitive.) I had the benefits waiting for me—and even I, the tax lawyer, didn't max out my contribution until the director of personnel called me and said, "Dorothy, you're leaving money on the table." I knew exactly what he meant: I was not contributing enough to get the maximum match from my employer. (Miss Dottie will be so disappointed when she reads this.)

Why? When I changed jobs, I sold my home in Ohio, which I'd bought with a thirty-year mortgage, and took out a different fifteen-year mortgage to purchase a new home in Virginia. Even though my salary increased with the move, my monthly mortgage payment increased as well. I was reluctant, as a single woman with my salary as my sole source of income, to max out on my retirement until I could see on the ground how my budget adjusted to the increased mortgage payment. I thought I'd change my retirement contribution after a year; that year stretched into two. I was touched, and frankly embarrassed, that the personnel director called me to push me to take full advantage of the benefit. I knew this wasn't the kind of nudge that many of my peers at other universities could rely on.

As for financial anxiety, there's some truth to that—but as

usual, the explanation that blames black people for bad choices isn't telling the whole story. The increased use of defined contribution plans, in which employees are responsible for determining where to invest their retirement funds, does put the burden of choice on the employee, and investing in the stock market is tied to higher retirement account balances because historically the stock market has provided the best return on investment.[43] And research shows that black Americans are far less likely than their white peers to invest their retirement funds in the stock market; more often they opt to buy life insurance or invest in real estate.[44] However, it's not as if the investment market has been equally accessible to black and white potential customers—and I'd argue that if the labor market has already devalued your education and experience, and asked you to accept less than your white peers, an aversion to the unknowns of the predominantly white stock market isn't unreasonable. (The racist financial system that hasn't seen black Americans as potential customers is examined in chapter 5.)

All the puzzle pieces that make up the racism in the labor market mean there's no simple solution to reducing the black-white wealth gap. However, we've seen the impact, good and bad, that individual companies can make with policy changes, and that's a good starting point. Instead of relying on HR to make individual phone calls, why not create an opt-in default for retirement accounts? The Ariel/Aon Hewitt study showed that when companies created automatic enrollment, black employee participation increased from 64 percent to 82 percent, with even more dramatic results for lower-wage workers. It also showed that as automatic enrollment with a default investment strategy like target-date funds increased, the percentage of black workers with stock investments in their retirement accounts also increased. After automatic enrollment, the funds would then be placed in appropriate investment vehicles that change over the life of the employee. If inertia wins, that employee still has a retirement account. More important, the default target-date funds investment portfolio will result in increased stock ownership by black workers, which can lead to higher account balances.

To counter the likelihood that enrolled black families—already facing marriage without a bonus, college debt, and lower salaries—will have to make early withdrawals, I'd also demand that the penalty for early withdrawal of retirement funds be repealed. It is paternalistic and ignores how societal racism continues to cause black workers to be financially disadvantaged compared with their white peers. Whether it's lack of parental wealth due to historic discrimination, higher taxes, or family members in need, black workers are forced to access retirement accounts more than white workers generally because of necessity. And repeal would also help those employees who default on their loans. (There is precedent for this: Legislation passed during the COVID-19 pandemic included relief from the 10 percent penalty for retirement withdrawals related to the pandemic.)

At the small-business level, more employers should do what the personnel director at Washington and Lee did for me years ago: let each of their employees know if they are not participating, and encourage them to do so. And if there are concerns that black employees will be unable to afford contributing to a retirement account, then it will be incumbent upon employers to ensure that black employees are not steered into lower-paying jobs and make sure they are paying their black workers fairly in whatever jobs they hold.

Of course, there is nothing to prevent employers from taking these measures under current law—but there's no incentive either, which is where the bigger shifts in tax policy come in. Corporations, like universities, receive major tax subsidies for employer contributions to health insurance and retirement accounts. And just as universities receive their tax subsidies regardless of how many black students they admit, how generous their financial aid packages are, or how many black students graduate, corporations receive the subsidies regardless of how many black workers they hire, or how many racial discrepancies exist when it comes to salaries and promotions.

In this case, similar obstacles require similar solutions: data collection and exposure. First, in exchange for tax subsidies applicable to retirement accounts, private employers should be required to publish information on all aspects of retirement accounts by race and ethnicity. The U.S. Government Accountability Office has already recommended such information be collected and published for retirement account withdrawals.

Second, existing "nondiscrimination" rules that prevent employers from getting tax breaks if they establish retirement accounts and limit them to their executives, or from favoring their "highly compensated employees" when it comes to the provision of benefits, must be expanded to include rules that require no racial gap in participation rates if they want to qualify for retirement account tax breaks. Adopting best practices (like automatic enrollment and target-date funds) will also go a long way toward minimizing racial gaps, as the Ariel/Aon Hewitt study demonstrated.

Finally, with new information and policies in place, we need to adopt another system like the one I propose for colleges and universities: Tax reform should require employers seeking any wage deductions to conduct their own audits, which would be made public, to determine whether similarly situated workers are being treated differently—either in the type of jobs they are offered or in the pay they are awarded. Nonprofits have to publish the salaries of their highest-paid employees to receive their tax exemptions; given the benefit-based tax breaks most employers are able to enjoy, regardless of internal bias or discrimination, why can't we require something similar from for-profit companies? If there are racial gaps, or if most black workers are concentrated in low-paying jobs, the employer should work to remedy the problem. After a period of doing such work, perhaps three to five years, if there are still gaps, then the employer would no longer be allowed to deduct employee wages on its tax return. Tax policy should be used to combat, not reinforce, market-based race discrimination.[45]

Even if all of these changes were implemented, they would not fix the racism baked into the labor market. A close examination of another benefit—health insurance—gives us some insight into why. Employer-provided health insurance provides a safety net against wealth depletion, guarding against huge medical bills and associated debt—or, alternatively, failing health because care is unaffordable, leading to missed work and job insecurity. While the majority of both white and black workers have health insurance through their jobs, the racial discrepancy is still significant—74 percent of white workers compared with 56.5 percent of black workers.

Insurance not provided through your job can be purchased, accessed through a spouse or parent, or received through Medicare or Medicaid. But disparities are clear here, too. Black Americans under the age of sixty-five remain more likely to be uninsured than white Americans:[46] 11.5 percent of them lack insurance, compared with 7.5 percent of white Americans. One possible explanation for the disparity is that black Americans are more likely than white Americans to live in one of the states (most of which are in the South) that have not expanded Medicaid under the Affordable Care Act. In these states, those who fail to qualify under the old Medicaid rules but whose income is not high enough (greater than the federal poverty level) to qualify for the Affordable Care Act subsidies fall into what's known as the Medicaid coverage gap. In 2018, 9 percent of white Americans and 15 percent of black Americans experienced this gap, and it's led to significant discrepancies in insurance rates between the states. Nationally, nearly 14 percent of nonelderly black women are uninsured. In Georgia, that number rises to 20 percent.[47]

We know that medical expenses can create serious debt for the uninsured. But even a high-cost out-of-pocket insurance policy inhibits savings. For example, if you get sick, and your health insurance plan has a deductible of $5,000, meaning you pay the first $5,000 of your medical costs, that's $5,000 you can't save for wealth building. And given the racial wealth gap, black workers are less likely to be able to absorb the expense of paying these out-of-pocket expenses.

As a result, medical debt is divided along racial lines, too: A 2017 Urban Institute report showed that 31 percent of black Americans have past-due medical debt compared with 23 percent of white Americans. "Past-due medical bills can end up in your credit report and lower your credit score, which means you may not be able to borrow for a mortgage or small business—or you may pay more when you do borrow," the report added. "Credit report information can also be used to determine whether you get a job or rent an apartment and how much you pay in insurance premiums."[48]

In that case, shouldn't the healthcare-for-all model touted by progressive political candidates be an effective tool in reducing the black-white wealth gap? Unfortunately, that model is only half-right. What it ignores is the reality that our healthcare system remains and has always been anti-black.[49] Moving uninsured black Americans into our existing healthcare system will only set them up for disparate treatment, which could prove fatal.

Take the case of tennis superstar Serena Williams; she and her husband have a combined net worth of $189 million.[50] She has access to the best healthcare that money can buy—but when she gave birth, her blackness undermined her care. As Williams told *Vogue,* she warned her attending medical team that she had a history of blood clots—only to be dismissed as "confused" when she told a nurse she thought she was experiencing a pulmonary embolism. (She was, and the delay in treatment set off a range of complications, including a hemorrhage.)[51] Her wealth alone could not overcome the system—it took her influence and determination, as well as her resources, to keep her from becoming another statistic in the maternal mortality saga in which black mothers in America are at least three times more likely to die as a result of pregnancy or childbirth than white mothers.

That's why it's not enough to provide access to a broken system—you have to try to move the system in the right way. Senator Elizabeth Warren and then-Senator Kamala Harris each had plans to deal with ameliorating racism in the healthcare field.[52] Warren's plan focused on financial incentives for hospitals, while Harris's focused on implicit bias training and a pilot program assigning a caseworker for Medicaid beneficiaries with high-risk pregnancies. The success of those approaches was far from proven, but they are significant because they recognized that access alone was insufficient to create better health outcomes for black Americans.

That's the model we need to replicate in the labor market: Recognizing that access to salaries and benefits alone won't guarantee better wealth outcomes for black Americans. Blacks graduate from college with more debt, do not get jobs as easily as whites, are not paid the same wages as their equally qualified white peers, are steered toward lower-paying jobs, and have an unemployment rate twice that of whites—yet are more likely to provide financial support for extended family. Once again, tax policy adds insult to injury, giving tax breaks to white workers already winning in the paid labor market while also levying heavy penalties for early withdrawal from retirement accounts against those black workers the paid labor market fails.

That's not to say that race-based labor market discrimination shouldn't be addressed directly—if we could eliminate opportunity and salary gaps tomorrow, that would definitely be progress. But this is where the difference between income and wealth comes into play—and when it comes to tax policy, the benefits that favor wealth preservation are some of the most inequitable in our entire tax system. A lifetime of lower earnings and fewer benefits in the workplace leads to disparities in savings, retirement contributions, and investment opportunities, of course. But that alone isn't the problem. When these opportunities are compounded with the tax treatment of inheritances and gifts—which affect each of these life-cycle events, such as college and homebuying, on a generational basis—we can truly begin to see how and why the black-white racial wealth gap remains so resilient. Those compounded opportunities are the topic of our next chapter, and a key means to understanding the obstacles to achieving a truly equitable system.

FIVE

LEGACY

At the end of 2018, *The Atlanta Journal-Constitution* ran a story about how black Americans were recovering from the Great Recession of a decade earlier. The findings were stark: Though average family wealth had dropped across the nation, black families and workers consistently experienced a bigger decline and slower recovery. Between 2007, when the recession began, and 2013, middle-income white families experienced a 31 percent decline as their median wealth fell to $131,900. Middle-income black families' median wealth, however, dropped a startling 47 percent, down to $33,600.

In Georgia, the economic decline had a profound impact on black homeownership rates. Before the recession, black homeownership across the state had reached a high of 53 percent; during and after the recession, the rate fell to below 45 percent for the first time in almost forty years.

Tia McCoy, a realtor and former homeownership center director for Atlanta's Resources for Residents and Communities, a community development corporation, told the reporter that throughout the recession and its aftermath, she saw one client after another—even a member of the Georgia state legislature—lose their homes to bankruptcy or foreclosure. The majority of those clients were black, McCoy said, and did not have generational or family wealth to carry them through a period of income loss or instability.

"Historically, we might not have the resources available," McCoy said. "Mom and dad couldn't save us."[1]

McCoy's answer—"Mom and dad couldn't save us"—is the story of black wealth, across generations, in America. We've already seen why getting married, buying a home, graduating from college, or getting a good job results in greater wealth for white taxpayers than black taxpayers. Under those constraints, one would expect white Americans to have greater wealth than black Americans, and they do—white families hold $171,000 in median wealth compared to $17,100 for black families. In 2016, 83 percent of black households had less net worth than the median for white households, and the top 10 percent of black households had average wealth of just over $1 million, compared to $6.7 million for the top 10 percent of white households.[2]

However, there's another key piece of the puzzle: how tax policies around investments, assets, and inheritances pave the way for wealth accumulation across decades and generations. If you can obtain any kind of financial security blanket—

whether it's a home in a predominantly white neighborhood, an investment account, or even an inheritance—tax policy works to help you preserve and pass along that security to your children or grandchildren. But if you can't obtain it, you're out of luck—and probably paying even more in taxes on your wage income than an investor is on their stock portfolio.

The policy discrepancy is only part of the picture. We can see, now, how white families have benefited from generations of wealth building: first gaining financial advantages throughout their lifetime, then using the tax policy surrounding asset ownership and gifts to build those savings into the kind of wealth that is passed down to both children and grandchildren. But those advantages are often rendered invisible by those who have benefited from them. Consider some of the white families interviewed for this book, most of whom declined to be identified by name, concerned about how their advantages would reflect on their reputations. These included a fourth-generation Ivy League graduate whose grandfather established trusts that paid for her college tuition, her sibling's, and her children's.

"I do have a family story that would be about whiteness and so forth," she said. "I would not be happy for that story to be publicly associated with my family."

The reality of how ordinary white Americans build wealth, then, is hidden—and leads to two distinct harms:

First, it leaves black families bewildered about their inability to achieve the financial security of their white peers. *How can they create a better future for their children,* they wonder, *while I cannot?*

Second, it causes white families who have benefited from significant tax-free family financial assistance to think of it as an insignificant factor in their success, which they go on to attribute only to hard work—not the luck of being born to white parents.

The result is an invisible safety net for white Americans, and yet another generation of black Americans wondering why they can't get ahead.

The tax code rewards and encourages generational wealth building in two major ways. The first is the preferential tax treatment that comes with asset ownership. The second is the provision for tax-free financial transfers to family members, both while the giver is alive and after they die, as part of their estate. In both cases, reduced or eliminated taxes result in increased savings and investment opportunities for the next generation. Each one dates back to the beginnings of our "progressive" tax system, and like many of the other shifts we've seen, each one has been influenced by the interests of the wealthy, white, and powerful.

Stocks and bonds have long been disproportionately held by the wealthiest white Americans, and a whole section of the tax code was developed when one man from a prominent family sued to avoid taxes on a bond sale. As we learned in chapter 4, stocks held inside of a retirement account, like a 401(k), are generally not taxed until an employee retires, withdraws an amount, or turns seventy-two. Stock investments outside of a retirement account, however—referred to as "capital assets"—receive very different treatment. If you buy stock and then sell it at a loss, you can take a tax deduction, which can be used to offset other gains or income. If you sell stock at a gain, you pay taxes on the income—but at the capital gains rate, which is different, and significantly lower, than the one that applies to wage income. (While the tax treatment for bonds is more complicated today, there are also significant tax subsidies associated with bond ownership. For example, state and local bonds pay interest that is often received tax-free by the owner.)[3]

The tax rate that applies to gains from stock and the sale of other capital assets, such as a home, is called the preferential rate. This rate varies depending on a taxpayer's total income and how long they have held the stock, but it's always better than the progressive rate, which applies to wage income: The maximum preferential tax rate is 20 percent, while the maximum progressive rate is 37 percent.[4] This means that taxpayers will pay a significantly lower tax rate on income from stock than they will on their wage income. (Remember, in chapter 2, our discussion of the tax breaks that come with selling your home? That's the preferential rate in practice, too—up to $500,000 of the gain tax-free, if you are married, and the remaining amount taxed at the preferential, not progressive, rate.)

To qualify for the preferential rate, an asset must be held for more than one year before it is sold. (Gain from the sale of stock held less than one year is taxed the same way as wage income.) After that, the greater a taxpayer's share of capital gains subject to the preferential rate, the lower their overall effective tax rate will be. The preferential rate can be 0, 15, or 20 percent, depending on the taxpayer's total income (including any capital gains) and their filing status. If the taxpayer's total income is more than $441,450, they will pay the maximum rate of 20 percent—which, you'll recall, is still 17 percentage points less than they'd pay if taxed according to the progressive rate system. A taxpayer whose only income is from capital assets of $50,000 will pay a preferential rate of 15 percent if single, and *zero* percent if married or filing as head of household. (That's another built-in marriage bonus.)

Let's compare two single taxpayers with $150,000 in taxable income (after all deductions) in 2020: Melissa and Michele. Melissa's $150,000 is all from her salary; Michele's is $100,000 from salary and $50,000 from the sale of stock. Melissa will pay $30,079.50 in taxes[5] while Michele pays only $25,579.50.[6] Why does Michele save $4,500 on her tax bill compared with Melissa? Because all of Melissa's income is subject to the progressive tax system, compared with only two-thirds of Michele's. Michele's salary income is taxed at the same rate as Melissa's, but her stock income receives the lower 15 percent preferential rate, while Melissa's last $50,000 of income is taxed at her highest progressive rate of 24 percent. This is why billionaire Warren Buffett's effective tax rate is lower than his secretary's: Most of his income comes from stock ownership and is subject to the preferential rate, while most of hers comes from wages and is subject to the progressive tax rate.

How did this happen, when the purpose of the progressive tax system is to ensure higher-income taxpayers pay higher tax rates? Just like the marriage bonus, the preferential rate was created through pressure from the wealthiest white taxpayers in the early days of our taxation system. In 1916, when capital gains were taxed the same as ordinary income, only the richest 1 percent of Americans filed a tax return.[7] Among them was Frederick F. Brewster, who (wait for it) was paying taxes on income from his enormous wealth, didn't like it, and decided to sue so he ultimately wouldn't have to.

Frederick and I do have one thing in common—both of our families arrived in America by sea. His, however, were aboard the decks of the *Mayflower,* and mine came chained in the bottom of a ship, and the differences in our American experiences only grow from there.[8] Frederick's father, Benjamin, was a business associate of the Rockefellers and earned his fortune in oil and railroads; for many decades he was considered the second-wealthiest man in America, right behind his colleague, John D. Rockefeller, Sr. When Benjamin died in 1897, Frederick, then around twenty-five, inherited a quarter of his father's fortune. He went on to become a director of the New York, New Haven and Hartford Railroad Company and build a twenty-five-acre estate in Connecticut for his bride, Margaret. *The New York Times* described him as "a wealthy young man in this city who is understood to have large interests in the Standard Oil Company."[9]

In 1916, Frederick sold more than $400,000 in bonds and did not include the profits—approximately $84,000—on his tax return, arguing to the Bureau of Internal Revenue (known today as the IRS) that because he did not regularly make such sales, the profits didn't count as income and weren't subject to taxation. The bureau disagreed and said he owed $17,756.79 in additional taxes. (In today's dollars, that's about $10 million in bonds sold, $2 million in profit, and a tax dispute of $400,000. The Brewsters make the Seaborns, our other wealthy white tax litigants from chapter 1, look like paupers.)[10] Brewster won the suit in district court, but the IRS appealed, and the case went to the Supreme Court in 1921.

The Supreme Court determined that income from the sale of property was required to be included in taxable income and reversed the lower court's decision.[11] But Brewster's defeat led to a major victory in Congress for the wealthy 1 percenters who occasionally sold stocks, bonds, and real estate.[12] Congress responded to the Supreme Court decision by enacting that *same year* a lower tax rate for this type of property. At the time, the highest marginal income tax rate was 73 percent; the new capital gains rate was set at 12.5 percent.[13]

Why so low? The legislative history noted that high tax rates resulted in tax avoidance strategies by the wealthy, who would put their money into alternatives like tax-exempt bonds, or give the stock to family members who were subject to lower tax rates. If all else failed, they would simply hold on to their stock longer than they wanted to, producing what's commonly called a "lock-in" effect.[14] The concern is that holding on to an unwanted investment precludes the investor from buying a different one that would stimulate the economy. (That said, there is a positive benefit to the lock-in effect: it tamps down on speculation in the market that could otherwise lead to widespread losses.)

By creating the lower capital gains rate, Congress found a way to discourage the richest Americans from using tax avoidance strategies, but kept them from protesting the change by offering them special treatment. Only eight years into the progressive tax system, a huge loophole was created for the wealthy; the richest Americans would not even pay the progressive tax rate on a portion of their income.[15] The effect has only grown over time; when the highest-income households didn't get any marriage-penalty relief in 2017, perhaps the reason they didn't protest was that the majority of their income was already subject to the low preferential rate, making a shift in the progressive system irrelevant for them. In 2019, roughly 85 percent of income subject to the low preferential rate went to the richest 5 percent of taxpayers, according to the Tax Policy Center, and almost 75 percent went to the top 1 percenters; this is how white wealth increases across a century.[16]

There are certainly legitimate policy arguments for why we should tax capital gains at a lower rate than wages, including the "lock-in" rationale provided at the time.[17] Another argument posits that since part of the gain is an effect of inflation, not a real increase in value, a higher tax is unfair. And some say that stock gains should be taxed at a reduced rate because such gains reflect corporate profits, which have already been taxed once.

None of the arguments, however, are persuasive. First, for most of the twentieth century our tax rates on capital gains were higher than they are now, and the markets functioned effectively, with minimal lock-in effect. Second, the potential effects of inflation may also be overstated, since you only have to hold stock one year and a day to get the preferential rate—and there is no inflation exception for any other type of income that accrues over a period of time. Take, for example, royalty income from books: If I write a book this year, it does not produce income until it is published; then it produces income every time a book is sold. The income I receive five years from the book's publication date is attributable to the labor of writing the book several years earlier, but no one ever argues there should be an inflation-adjusted amount of royalty income included as taxable income.

As for the double-taxation argument, it's interesting that it comes from corporate shareholders as opposed to small-business owners. When I pay taxes on my wages, then pay the electrician to fix some wiring in my home, the electrician pays taxes on the payment received from me. It's how most retail and service transactions work—yet no one ever argues that the electrician is being taxed twice. Meanwhile, with the corporate tax rate now at 21 percent (down from 35 percent in 2017), it's hard to believe that corporations and their shareholders are shouldering an undue burden.[18]

When we examine asset ownership in America by race, however, we see plenty of unfairness. We've seen already why black Americans are less likely to own property or reap significant gains from its sale or transfer. When it comes to other assets, like stocks, there are similar obstacles to access. As was the case with real estate, this isn't simply a question of income: Research shows that at every income level, white Americans are more likely to own stock than black Americans.[19] White middle-class families are more than twice as likely as black middle-class families to own stock.[20] Even white families in the bottom quintile of the income distribution are more likely to own stock than black families in the second-highest quintile.[21]

You don't need to have *Mayflower* ancestry to benefit from the disparity either. Take Susan, a white woman in her sixties who had a long career as a corporate executive. Susan bought herself three shares of stock when she was in middle school, using her babysitting money. She doesn't remember her parents ever encouraging her to buy stock, but she does remember learning about the stock market at her junior high school outside of Evanston, Illinois—which she describes as "a public school in the whitest, least diverse suburb in the world."[22] After learning about the market, she purchased three shares of stock: one in a now-defunct company, one in Marshall Field's (the former department store now owned by Macy's), and one in McDonald's.

"I could look at the paper every day to see how my stock was doing," Susan recalls. "And eating McDonald's, I'd feel like I was helping my investment."

That single share of McDonald's stock, purchased in the 1960s, is worth $60,000 as of early 2020. But that's not the end of Susan's stock market story. She graduated from college without debt, thanks to her grandparents, and then struck out on her own financially, working a variety of jobs to help put her husband through law school. A divorce in her twenties left her with a $5,000 settlement, and she had several lean years of working on commission, but by her midthirties, she felt financially stable enough to consider the stock market again. She knew she couldn't afford a financial planner, and she didn't think she understood the market well enough to invest on her own. The solution? Use her personal network of friends, classmates, and colleagues to improve her financial literacy.

Through friends—she jokes that her broker was someone "a girlfriend's sister's brother knew"—she found a professional to teach her about the market. "The deal there was that he would teach me about stocks," she says. "I had divvied up whatever small pot of money, he could invest that half or three-quarters of it, and I would take a percentage of it, and invest it. And we would discuss why we were doing what we were doing, and what was working, so I could learn." That single share of McDonald's, combined with the starter port-folio Susan established in her thirties, seeded an investment portfolio that grew to more than $8 million by the time she reached her sixties. Susan's story illustrates how financial privilege can start with something as small as an access point—one share of McDonald's stock and a friend who "knew a guy"—and balloon into extraordinary wealth.

Stock ownership disparities transcend income, education levels, and many of the commonly held ideas about what lim-its black wealth building. A study of households with compa-rable wealth of at least $356,900 (which represented the top 5 percent of black households versus the top 28 percent of white households) analyzed stock holdings outside of retirement ac-counts.[23] That research showed 30 percent of these wealthy black Americans owned stock compared with 41 percent of whites with similarly high incomes. When you look at mean, or average, stock ownership values, black stock owners in the top 5 percent own $185,000 in stocks, and white stock owners own $449,000. But averages can be skewed by a single indi-vidual with an enormous amount of wealth—like Robert Smith, the black billionaire who pledged to pay the student loan debts for the Morehouse class of 2019. If you look at the median value, which means half the study participants have less, and half have more, white stock ownership drops to $140,000—but the black median doesn't even reach $100,000.

Part of the problem is attributable to the reality that even high-income black Americans have less money available to invest; remember, income and wealth are not the same, and even black and white Americans with comparably high incomes don't have the same amount of wealth, for all of the reasons we've already explored. But there is more to the story than just cash flow: Access, trust, and history have all shaped today's black and white investment practices.

I first began exploring how and where black families invest their income for a paper about pensions and the retirement packages black professionals chose when they were offered plans at work.[24] What I found is that while investing in the stock market is a "rite of passage for white investors" like Susan, for whom it was part of the curriculum at her predominantly white middle school, a lack of diversity in the financial services market makes black Americans' lack of investment a self-fulfilling prophecy.[25] A 2017 study of asset management firms showed that firms owned by minorities and women manage only 1.1 percent of the industry's total $71.4 trillion in assets under management. It's no wonder, Mellody Hobson, a black woman and the co-CEO and president of Ariel Investments, told *Investor's Business Daily* in 2019, that potential black investors don't necessarily feel welcome.

"Does that person of color feel comfortable walking into that brokerage firm office or that financial advisor's office? Do they see people that they think represent the diverse society that we live in? Do they feel that somehow there are barriers to entry for them, because of just the environment?" she asked.

"While the market itself may not discriminate—and I'm using that term intentionally," she said, "the environment by which someone might come to invest can be discriminating."[26]

A natural outgrowth of this explanation is a lack of trust in markets that have not historically worked to build trust in the black community. For example, it took until 1970 for the first black American to make a trade on the floor of the New York Stock Exchange.[27] In contrast, the real estate and insurance industries have a history of employing black real estate and insurance agents.[28] Insurance, in particular, was a thriving field for black Americans: Historian Christy Ford Chapin describes how "during the early twentieth century, black-operated insurance firms experienced great success even as they competed vigorously alongside white-operated insurance companies for the business of African American consumers."[29] This history helps explain why, for more than a decade, black Americans earning more than $50,000 have consistently said they prefer to invest in housing and life insurance, according to a yearly survey by Ariel Capital Management and Schwab—even though these forms of investment are more conservative and bring lower returns than the stock market.[30]

Does this preference for conservative investment options reflect an aversion to risk in the black community? Or is it simply a matter of financial literacy, and if black Americans knew more about the stock market, they'd invest more? I find both of these lines of questioning flawed at best. Financial literacy training has been proven to be ineffective: A study found that financial literacy accounts for only one-tenth of 1 percent of differences in behavior when it comes to financial decision-making.[31] It's not a matter of education more generally either—in the comparable wealth study, the black Americans tended to have higher education levels than their white peers.

As for risk aversion, it carries a taint of victim blaming, and the victim blaming ignores the significant role played by the predominantly white financial services industry. If, as we've seen, only 1 percent of the asset management industry is managed by minority- or woman-owned firms, can we genuinely suggest that the industry is courting black clients, but the black clients are too risk-averse to respond?

I personally reject the risk aversion theory based on my own experience working on Wall Street. Years ago, in the late 1980s, I switched, briefly, from practicing law to working as an investment banker in municipal finance. Why? Because of Maynard Jackson, Atlanta's first black mayor. After years of dealing with exclusively white investment-banking clients at my law firm, I was excited to work on a deal, based in Atlanta, with my first black client. I soon learned that it wasn't a coincidence: Under Jackson's leadership, it was understood that to do business with the City of Atlanta meant deals had to include black professionals. Other black elected officials around the country followed his lead, and the municipal finance section of investment banking became a place where you could work with other black bankers. When I went to work with my former client on the banking side, I recall four other black bankers in my department in New York. In contrast, on the corporate finance side, I only met one black investment banker during my almost two years on Wall Street. I had access to that municipal finance space because black politicians used their clout to pry open the door for others; there is no counter on the corporate finance side as those making the hiring decisions, CEOs and corporate boards, remain largely white and male. When I think about the power and political muscle that

explaining how the policy came to be, and tax scholars agree that it defies logic, citing "no good tax policy reason for excluding gifts, or inheritances" from taxable income.[33] Nonetheless, it has contributed to more than a century of wealth building for those whose family members have ample resources to share with them. When considered alongside the basis rule, which limits taxation on gifts and inheritances of stocks and bonds, it becomes clear how white family wealth building has relied on tax policy designed with it in mind. (I would be remiss if I didn't also point out the boost to wealth building provided by our federal estate and gift tax regime, which allows family members to gift a certain amount [$15,000 per person in 2020] annually to as many individuals as they want without having to report the gifts to the IRS. While gifts over that threshold do need to be reported to the IRS, there's a very good chance they'll never be taxed. After the 2017 Tax Cuts and Jobs Act, individuals can give away up to $11.58 million during their lifetime or at their death that neither they nor the recipient will ever have to pay gift and estate taxes on. Married couples can give away twice that amount.)

There aren't, of course, different tax rates in place for black and white families. But the way wealth typically flows in black and white families is dramatically different, and tax policy favors a predominantly white wealth pattern. In white families, wealth is more likely to increase from generation to generation, and tax-free gifts are likely to travel from parent to child, or grandparent to grandchild. In black families, however, tax-free gifts often travel in the opposite direction, like Racheal's financial gifts to her grandmother. This both limits black households' potential to save and invest, and reduces the likelihood that a black parent will be able to leave an inheritance to be passed down to the next generation tax-free. Proportionately, almost three times as many college-educated black households provide financial support for their parents as their white college-educated peers, and those transfers have a significant impact on net worth. Researchers have found that "financial transfers to parents (much more common among Black college-educated households) significantly decrease household net wealth by more than 25 percent."[34]

White households, in contrast, are four and a half times more likely than their black peers to receive a gift or an inheritance. A study that tracked black and white families over twenty-seven years, from 1984 to 2011, showed that almost half (46 percent) of white households received some type of financial transfer, while only one in ten black households did.[35] All the households receiving family financial resources built more wealth over the period studied; however, the white households experienced growth at a far higher rate than their black counterparts. The white Americans who received a financial transfer—46 percent of the white Americans in the study—received a median of $83,692. But what's perhaps even more astonishing is that, for these families, wealth grew to $282,000—more than three times the amount of the gift they'd received.[36]

Take one middle-class white family from the study: Jessica and Nicole Bzdell, urban homeowners who held nonprofit jobs and had a combined household income of $80,000. They borrowed money from Nicole's mother for a new rural home; then, when Nicole's mother passed away, Nicole inherited about $1 million in stocks and at least $300,000 in cash. When their urban home sold, they received $200,000 more—likely tax-free. Jessica and Nicole owned their farm debt-free, had annual income of $40,000 from the stocks, and cash in the bank. From a tax policy perspective, Jessica and Nicole had very little taxable income from wages, greater preferential income from capital gains likely subject to a 0 percent tax rate (because of their low taxable income), and of course a tax-free inheritance of more than $1 million. "This inheritance shifted the family into the top decile of wealth holdings in the U.S.," the study's authors noted. "Jessica and Nicole inherited Nicole's mother's wealth status, moving them beyond their own achievements in work and education."[37]

In contrast, over the twenty-seven-year period of the study, only 10 percent of black Americans received a financial transfer, with a lower median value of $52,240. Those families saw their wealth grow by only $20,000—more than the black families who didn't receive transfers at all, but still less than the white families who didn't receive transfers either. For white households, the median wealth growth for those with and without financial transfers was $282,000 versus $72,000; for black households, the median wealth growth for those with and without financial transfers was $20,000 versus $12,000. Where white families saw their wealth tripled, black families saw it drained. The study concluded that financial transfers did not create wealth for black Americans the way they did for white Americans, and this difference was a significant contributor to the racial wealth gap.

How does that happen? It's a question of whether the financial transfer goes toward a wealth-building activity, like college tuition or a down payment on a home, or toward a basic need or an emergency. And black families are far more likely than white families to be making financial transfers that are used to help family members cover daily expenses—like Racheal's mother paying for her to go to the dentist as a Christmas gift. Earning a higher income does not protect black families from such wealth depletion; in fact, it makes them more vulnerable. "As income increases, blacks are increasingly more likely than whites to report having provided financial assistance to friends and family," one study found. "Middle-income blacks are significantly more likely than middle-income whites to report having provided informal financial assistance in the past year."[38]

That conclusion was consistent with earlier research showing "the middle-class black families in [the study] suffered about a 27 percent reduction in their wealth relative to white families as a result of the kin networks into which they were born."[39]

In other words, all tax-free gifts are not created equal. When we look at the tax treatment for inheritances, it becomes clear why simply canceling student loan debt or encouraging black families to invest in stocks won't solve the problem. When black families use the tax advantage created by the gift exemption but give the money to their parents to use for necessities instead of their children to use for investing (including in education or real estate), both parents and children are disadvantaged when it comes to building wealth.

One of the reasons why is the tax concept called *basis,* which typically refers to the cost of acquiring property. When I buy property, my basis is whatever I paid for it, and that basis will be used to measure the taxable gain or loss when I sell it. But if I don't sell that property during my lifetime, leaving it for my children or another relative to inherit, there is a different basis rule that will help them keep more of it tax-free.

Who's most likely to benefit from this rule? A family like the Brewsters, of course. When Frederick Brewster died in 1958, at the age of eighty-six, he left significant property to his heirs, including a sixty-six-room Tudor mansion on twenty-five acres of land in New Haven, Connecticut, as well as a second home in Dublin, New Hampshire, and a third in Durham, Connecticut. Brewster's will was very specific about how his estate should be used: The New Haven property, known as Edgerton, was to remain his wife's until her death, when it would be left to the city as a public park—on the condition that the mansion be razed. He also gave a bequest of twenty-four paintings to Cornell University, on the condition that they re-create the study in his home where they once hung, because he considered it a "suitable contemplative setting" for the art.

The Brewsters, you'll recall, were among the wealthiest families of their era—part of the reason Frederick Brewster wanted his mansion razed was that the upkeep alone was $100,000 per year—but to keep it simple let's say that Frederick purchased his property for $20,000, and it had grown in value to $100,000 at the time of his death. If that happened, his children would inherit $100,000 of property tax-free—and could sell it for full value, the very next day, without paying any federal income taxes. Why? Because for inherited property, the basis rule is fair market value at death. If they sell for exactly the fair market value (what a typical buyer is willing to pay), the entire amount is not considered a taxable gain—and they keep all of that wealth.

If he'd given his children the estate during his lifetime, the rule is a little different—but still offers significant wealth-building potential. First, if the beneficiary keeps the property, it's excluded from taxable income—so his children would gain a property valued at $100,000 and not pay any taxes on the gain. If they sold it at fair market value, their basis would be the same as their father's basis—$20,000—and they'd pay taxes on the $80,000 gain. But thanks in part to their father's lawsuit, they'd pay the preferential rate, not the progressive rate, on that $80,000.[40] And if the property is their personal residence, the entire $80,000 would be tax-free because it's less than the $250,000/$500,000 exclusion.

Again, you don't have to be a Brewster to benefit from these policies. In the life cycle of white wealth, sometimes a single gain leads to the next, and the next, and the next. Take Susan, who started out with a debt-free education and a connection to a stockbroker, and has built it into a multimillion-dollar portfolio. Or Kathy, another white Atlantan, who used an inheritance of $30,000 from her mother, plus a loan from her husband's brother, to buy a Manhattan apartment in the early 1990s. When she and her husband sold the apartment for a profit a few years later, they used the money to buy a larger home in less expensive Atlanta. That home, which is located in a largely white neighborhood, has seen its value multiply by a factor of six in the last two decades, from $146,700 in 2000 to $955,000 in 2019. Or Beth, a teacher-turned-consultant, who graduated from college debt-free and borrowed money from family to raise the down payment on a house in a different but still overwhelmingly white neighborhood, and has seen her home value multiply by a factor of seven. The house, valued at around $94,000 in 2000, was assessed at $667,600 in 2019. (The median home value in Atlanta is just under $300,000.)

When families have enough disposable income to purchase stock, the tax-free treatment of family financial transfers enables their children to sell the stock, keep more of their after-tax dollars, and build up their own nest egg. Both gifts and inheritances receive advantageous tax treatment; if it's a gift, the children receive the low preferential rate on any profit above the basis. If it's an inheritance, the basis is based on value at death, and they receive the income tax-free. Those children can use that money to pay their own children's college tuition, enabling them to graduate debt-free. Perhaps the grandchildren will also receive assistance with a down payment on a home. That would make it more likely for them to be offered a competitive interest rate because they are white with a high down payment, compared with the subprime rates targeted to black homebuyers. That home will likely be located in a homogeneous white neighborhood, where it will grow in value much more quickly than it would in a diverse or majority-black neighborhood. Then, the cycle is poised to repeat for the next generation.

In contrast, a single setback can eliminate the possibility of generational wealth for black families—and often, that setback occurs when these families are trying to conform to conventional wisdom about how to close the black-white wealth gap. Whether it's pursuing an advanced degree and ending up with debilitating student debt, or buying a starter home that ends up selling at a loss, the white paths to wealth don't work the same way for black families. A 2015 Brookings Institution report titled "Five Bleak Facts on Black Opportunity" found that not only did most black American families fail to rise out of the middle class but their children were actually more likely to fall out of the middle class than they were to remain there.

"In some ways, this is an even more depressing fact than the poor rates of upward mobility," the authors wrote. "Even black Americans who make it to the middle class are likely to see their kids fall down the ladder."[41]

Doesn't this mean that black parents simply need to focus their efforts on supporting their children? To that I'd say, how? If black parents deplete their wealth to support their children, they risk becoming a financial burden to those very same children, leaving them in a catch-22. They can sacrifice a lot to help their children pay for college and graduate with less debt. Later in life, however, those same black parents, having used their own nest egg to help their children, will now need those children to provide financial assistance, leaving them less able to provide for their own children. Remember John, who worried about filling out his sons' college financial aid applications? He was concerned that the income reported on his tax returns would disqualify his sons for certain financial aid packages—when, in fact, a significant part of that income already goes to support his mother. Which family member should John cut off to ensure the well-being of the other? The black-white wealth gap pits grandparent against grandchild, and no one wins.

———

The wealth gap is gaining political traction as a critical issue for voters, and Democratic politicians and think tanks have proposed reforms, including increased black homeownership and with targeted enforcement of antidiscrimination in mortgage lending laws. But these are limited in their ability to truly reduce the black-white wealth gap. We saw in chapter 2 how the Democratic presidential candidates' plans to increase homeownership included down payment assistance or a homesteading approach. But in that same chapter, we saw that there's another factor few progressives openly discuss: how white homebuyer preferences dominate the market and eliminate black opportunity.

Consider Richard Rothstein's proposal to address the historical government discrimination that prevented black Americans from buying homes in Levittown, New York: He suggests that the government purchase the next 15 percent of homes for sale in Levittown and sell them to black Americans at a reduced price in order to provide them with instant homeownership wealth.

Though a laudable effort, it fails to consider one key neighborhood attribute: white homeowners in Levittown live with a less than 1 percent black population, and they must be comfortable living with very few black neighbors—or they would live elsewhere. Rothstein's proposal, which would bring more black neighbors in Levittown, would likely make it much less appealing to current and prospective white homeowners. Existing Levittown homeowners would put their homes on the market, and as the percentage of black homeowners increased, their home values would fall further. When the dust settled, black homeowners who purchased homes at reduced prices in order to get "instant" wealth would have much less of it because "too many" black homeowners moved in. Rothstein's proposal ignores twenty-first-century systemic racism operating through the *private* decision-making of white homebuyers.

Once again, one truth—that black homeowners have a higher net worth than black renters—doesn't yield a simple prescription for wealth-gap relief. Any proposal that only focuses on increasing black homeownership fails to take into account how fraught the issue can be for black families. It also fails to recognize that homeownership does not necessarily increase generationally for black families: Today, white Americans whose grandparents were *not* homeowners have a higher rate of homeownership than black adults with grandparents who *were* homeowners. Policy reforms around black students and higher education or black employees in the labor market are similarly flawed. Increasing access to a system designed to build white wealth will ultimately not work to build black wealth.

Another progressive plan, to focus on the income gap, is similarly limited in its scope. Recent research out of the Roosevelt Institute, a progressive think tank, argues that current tax policy is unfair because the benefits "accrue disproportionately to high-income households."[42] Because most black Americans are not high-income, they say, most are ineligible for the most valuable tax breaks. That's true, and as we established in our exploration of the job market, racial income disparities absolutely need to be addressed with focus and intention by all employers, for-profit as well as not-for-profit, with a particular focus on the role the federal government can play in helping those efforts. However, even if the income gap were to close, the wealth gap would still exist. Black Americans are still black even when we have high incomes, and the tax code doesn't recognize how our family structures and needs have grown around different circumstances than those of our high-income white counterparts. For example, the tax code does not provide deductions for payments to extended family, and we've seen that this practice is not just common but standard among many contemporary black families like those from Atlanta profiled in earlier chapters.

Two black members of Congress—New Jersey senator and former presidential hopeful Cory Booker and Massachusetts representative Ayanna Pressley—have introduced legislation proposing another solution to the wealth gap: baby bonds. Under their proposal, which was central to Senator Booker's presidential campaign, the federal government would create a $1,000 trust fund for every child born in America. Every year, the federal government would contribute up to $2,000 to the account, depending on the parents' income. By the time the child reached eighteen and gained access to the account to buy a home or to pay for higher education, the poorest children would have about $46,200, and children in the highest-income homes about $1,700, according to Booker's analysis.[43] Black and Latinx children are projected to collect almost twice what white children would, on average.

Baby bonds have more advantages than disadvantages. But the baby bonds solution, too, fails to recognize that income and wealth are not the same.[44] There are low-income white Americans who have more wealth than their higher-income black peers, and their children will receive a more valuable trust fund than a high-income, low-wealth black child. Compare Jessica Bzdell, who, through her wife's inheritance, was able to own a home and work at a low-paying dream job, with John, who has a prestigious job and a higher income, but lost money on his first home and is supporting his extended family. And it doesn't change the fact that once black children turned eighteen and gained access to their accounts, they'd still be using the money in a system designed to produce white wealth and drain black wealth.

Why not simply tackle the problem from a tax perspective and tax all gifts? If gifts contribute to the racial wealth gap, an easy solution might be to include them in the recipient's taxable income. But taxing *all* gifts is once again creating tax policy with white experiences in mind to the detriment of black families. Gifts that lead to white wealth building are different from gifts that diminish black wealth building. Those giving and receiving them do not have the same ability to pay and should not be treated the same. Gifts that lead to wealth building, like money for a down payment on a home, should be included in taxable income; gifts that provide support for basic necessities and do not lead to wealth building should not. Horizontal and vertical equity should require nothing less.

However, there is one suggestion from progressive scholars that seems an easy and obvious first step: repeal the preferential rate for capital gains. The Tax Reform Act of 1986, heralded by Republican president Ronald Reagan, had as its centerpiece the idea that income from stocks should be taxed exactly as income from wages. Both wages and capital gains were taxed equally under the progressive tax system; there was no preferential rate.

Unfortunately, that legislative compromise was short-lived. In 1990, Congress increased the marginal tax rate on ordinary income like wages to 31 percent but kept the preferential rate at 28 percent.[45] President George H. W. Bush had campaigned for president in 1988 vowing to keep a tax preference for capital gains rates, and he continued to push for that as he sought reelection in 1992.[46] Senator Bill Bradley, one of the chief architects of the 1986 Tax Reform Act, described the political landscape around the decision:

> Half of the witnesses coming before the Finance Committee were willing to give up the capital gains preferences if the top rate were cut to about 28 percent, but the "other half of them said that even if you get the rate down to 12, we still want a capital gains differential."
>
> . . . Instead of leaving the rates low and not having a differential, the people who wanted to [have a] special capital gains rate came in and *pushed, pushed, pushed, pushed, pushed*. And what we are seeing today is the inevitable result of that: [Ordinary income rates] going up, up, up, up, up until we are almost back to the old system.[47]

Once again, we see how special interests "pushed, pushed, pushed, pushed, pushed," in Bradley's words, to get the loophole they sought. But what is important to remember is we had a time in the not-too-distant past when income from wages was taxed the same way as capital gains income. All the arguments about indexing gains for inflation or the harm of locking in investors did not prevent Congress from lowering tax rates for more Americans by taxing all income equally. Civilization as we know it did not come to an end. We should follow the most practical reform progressives have put forth, and repeal the preferential rate for capital gains.

Now, when you ask conservative scholars how to reduce the wealth gap, they have a different take: If only black Americans acted more like white Americans, they argue, the gap would shrink. Black Americans should go to college, get a good job, work hard, get married, buy a home—and then we would have pretty much everything our white peers have. So let's see how it would play out if every black American could truly replicate white behavior (assuming, of course, that all of us would want to).

Do black Americans want the marriage bonus? Great—let the husband work in the paid labor market, and let the wife stay at home. They will get a tax cut. Do black Americans want tax-free gains on their home sales? Then they should buy in the homogeneous white neighborhoods with high home values. Do they want colleges' tax-free endowments to work in their favor? They should send their children to excellent K–12 schools so they can earn admission to highly selective colleges that use their tax exemptions to provide resources for their students. Do they want tax-free benefits like health insurance and a retirement account or an investment portfolio? Get a good job, and find a friendly stockbroker.

This advice presumes that the white way of doing things is

either the only way to do them—or the best way. But as we've seen, following it is simply impossible: Most black Americans can't "act white" and receive the same rewards as a white person, even if they wanted to. What conservatives miss is the benefit comes from *being* white, not simply *acting* white.

Black Americans cannot do marriage like white Americans. Why? Because neither black husbands nor black wives have the same job opportunities and earning potential as their white peers, making it harder for them to support a stay-at-home spouse. (We also can't presume that black Americans *want* to do marriage like white Americans—my research showed that even in high-income households, where presumably black wives could be stay-at-home spouses, they instead contribute significant amounts to household income. It's possible that the precarious position of black men in the labor market is part of their motivation—but it could also be that black Americans prefer a more egalitarian marriage, financially and otherwise.)

Black homeowners cannot do homeownership like white Americans. Why? History shows us that if all black homeowners bought homes in all-white neighborhoods, white flight would result, driving values down. This pattern isn't just a relic from the past either: A 2019 *Newsday* investigation of realtor practices on Long Island found that white homebuyers were warned of crime in racially diverse neighborhoods, while black homebuyers were encouraged to buy in the same neighborhoods.[48] Also, black homeowners in virtually all-white neighborhoods cannot stop police or their neighbors—or even their children's teachers—from racially profiling them.

Black Americans can't replicate the white experience in

college, or in the labor market, or even in the stock market. Ultimately, only a select few black Americans can "act white" and get white rewards. It takes more work and requires racism triage at every turn.

The way the conservative policy prescription is designed means that only a few black Americans will succeed. This won't reduce the overall racial wealth gap, but it will help a select few black Americans build wealth—and then, perhaps, allow conservatives to blame all the other black Americans who haven't managed to do the same on an uneven playing field.

Still, such black exceptionalism is seductive: It leads white Americans (and even some black Americans) to think if one made it, then all can. The failure lies not in the system but in the individual.

A recent study shows just how wrong this narrative is. It concluded that if blacks had the same levels "of income, business ownership, stock ownership, and home ownership and other characteristics as whites, the wealth gap would be cut in half. However, the mean racial wealth gap would still be more than $155,000." The authors correctly describe their results as demonstrating how "cultural and behavioral factors explain less of the racial wealth gap than structural and ownership opportunity variables."[49] But where they missed the mark was in their ahistorical approach.

"It has never been the case in America that we have had a race-neutral structural and policy infrastructure in which blacks have been permitted to translate their income into wealth at the same rates as whites," says Darrick Hamilton, Henry Cohen Professor of Economics and Urban Policy and director of the Institute for the Study of Race, Stratification and Political Economy at The New School. "Nor has it ever been the case that income itself was structurally generated in a similar fashion for blacks as it has been for whites in America."

Put another way: Hard work alone will never enable black Americans to get the benefits that our white peers receive. We might be able to mimic white behavior—getting married and filing jointly, buying homes, trying to get our children into the best colleges—but we do not become white and benefit from the decades, or in some cases centuries, of opportunity that white Americans have enjoyed. White children receive financial support from their parents and grandparents to assist with their own wealth building through home purchases and debt-free college and/or graduate school. Tax subsidies provide an extra boost. Income from investments in the stock market—disproportionately held by white Americans—are taxed at a lower rate than ordinary wages, which enables even more savings and wealth building. Homes in overwhelmingly white neighborhoods appreciate astronomically, raising their owners' net worth—and snagging them up to half a million dollars tax-free when they sell. The typical white adult is not making early withdrawals from their retirement accounts or supporting financially strapped relatives. When their parents and grandparents die, they inherit property tax-free. And the cycle repeats, but now with even more tax-subsidized assets that they can leave to their heirs.

Whiteness itself, and the legacy of advantages that come with it, is the magnet that attracts wealth.

The American system for building wealth has always taken

wealth away from black Americans and given it to white Americans—beginning when enslaved blacks were stripped of their humanity and counted as the property that became the white wealth that still benefits white Americans and corporations today. I think back to Jerome Culp's original question: "To what extent have our tax laws been distorted . . . by the question of slavery and continuing racism?" What I have learned is that the distortions go back to the very beginning of our tax system, and that they persist today. Barriers to black wealth building are deeply embedded in our tax code and result in an ever-increasing racial wealth gap. Bold solutions are required. It is time that we make a change—a radical, hold-on-to-your-seat type of change.

SIX

WHAT'S NEXT?

In the April 1993 issue of *Essence,* journalist L. G. Sherrod wrote a column called "40 Acres and a Mule" that tackled the question of reparations through a tax lens. There were two issues at hand, Sherrod argued: first, the reparations owed for more than two centuries of enslavement; and second, compensation for the continued legal discrimination inflicted on black Americans during the Jim Crow era. "Although we were consigned by law to second-class citizenship," she wrote, "we were still forced to pay first-class taxes."

In the sixty years between *Plessy v. Ferguson,* which approved the doctrine of "separate but equal," and the end of the Jim Crow era, Sherrod noted, black taxpayers had been making the same payments as white taxpayers without receiving the same benefits. This added up to $43,209 in rebates due.

"So when income-tax time rolls around," she concluded, "on line 59 of form 1040—which asks you to list 'other payments'—simply enter $43,209 in 'Black taxes' and compute accordingly."[1]

To state the obvious: There was no such tax credit. But almost a decade later, between 2000 and 2001, the IRS paid out an estimated $30 million in bogus claims, many of which claimed $43,209 as other taxes paid.[2] While many of the rewards were reaped by unscrupulous tax preparers, who claimed fees from black clients up front[3] for refunds that would never come, one taxpayer—Crystal Foster, of Richmond, Virginia, whose taxes were prepared by her father, Robert—claimed that she'd overpaid capital gains on a fund called "Black Capital Investments" and received a $500,000 refund check.

Again, there was no such fund; Foster's father said he'd filed the return to make a statement about black life and wealth in America. "Black people are not treated as humans, but as things by the U.S. government," he said in an interview with the Associated Press. "We were used as resources to enrich this country and we get no inheritance from the wealth we brought."[4]

However, the IRS didn't agree. When the payout was discovered, Crystal Foster was ordered to refund the money and sentenced to three years in prison for fraud; her father, Robert, was sentenced to thirteen. A tax lawyer interviewed by NPR about the case said he would have expected a six-month sentence at the most.[5] Though the case was appealed several times, and Robert Foster's sentence was eventually reduced, no court ever found in favor of the Fosters and their protest.

The Fosters weren't the first Americans to try to challenge

the tax system by filing a deliberately fraudulent return; the Seaborns, you'll recall, did something similar in 1927 when they split Henry Seaborn's income between their tax returns and invented a married-filing-separately exemption amount, putting them in a lower tax bracket. While the IRS also challenged their returns, they didn't end up in jail; instead they paid the taxes, hired lawyers, and took their case to the Supreme Court, where they won and their fraudulent claim paved the way for the joint filing benefit.

The story of these two families, their tax protests, and their outcomes demonstrates the different ways in which white and black Americans need the tax system to change. The Brewsters and the Seaborns needed a single provision changed; the Fosters needed an entire tax system overthrown. Even if a single black family could successfully sue to change one piece of tax policy and reduce their own taxes, there's no one shift that would close the black-white wealth gap. Litigation is designed to impact the individual taxpayer; we need a solution for an entire population.

That doesn't mean, however, that the black-white wealth gap can't be closed. It will take intentional changes, by policy makers motivated to take societal racism into account, and by individual black and white Americans. Tax policy alone can't solve the problem. But it can help. In fact, the changes to tax policy that will help reduce the racial wealth gap will also more accurately reflect the way our tax system was intended to operate in the first place, before rich and powerful influencers demanded conditions and loopholes that would benefit them and help preserve their wealth. I propose three key tax measures that would both reduce the existing gap and prevent

ministration also collected data on race—so why wasn't that information matched with tax returns as well? It's an unexplained policy choice, according to Associate Professor Jeremy Bearer-Friend of the George Washington University Law School, and a strangely uniform one when it comes to excluding racial data, spanning the IRS, the Treasury, and the Joint Committee on Taxation. "Isn't it curious," he asked me, "that a policy area so centrally concerned with the redistribution of wealth is also one where race and ethnicity data are so persistently excluded?"

I'd never ask taxpayers to identify themselves by race on their returns—it seems far too likely that individual taxpayers would fall victim to cases of implicit or explicit bias from federal employees, resulting in more audits—and today's Social Security matching offers less data than it used to, thanks to new procedures that assign a number at birth or upon qualified entry to the country and don't collect racial data. Fortunately, there are other ways to get this information. Bearer-Friend's research proposes matching taxpayer data with nontax data sets, and using the results to gain race-based insights into taxation.[6] For example: sort tax returns by zip code and run an analysis based on which returns come from majority-black versus majority-white neighborhoods reported in census data. In neighborhoods where the racial demographics are starkly disproportionate, the IRS could treat those tax returns as from white or black residents with a great deal of confidence that their analysis would be pretty close to accurate. The Tax Policy Center is currently doing just that kind of work (some of which I've relied upon to write this book), but we need much, much more.[7] And the best tax data are actual tax return data.

One of the simplest, if imperfect, ways for the IRS Statistics of Income division (SOI) to access this information would be to apply a zip code analysis coupled with a surname analysis, where last names are used to broadly classify taxpayers by ethnicity, to impute race and ethnicity data. Another option is to add questions about race and ethnicity to existing surveys—the Comprehensive Taxpayer Attitude Survey, which collects opinions on taxpayer compliance and trust in the IRS, is already conducted regularly (though the SOI would have to ask for Social Security numbers if the answers were to be matched with specific tax returns). However, even without IRS participation, we could take advantage of other data collection that is currently in place—the Survey of Consumer Finances, for example, conducted by the Federal Reserve, already collects race and ethnicity data. They'd simply need to begin including tax return (1040) items in their own survey and publishing the results.

Each of these methods, of course, has advantages and disadvantages. Relying on data imputed from proxies inevitably means that some classifications will be inaccurate—just because most people in the zip code are black and have a black-sounding surname or are white with a white-sounding surname doesn't mean everyone is. But they are a thousand times better than nothing, which is what we have now.

Obtaining this information would counter the fallacy that our tax system affects everyone equally, regardless of race, or that only white Americans pay taxes. That data could then be brought before Congress when new rates and preferential loopholes are introduced as part of reforms. It's also a critical part of the case for a reparations-based tax credit; legal precedent (which we'll discuss later on in this chapter) requires proof of both discriminatory effect *and* intent to award any kind of race-based compensation. We may not have that data for the past, but if we begin collecting it now, it will become harder for lawmakers to claim ignorance of how the same tax policies have different racial impacts in the future.

However, even without the data, we already know the outcomes for our black families. That's why we need to create a new tax system—or rather, return to our old one, but with a twist. Our original system benefited black Americans as a side effect of excluding most white Americans from the tax rolls—if they didn't earn enough to pay income tax, few black Americans would either. This new tax system will benefit black Americans with intention, by recognizing the racism they endure in every walk of life. A truly equitable tax system would contain elements of the one created by the Revenue Act of 1913, such as individual returns, and address the racism that has shaped the housing, college, and labor markets in the decades since. Eliminating exclusions, reducing deductions, and returning to a single progressive rate system would go a long way toward closing the future wealth gap every April 15.

The no-exclusions rule is straightforward: All income is taxable. If you sell your home, you pay taxes on the gain from the sale; if you inherit a piece of property, you pay taxes on its fair market value. You are taxed on your total wage income, including whatever portion goes into a retirement account (whether employer-provided or self-funded). Current exclusions, as we've seen, privilege white taxpayers with existing wealth at the expense of black taxpayers without it. Huge federal deficits are created even as the preferential rate remains low. By eliminating all exclusions, we can halt the cycle in which established white wealth continues to grow, and black wealth continues to diminish.

Repealing all existing deductions has a similar effect, and is likely to have the greatest impact on only the wealthiest taxpayers. Remember, as we saw in chapter 2, taxpayers in the highest-income zip codes have historically claimed the most deductions, while taxpayers in lower-income zip codes typically take only the standard deduction. Before the 2017 Tax Cuts and Jobs Act, about two-thirds of taxpayers took the standard deduction; now that number is closer to 90 percent, and the remaining 10 percent is statistically likely to be the wealthiest Americans. (If you are wondering why I'd eliminate the student loan interest deduction, given the debilitating effect college debt has on black families, I would argue that the relief it offers is so low compared with the debt load—a maximum of $2,500 in deductions versus an average of $53,000 in debt for black college graduates just four years after graduation—that it's preferable to eliminate it along with the rest.)

In exchange, however, I'd add one new deduction that, again, revisits our earliest tax system, where the greatest burden is levied on the wealthy. A living allowance deduction (often seen in flat tax proposals like those favored by some Republican lawmakers) would reduce or eliminate income taxes for those taxpayers who earn less than the living wage in their geographic region. If you earn less than the living wage in your area, as measured by what it takes to actually make ends meet, you are paid the difference at tax time. If you earn more, you pay taxes on that difference.

That leaves our overall tax rate, which I believe should be completely progressive: Rates rise as income rises. All wage income that is over the living allowance deduction would be taxed at the progressive rate, and investment income, inheritances, and property sales would be taxed the same way—no more preferential treatment. I used to believe that vertical equity, based on ability to pay, could include a flat-rate system, where everyone pays the same percentage rate in taxes regardless of income, because those with greater incomes would still pay more in taxes. But I've come to value the symbolism of a *progressive* tax system that does more than just require higher-income Americans to pay more taxes (which could happen with a flat tax); they need to pay taxes at a higher rate. As I once explained to my tax class, rich people take up an inordinate amount of services. For example, the entire judicial system benefits them when contracts they enter into are upheld. (Indeed, we've already seen how litigation has led to white taxpayers paying less in taxes.) Even if we've eliminated the preferential rate that can allow the head of a multinational corporation to enjoy a lower tax rate than its salaried employees, billionaires like Warren Buffett (who has released his taxes, which is why we know his rate is lower than his secretary's) or Amazon's Jeff Bezos (who has not) shouldn't be taxed at the same rate as people who earn a fraction of what they do.

The good news? If we repeal all existing deductions and exclusions, we'll actually be able to make the progressive tax rates lower, because more income will be subject to tax

overall—even taking into account my proposed living allowance deduction. A 2010 report by the bipartisan Simpson-
Bowles Commission estimated that if all exclusions and
deductions were repealed, the tax system could have three
rates: 8 percent at the lowest-qualifying income levels, 14 percent in the middle, and 23 percent at the top. (By comparison,
the lowest tax rate is currently 10 percent and the highest is 37
percent.) The Seaborns and the Brewsters and their children
will pay higher taxes on their investment income and their inheritances; my parents, the Browns, and their contemporary
counterpart, the Galloways, will pay less.

The more I think about horizontal and vertical equity, the
more I think we've gotten the basic notion of equity wrong.
They assume away the impact of societal race-based discrimination. Black and white households with the same income
simply do not have the same ability to pay. A black household
with the same income as a white household is statistically
more likely to need two working spouses to earn that amount,
to have less home equity, and to be supporting family members who were overtly and legally prohibited from the same
wealth-building opportunities available to the family members of white workers. Those two households are in completely different financial situations, and federal policies
created that discrepancy. True equity demands that they *not*
pay the same amount in taxes.

I believe a fully progressive taxation system—with no exclusions and a single living allowance deduction, along with a
single wealth credit that I'll describe later in this chapter—
would not only intentionally create a more level playing
field for black American taxpayers but also benefit the major-

ity of American taxpayers of all races, just like the Revenue Act of 1913 did. The very wealthiest Americans—the ones who are more likely to itemize, claim the mortgage interest deduction on both their first and second homes, have more income from stocks than wages, and receive wealth-building family financial transfers—may be predominantly white, but that doesn't mean their experience reflects that of the majority of white Americans. The median wealth of white households is $171,000, which means half of white America have less than that. Reducing and eliminating the tax loopholes by which the wealthiest Americans protect and increase their wealth means a reduced federal deficit and a better progressive tax rate for the majority of working Americans.

However, as we've seen throughout history, tax policy changes are most often steered by powerful lobbyists and special interest groups. Shifting the system to benefit the many, instead of the few, will take a lot of work and require the vocal and bipartisan support of the public. While we're working toward systemic change, what do we do in the meantime?

There are steps both black and white taxpayers can take, starting today, to improve the circumstances of black Americans. For black Americans, many of these are simply best practices to work within a system that's not designed for your benefit. In contrast, for white Americans, many of these steps are a critical part of reducing, and ultimately eliminating, the black-white wealth gap, because white American preferences and practices influence all of our marketplaces, from housing to investments.

In our current system, if you are a black American, the best way to get ahead is *either* by aligning your behaviors with white preferences and practices or by listening to your own preferences, but taking precautions. If you choose to mimic white behavior, do not expect to have the same freedom of choice that your white peers have. (And remember, there's a good chance your white peers have a safety net, in the form of family support or gifts, that they've never told you about.) If you are a black two-income couple planning a wedding, plan it early in the year—if you get married on December 31, you'll lose your student loan deduction for the entire previous year, whereas if you get married the next day, on January 1, you'll be able to retain the deduction for that prior year's taxes. If you're buying a home, never spend your maximum housing budget in a predominantly black neighborhood—you simply won't get a good return on your investment. (That also makes home equity loans riskier, so avoid those as much as possible in predominantly black or diverse neighborhoods.) Either spend less in a diverse neighborhood, making sure that you have disposable income remaining to invest in retirement, 529 plans, or stocks after your mortgage payments, or use your full budget to buy a smaller home in a white neighborhood. If you do this, your home value is likely to grow, though your day-to-day experience might involve more of the "racism triage" we've discussed.

When it comes to your own or your children's education, avoid for-profit colleges whenever possible: They're designed to prey on you, and they have shareholders' best interests in mind, not yours. Focus instead on prestige and affordability. Look at endowments and graduation rates when you make your choices, and if you can, go to an institution that has the resources to see you through. When you enter the labor market, if your company offers a retirement plan with an employer match, invest in it immediately and max out whenever possible; it's part of your salary, and you're leaving money on the table, as I did, if you don't take advantage of it. If your company doesn't offer retirement benefits, start your own IRA, like Racheal, the young woman we met in chapter 3. (In fact, if you have a Racheal in your life who's making fiscally conservative, long-term decisions, follow her around and do whatever she does. She is one of the most financially savvy people I have ever encountered.)

Start your retirement savings while you're young—but if you didn't, don't forget that *it is never too late*. Also, while you're at it, start 529 plans for your children as well. *With what money?* you might ask. I do understand that for many black families, especially those supporting siblings or elders, these prescriptions may already seem out of reach. However, I urge you to look anywhere you can in your life to find money for a contribution, no matter how small. I'd recommend my mother's approach to every raise she ever got: "You didn't have the money the day before you got it—so act like you still don't have it." This is one area where tax treatment will benefit you, if you can find a way to participate.

In the same vein, try to find a way to invest in the stock market—although it is a long-term investment and risky, for black Americans, it can actually be less risky than homeownership. Why? In the housing market, white preferences against "black" neighborhoods (those with more than 10 percent black neighbors) yield a lower return for most black homeowners. While the stock market has obvious barriers to entry for black investors (you'll need money, and the willingness to deal with a predominantly white workforce), once you do invest, white preferences don't have the same influence—there are no "black" stocks that white stock owners can avoid en masse, lowering the price of the stock.

When the stock market loses money—and it will—do not panic. Keep your funds invested and wait for the market to come back—it always has, and white stockholders have been relying on those rebounds to build wealth for generations.

Meanwhile, as I encourage black Americans to be intentional about choosing their behaviors, I'll call on white Americans to consciously shift theirs. If you are a white American taxpayer, no matter your income level or family history, the system has benefited you at the expense of black Americans, and you, too, must be intentional—about dismantling it. Support individual filing and the repeal of the joint tax return. It may cost you more in taxes, but black Americans have been paying more taxes for years; it's only fair. If you want to live and raise a family in a diverse neighborhood, where the housing stock is still affordable, fine—but make sure you don't move in and center yourself in the experience, complaining that the corner store plays its music too loud (as a resident of a new luxury apartment in a Washington, D.C., neighborhood did) and the schools aren't good enough.[8] Instead, take the time to learn about how the neighborhood has functioned without you, and make yourself a part of its established values and customs.

White parents should consider their biases when choosing neighborhood schools as well. Remember, research shows that white parents are more likely to make a snap decision about a school's quality based on how many other white families send their children there.[9] This perpetuates equating blackness with inferiority—and passes that perception on to the next generation. Conduct real research to determine if your neighborhood schools are good—and if they really aren't, use your power to help advocate for them. Individual white voices shaped many of the policies that created these inequities, and individual white voices can speak out against them now.

If you are helping your child apply to college, examine the institution's overall graduation rates and graduation rates by race, if available. Look at which students are positioned for success, and see if it comes at other students' expense, and ask yourself what kind of educational system you want to support. If you are in a management position at your company, be a vocal advocate for equal compensation, and make sure that black and white employees working at the same levels are receiving it. And if you work in financial services in particular—which means you know why stocks are a smart investment, and how to make them work to your client's benefit—make outreach to black clients a priority. Think of Susan, and the broker-client relationship that ensured her prosperous future.

There is one more critical step that white taxpayers need to take: Be honest about the advantages you have received, and recognize that even if they don't seem like much to you, they are very likely more than what your black peers have. As long as white families downplay and dismiss the generational advantages they've received, there is no way to make an honest comparison between opportunities and outcomes. Dismantling the anti-black nature of the system requires both radical policy change and radical transparency from white Americans.

In writing this book I was struck by how the white families interviewed downplayed the inheritances and gifts they received, or the significance of graduating from college without debt because a family member paid their way. I was also struck by how they did not want to go on the record to discuss their good fortune. The way whiteness attracts wealth is a well-kept secret—and one that perpetuates over time. A recent study by a team of researchers at Yale University surveyed a group of one thousand Americans and found that the majority believed that black families in 1963 were about half as wealthy as white families, and black families in 2016 were about nine-tenths as wealthy as white families. In fact, in 1963 black families had less than one-tenth of the wealth of white families—and that was still true in 2016.[10]

I hope this book will teach white Americans how to look for luck in their stories and talk about it when they find it— even something as seemingly small as a low-interest loan from a family member. I hope it will help to stop them from thinking that our system is a meritocracy and they've earned everything they have through hard work alone. I hope, over time, more will be willing to tell their stories out loud.

One more piece of the wealth gap still needs to be addressed: the decades of historical discrimination against black taxpayers that L. G. Sherrod demanded compensation for back in 1993. The sixty years of legalized second-class citizenship she referenced span from approximately 1896, when the Supreme Court decided *Plessy v. Ferguson*[11] by a 7–1 majority and made "separate but equal" constitutional, to 1954, when the Supreme Court unanimously reversed it in *Brown v. Board of Education*.[12] Not only are many of the black taxpayers who suffered under that legalized discrimination alive today, but they are without the financial security that their white peers were able to obtain through education and homeownership. They, in turn, are being supported by children and other extended family members, who deplete their own resources to care for them. The legal discrimination may be history, but its effects remain very present, and continue to influence downward social mobility for black families. And each April 15, the victim class continues to grow.

For this reason, a reparations credit is the final piece of closing the black-white wealth gap. The reasoning is simple: The overtly racist policies of the past aren't truly behind us, and not just because the taxpayers held back and victimized by them are still part of our society and members of our families. Our racist tax policies disadvantage black Americans who were born after Jim Crow was legally invalidated, too. Today, black taxpayers are still paying too much, and our current tax policies are still "separate but equal." The victims need to be compensated.

My first choice for race-based reform would be a refundable tax credit—like the earned income tax credit discussed in chapter 1 but simplified. Under this plan, Congress would assign a single fixed credit to *all* black taxpayers. If your tax liability is lower than the credit, you'll receive the difference, in the form of a refund, every year. (If your tax liability is higher, you'll still pay the difference, but you'll pay less than white taxpayers with the same household income, which would satisfy a definition of horizontal equity that took societal racism into account.) The fixed credit makes this a more effective plan than the EITC—which, as we've seen, varies credits based on income and children in the household for added complexity, leading to increased taxpayer audits and high error rates.[13]

If you are wondering what amount the credit should be, a recent estimate on reparations limited to descendants of enslaved Americans, and focused on eliminating the current racial wealth gap, would be $10.7 trillion, or an average of $267,000 per person for the forty million eligible black descendants of American slavery. Given that black Americans currently hold 3 percent of the nation's wealth but represent 13 percent of the population, is $267,000—a proportional redistribution based on population—really out of line?[14]

I'd argue no. But this, or any tax reform designed to compensate black Americans for years of higher taxes, is unlikely to be found constitutional under the current Supreme Court. With that in mind, I propose a different shift to our tax system that will help close the racial wealth gap and that would be found constitutionally sound: a wealth-based tax credit that offers relief for the lowest-wealth Americans. This will not exclusively help the black taxpayers who suffered under Jim Crow or who continue to suffer today *because* they are black, which is why it is my second-best choice. But it will disproportionately aid those taxpayers, since 83 percent of black households have household wealth below the white median, and still withstand any charges of unconstitutional race-based policy.

Why is race-based tax reform unconstitutional? Remember our friend Charles Dickens: "The law is a ass." If Congress were to pass legislation to compensate black taxpayers for their decades of paying higher taxes, you know what would happen next: A white taxpayer would file a lawsuit. And the Supreme Court would once again side with the white taxpayer.

As recently as 1996, the Supreme Court has held that in order for a law with a racially disparate impact to be unconstitutional, the law has to have a racially discriminatory purpose.[15] Put another way, if a case for race-based tax relief went to the Supreme Court, you'd have to prove that tax policy was created with the explicit intent to make black taxpayers pay more.[16] To say that Congress may have been aware that a particular tax provision would help white taxpayers more than black taxpayers is simply not enough to hold up under current precedent.

The legal precedent for this is the 1976 landmark Supreme Court decision of *Washington v. Davis,* which held that in the absence of discriminatory intent, it is almost impossible to prove that discriminatory impact alone will cause a statute to be invalidated. In *Washington v. Davis* the issue was whether a test that was used to screen applicants for hire as police officers was discriminatory; a higher percentage of blacks failed the test than whites, and as a result, blacks were underrepresented on the police force. The Supreme Court rejected the argument that discriminatory impact alone is sufficient to strike down a law as unconstitutional. The court stated:

> A rule that a statute designed to serve neutral ends is nevertheless invalid, absent compelling justification,

if in practice it benefits or burdens one race more than
another would be far reaching and would raise serious questions about, and perhaps invalidate, a whole
range of **tax,** welfare, public service, regulatory, and
licensing statutes that may be more burdensome to
the poor and to the average black than to the more
affluent white. (emphasis added)[17]

Even though our income tax system penalizes black Americans more than white Americans (or has a racially disparate
impact), in other words, that is not enough to find the system
unconstitutional. The opinion both acknowledged the existence of racially disparate treatment and said that it was constitutionally protected.

That's not even the whole story. Even if I could show evidence of a discriminatory purpose, all Congress has to do to
counter my claim is to show that it would have taken the same
action without the discriminatory motivation—arguing that
the laws were intended to help the majority of taxpayers, not
to hurt black taxpayers specifically. If that argument were accepted (as it likely would be, given the current composition of
the Supreme Court), any evidence of past discrimination
would be insufficient to support a remedy.

There is, however, early Supreme Court precedent from
1886 that invalidates laws that penalize *only* racial minority
groups: *Yick Wo v. Hopkins*.[18] In that instance racist intent
can be presumed. The city of San Francisco required all laun-
dries in wooden buildings to get a permit from its board of
supervisors before they could open. The stated reason for the
law was that these businesses posed a fire risk. In practice,

however, more than two hundred petitions by those of Chinese ancestry were denied, while all but one of the petitions filed by non-Chinese individuals were granted.

The court found the law unconstitutional, because it had been administered in a racially discriminatory manner. What was the difference here? Access to information. The favorable ruling was only possible because the plaintiff was able to gain *access* to the information about the petitions granted and denied by the board of supervisors. However, this kind of finding—and the evidence it's based on—is rare; you'd have to prove a pattern as stark and discriminatory as that in *Yick Wo*. In other words, you'd need to show that no black taxpayers have received the marriage bonus, claimed the mortgage interest deduction, or sold their home and received tax-free gain. Targeted tax relief for black Americans is simply not available—for now.

That leaves the second-best option, which would also reduce the racial wealth gap: Ask Congress to create a wealth-based refundable tax credit for individual taxpayers whose wealth is below the median. A wealth-based credit will disproportionately benefit black Americans *because* of the racial wealth gap—which, as we've seen, is substantially different between black and white Americans at all income levels, differentiating it from the EITC, which is based on income.

Why is a wealth-based credit legal, but not a race-based one? In a closely divided 5–4 decision in *San Antonio Independent School District v. Rodriguez*, the Supreme Court found that conditioning government benefits on wealth only requires a logical or "rational" basis. (Conditioning benefits based on race requires a much higher standard.) That 1973 case found that funding school districts by local property taxes was constitutional—even though it meant wealthier (and disproportionately white) school districts got more funding than poorer school districts, which had a negative effect on students of color who disproportionately lived in those poorer school districts. The court's decision was based on a finding that linking funding to local property values was "reasonable"—paving the way to make any decision rooted in wealth-based conditions logical and therefore constitutional.[19] All you need for a law that creates wealth disparities to be upheld is to have a reason the court will respect. (Although *San Antonio v. Rodriguez* is helpful in mounting a defense for a wealth-based tax credit, it's considered a major civil rights setback for its failure to uphold the right to a quality education for families living in low-wealth districts simply because the wealth disparity didn't result in an "absolute denial" of their education.)

A tax credit for all individuals with below median wealth—just under $100,000 for the average U.S. household—would help low-wealth taxpayers of all racial and ethnic backgrounds, making it likely to pass the "reasonable" threshold set by *San Antonio v. Rodriguez*.[20] Congress could also decide that in a world with deficits, only the neediest should benefit and limit all individual tax breaks to low-wealth individuals. Either option would disproportionately help black taxpayers who have been disproportionately harmed under the current system.

This kind of compensation, whatever form it takes, is controversial. But I believe we can't close the wealth gap without it, because of the established differences we've seen in black and white family structures. A wealth credit for John's mother would mean he could send his sons to college without worrying about who will support her; a wealth credit for Racheal's grandmother would relieve a young woman, just out of college, of the burden of helping to support her family while starting her own career. A wealth credit could help black homeowners like the Hancocks stay in place against the forces of gentrification, and help Chris and Je'lon pay down the debts they incurred to get advanced degrees. It would answer Greg Galloway's question: "How can we ever get ahead?" Each of these black Atlanta families reminded me how hard most of us will work in pursuit of an American dream that was never designed with us in mind.

As for me, I've been lucky—and the luckiest thing that ever happened to me was having James and Dottie Brown as my parents. And James and Dottie, who faced overt and legal discrimination throughout their lives, were lucky, too: My father, prohibited from entering the plumbers' union, found a job with Mr. Gelman, who helped my parents buy their three-family home. When he did get a job with the union (once legal discrimination was outlawed), it provided him with a pension that supports my mother to this day. At this point in my life I won't benefit from a wealth credit, and now, neither will Miss Dottie. When I think about all the years she balanced budgets, made money stretch, and saved for rainy days, all so my sister and I could succeed, it's hard for me to advocate for a tax credit that she will not get. Maybe someday, a different Supreme Court will decide that disparate impact alone will be enough to declare a government policy unconstitutional and allow for a race-based remedy. But for now, I'm content with a wealth tax credit that other black Americans who simply weren't as lucky will receive as some compensation for the years they struggled as second-class citizens.

Miss Dottie, like so many of her generation, isn't one to complain about her past or her present. But when I let her read chapter 1, on the marriage penalty, she got very quiet and said, "They owe me and James reparations." It was the first time I remember ever hearing her say the word.

How many black taxpayers have a Miss Dottie in their lives to this very day—someone who was denied their fair share for most of their lives, but still managed to support us when we needed it? How many of us have someone who made those "nonmonetary" investments in our education that are a hallmark of black families? How many of us have someone who worked "triple time" like my father, thinking that it would get them ahead—and never knowing that it was putting them further behind?

That's why I was wrong, all those years ago, when I went into tax law thinking that race wasn't a part of it. The truth is, there's nothing in this country that race and racism aren't a part of—the very foundation of the United States emerged on the premise that black people weren't fully human, and despite the progress since the civil rights era, the stories here show us how much work is left to be done. At first glance, tax policy may not be an obvious way to fight systemic racism. But as we've seen, its effects on black families are, by and large, insidious, debilitating, and ubiquitous.

Fortunately, today's Congress has many more black members and allies, and today's electorate has many more black

voters. We are well positioned to start making the kind of demands that the wealthiest white Americans have made for decades. What we need now is greater understanding of *why tax
policy matters*. When you vote at the federal, state, and municipal levels, remember that the people who created and upheld the racist policies that set black Americans behind rarely
said outright that that's what they were doing. Just look at the
voter suppression efforts taking place today, which consistently make it more difficult for black Americans to vote, but
never acknowledge that that's the explicit purpose. Even as we
seek justice, we are once again dealing with societal racism
that our white peers simply do not face. You need to watch out
for their tricks.

You need to look at what exemptions and loopholes your
elected officials uphold, what data they demand and what
they're willing to overlook, and which lobbyists fighting to
preserve the status quo have their ear.

On that long-ago day, when I saw the white police officer
beating up a black citizen, and Mommy told me that it just
"happens sometimes," she wasn't wrong—and she still isn't.
Police brutality continues to this day, often without justice or
repercussions. But decades later, there has been a small shift:
As such acts are now caught on camera and widely viewed,
more white allies discover what black Americans have long
known—and are demanding reforms. If you'd told me, in
2016, that Americans would be marching in the streets of
every major city, during a global pandemic, calling for de-
funding the police and other systemic reforms, I wouldn't
have believed you. Neither would I have thought that 71 percent of white Americans would call racism "a big problem."[21]

But I'm glad that the summer of 2020 proved me wrong and made me hopeful about change.

Writing this book has caused me to veer between pessimism and optimism. The lack of significant black economic progress since the civil rights reforms of the 1960s makes me pessimistic, but the thought that my research could lead to change gives me some hope. As in the fight against police brutality, persistence and vigilance must be our constant companions. And while you can't take a picture of this harm and post it to social media, all of you, black and white, can go public with your stories. It's long past time to have a conversation about the racist acts buried deep in our tax returns.

In other words, you are in charge. And, taking inspiration from Miss Dottie and the beautiful clothes she made, it's time to tailor an American dream that includes each and every one of us.

AUTHOR'S NOTE AND ACKNOWLEDGMENTS

Writing this book made me so aware of how much luck plays a part in everyone's financial success. My lucky break came from being born to James and Dottie Brown. Not just because they sacrificed for me—lots of black parents sacrifice for their children, and their children do not have the financial success I have—but also because they were lucky, too.

It's because of luck that my parents were able to buy our home. It's because of luck that nobody found out about the lie that allowed my mother to move me to a less racist public elementary school. That school led me to my sixth-grade teacher, Mrs. Gertrude Bertinthol, who selected me to take the entrance exam for Hunter College High School. I passed (taking the exam with a 104-degree fever—Miss Dottie was *not* going to let me sit it out), and it secured my future.

Yet my family was one incident away from my future trajectory being markedly different. What if my parents never had a Mr. Gelman to help them buy a home? What if my mother was charged with a crime for her lie about our residence? What if I, or any member of my family, had become seriously ill when we didn't have health insurance?

I would not have the financial success I currently have. My wealth, like the wealth of most black Americans, is really a story about luck and exceptionalism. My success does not reveal a level playing field—just the opposite. My story is not that if I can do it, anyone can do it if they try; my story is that I and my parents beat the odds in a system designed for white wealth.

I started down this journey because of a question from my friend and mentor Jerome Culp. My research proved him right, but it is a bittersweet revelation because Jerome is no longer with us. He passed away on Thursday, February 5, 2004, at the age of fifty-three from kidney disease. It fills me with sadness that I cannot pick up the phone and talk to him about my book, but I am comforted knowing that his work will live on.

I owe a debt of gratitude to my wonderfully brilliant and fierce agent, Alia Hanna Habib, without whose guidance and insight this book never would have happened. To Emma Berry, who has been the best intellectual partner I have ever had, words can never express my heartfelt gratitude for all of your tireless efforts on this project. A special thanks to Stacey Stein, Lydia Morgan, and the superb marketing team, along with everyone else at Crown for the amazing job they have done.

Tressie McMillan Cottom always encouraged me when I needed it and gave me a reality check when I needed that, too. She never doubted that I could get this done, even when I did. A special shout-out goes to Justin Driver for his early encouragement when serendipity put us next to each other at a dinner table and in the course of the evening he told me: "Dorothy, if you don't write this book, who will?"

To my current and former Emory University colleagues and students too numerous to thank individually: Your support has meant the world to me. I am grateful to all the librarians at Emory University, but especially this book's champion, Elizabeth Christian, for her wonderful work unearthing the materials on the Seaborns and the Brewsters, along with Dr. Melissa Hackman and Dr. Robert O'Reilly for their outstanding work on any project I needed help with. My deepest gratitude goes to the many law professors throughout the years who have helped sharpen my thinking and who graciously read draft chapters. A special thanks to Dr. William A. ("Sandy") Darity, Jr., Samuel DuBois Cook Distinguished Professor of Public Policy at Duke University, who encouraged me to move beyond my comfort zone and welcomed me into other intellectual spaces.

I would like to especially thank Dr. Ryan Gibson, Postdoctoral Scholar in Innovation and Diversity at the University of New Hampshire, for his excellent data preparation and analysis in chapter 1. In addition, a special thank-you goes to my brilliant and talented colleague Joanna M. Shepherd, Thomas Simmons Professor of Law, for letting me pick her brain about all things—but particularly about economics. And my unending gratitude goes to Dr. Darrick Hamilton, Henry Cohen Professor of Economics and Urban Policy at The New School, for numerous conversations about my ideas while always remaining accessible and cheerful.

For my posse: Lynell, Mechele, Melissa, and Michele. You always have my back and I love you forever.

A sincere thank-you to the Atlanta families—Chris, John, Racheal, Susan, Kathy, Beth, Je'lon Alexander, Veronica Alexander, Kristen and Greg Galloway, Mary Hancock, and Ursula McCandless—for your willingness to share your stories in order for us to learn a little more about how racism and tax policy intersect in the lives of ordinary Americans. Your courage and resilience inspired me. I am especially appreciative of Wayne Early, Jim Wehner at Focused Community Strategies, Mike Schwartz, and Reed Kimbrough for all of their assistance. And last but certainly not least I want to thank Jessica Ullian, reporter extraordinaire, who found and interviewed the families (and Miss Dottie) and helped me bring their stories to life.

NOTES

INTRODUCTION

1. *Nomination of Judge Clarence Thomas to Be Associate Justice of the Supreme Court of the United States: Hearings before the Comm. on the Judiciary,* 102nd Cong. 265–67 (1991) (testimony of Joe Broadus, Professor, George Mason Law School).
2. Brooke A. Masters, "Classroom Slur Brings Protests," *Washington Post,* Sept. 10, 1993.
3. Jerome Culp, "Toward a Black Legal Scholarship: Race and Original Understandings," *Duke Law Journal* 40, no. 1 (1991): 39, 67.
4. Culp, 101.
5. U.S. Department of Agriculture, *2012 Census of Agriculture Highlights: Black Farmers,* Sept. 2014, 1, https://www.nass.usda.gov/Publications/Highlights/2014/Highlights_Black_Farmers.pdf.
6. PeopleForBikes and Alliance for Biking & Walking, *Building Equity; Race, Ethnicity, Class, and Protected Bike Lanes: An Idea*

Book for Fairer Cities, 2017, 11, https://nacto.org/wp-content /uploads/2015/07/2015_PeopleForBikes-and-Alliance-for-Walking -Biking_Building-Equity.pdf; Jerry J. Vaske and Katie M. Lyon, "Linking the 2010 Census to National Park Visitors," U.S. Department of the Interior, June 2014, 20, https://irma.nps.gov /DataStore/DownloadFile/495294#:~:text=People%20in%20 the%202010%20Census,%25)%20of%20national%20park%20 visitors.

7. Vaske and Lyon, 20.

8. U.S. Commission on Civil Rights, "The Economic Status of Black Women: An Exploratory Investigation," 100 (1990).

9. Eric S. Yellin, *Racism in the Nation's Service: Government Workers and the Color Line in Woodrow Wilson's America* (Chapel Hill, N.C.: University of North Carolina Press, 2013), 135.

10. Carolyn Jones, "Class Tax to Mass Tax: The Role of Propaganda in the Expansion of the Income Tax during World War II," *Buffalo Law Review* 37, no. 3 (1988): 685, 688.

11. Cheryl L. Greenberg, *To Ask for an Equal Chance: African Americans in the Great Depression* (Lanham, Md.: Rowman & Littlefield, 2009), 25.

12. Greenberg, 29.

13. Greenberg, 26.

14. Lily Rothman, "How World War II Still Determines Your Tax Bill," *Time,* April 14, 2016.

15. Mary S. Bedell, "Employment and Income of Negro Workers— 1940–52," *Monthly Labor Review* 76 (1953): 596, 600. The nonwhite category is roughly 90 percent black.

16. Office of Management and Budget, *Fiscal Year 2017 Historical Tables,* 36, https://www.govinfo.gov/content/pkg/BUDGET-2017 -TAB/pdf/BUDGET-2017-TAB.pdf.

17. Ira Katznelson, *When Affirmative Action Was White: An Untold History of Racial Inequality in Twentieth-Century America* (New York: W. W. Norton, 2005), 113.

18. F. John Devaney, *Tracking the American Dream,* Current Housing Reports, Series H121/94-1 (Washington, D.C.: U.S. Government Printing Office, 1994), 29.

19. In *Shelby County v. Holder,* 570 U.S. 529 (2013), the U.S. Supreme

Court declared unconstitutional parts of the Voting Rights Act, which has led to voter suppression efforts in North Carolina and Georgia, among other states.

20. Chuck Collins, Dedrick Asante-Muhammad, Josh Hoxie, and Sabrina Terry, *Dreams Deferred: How Enriching the 1% Widens the Racial Wealth Divide*, Inequality.org, Jan. 2019, 11–12, https://inequality.org/wp-content/uploads/2019/01/IPS_RWD -Report_FINAL-1.15.19.pdf.

21. Michael W. Kraus, Julian M. Rucker, and Jennifer A. Richeson, "Americans Misperceive Racial Economic Equality," *PNAS* 114, no. 39 (Sept. 26, 2017): 10324–31.

22. Collins et al., *Dreams Deferred*, 4.

23. Tatjana Meschede, Joanna Taylor, Alexis Mann, and Thomas Shapiro, " 'Family Achievements?': How a College Degree Accumulates Wealth for Whites and Not for Blacks," *Federal Reserve Bank of St. Louis Review* 99, no. 1 (First Quarter 2017): 121–37.

24. Aaron Blake, "Republicans' Views of Blacks' Intelligence, Work Ethic Lag Behind Democrats at a Record Clip," *Washington Post,* March 31, 2017.

25. David Neiwert, "Bill Bennett: Obama's Win Means 'You Don't Take Excuses Anymore' From Minorities," Crooks and Liars, Nov. 5, 2008, https://crooksandliars.com/david-neiwert/bill -bennett-obama-wins-means-no-mor.

26. Ryan Sit, "Trump Thinks Only Black People Are on Welfare, But Really, White Americans Receive Most Benefits," *Newsweek*, January 12, 2018.

27. Jessica Semega, Melissa Kollar, John Creamer, and Abinash Mohanty, "Income and Poverty in the United States: 2018," Current Population Reports (issued September 2019, revised June 2020), 15, https://www.census.gov/content/dam/Census/library /publications/2019/demo/p60-266.pdf.

28. Bethany Romano, "Racial Wealth Gap Continues to Grow between Black and White Families, regardless of College Attainment," Brandeis, July 16, 2018, https://heller.brandeis.edu/news /items/releases/2018/meschede-taylor-college-attainment-racial -wealth-gap.html.

29. William Darity, Jr., Darrick Hamilton, Mark Paul, Alan Aja,

Anne Price, Antonio Moore, and Caterina Chiopris, *What We Get Wrong about Closing the Racial Wealth Gap,* Samuel DuBois Cook Center on Social Equity, Duke University, April 2018, 63, https://socialequity.duke.edu/wp-content/uploads/2019/10/what-we-get-wrong.pdf.

30. Edward Rodrigue and Richard V. Reeves, "Five Bleak Facts on Black Opportunity," Brookings Institution, Jan. 15, 2015, https://www.brookings.edu/blog/social-mobility-memos/2015/01/15/five-bleak-facts-on-black-opportunity/.

31. Raj Chetty, Nathaniel Hendren, Maggie R. Jones, and Sonya R. Porter, "Race and Economic Opportunity in the United States: An Intergenerational Perspective," *The Quarterly Journal of Economics* (2020), 733, 736.

32. Kevin Kruse, *White Flight: Atlanta and the Making of Modern Conservatism* (Princeton, N.J.: Princeton University Press, 2005).

33. Paul Crater, "Atlanta's 'Berlin Wall,'" *Atlanta,* Dec. 1, 2011.

34. Aiyana Cristal, "Atlanta's 'Berlin Wall' Built to Keep Black Residents Out of All-White Community," CBS46, Feb. 14, 2017, https://www.cbs46.com/news/atlanta-s-berlin-wall-built-to-keep-black-residents-out/article_2bdee5d6-8bd4-5ef0-bfc5-61ea542dd482.html.

35. Sheffield Hale, "An Award for All Mankind, a Dinner for One—the Atlanta Nobel Prize Party for MLK, Given by the City's Image-Conscious White Leadership," Georgia Humanities, Nov. 2, 2016, https://www.georgiahumanities.org/2016/11/02/an-award-for-all-mankind-a-dinner-for-one-the-atlanta-nobel-prize-party-for-mlk-given-by-the-citys-image-conscious-white-leadership/.

36. Argosy University—Atlanta Data Overview, College Factual, https://www.collegefactual.com/colleges/argosy-university-atlanta/student-life/diversity/.

37. Robert Siegel, "Black Atlantans Struggle to Stay in the Middle Class," NPR, Dec. 8, 2011, https://www.npr.org/2011/12/08/143378702/black-atlantans-struggle-to-stay-in-the-middle-class.

38. Siegel, "Black Atlantans Struggle to Stay in the Middle Class."

39. Rakesh Kochhar and Anthony Cilluffo, "How Wealth Inequality Has Changed in the U.S. Since the Great Recession, by Race, Eth-

nicity and Income," Pew Research Center, Nov. 1, 2017, https://www.pewresearch.org/fact-tank/2017/11/01/how-wealth-inequality-has-changed-in-the-u-s-since-the-great-recession-by-race-ethnicity-and-income/.

40. Sammi Chen, "Racial Wealth Snapshot: Asian Americans," Prosperity Now, May 10, 2018, https://prosperitynow.org/blog/racial-wealth-snapshot-asian-americans.

ONE: MARRIED WHILE BLACK

1. Preeti Varathan, "Does It Make Financial Sense to Get Married?," Quartz, May 5, 2018, https://qz.com/1262993/does-it-make-financial-sense-to-get-married/.

2. Robin Fisher, Geof Gee, and Adam Looney, "Joint Filing by Same-Sex Couples after Windsor: Characteristics of Married Tax Filers in 2013 and 2014," Department of the Treasury Office of Tax Analysis, Working Paper 108, Aug. 2016, 4, https://www.treasury.gov/resource-center/tax-policy/tax-analysis/Documents/WP-108.pdf. Another reason is if one spouse has student loans and they are trying to qualify for income-based repayment plans, filing separately allows them to qualify based on their income only.

3. Ralph Vartabedian and Maeve Reston, "McCain Shares Tax Returns but Withholds His Wife's," *Los Angeles Times*, April 19, 2008.

4. Dana Bash, "McCain Releases His Taxes, Not Wife's," CNN, April 18, 2008, http://www.cnn.com/2008/POLITICS/04/18/mccain.taxes/index.html.

5. Alice Kessler-Harris, *In Pursuit of Equity* (New York: Oxford University Press, 2003), 198.

6. As a married taxpayer filing a joint return, he would subtract the personal exemption, which for 1927 was $3,500, and have taxable income of $22,776.72 ($11,500). That would result in a $370 tax bill—roughly $5,300 in today's dollars. Author's calculation as follows: $4,000 × 1.5% = $60; $4,000 × 3.0% = $120; $2,000 × 5.0% = $100; and $1,500 × 6.0% = $90 = $370.00. The progressive tax system is designed to tax income at different rates as in-

come increases. So here, the taxpayer's first taxable dollars are taxed at 1.5%, and their last dollars are taxed at 6%. The taxpayer's marginal tax rate here is 6%.

7. That would put their taxable income at $5,750 ($7,500 - $1,750 = $5,750) and a resulting tax bill of $112.50 for each Seaborn. Author's calculation as follows: $4,000 × 1.5% = $60; $1,750 × 3.0% = $52.50 = $112.50.

8. Today only nine states are community property states: Louisiana, Arizona, California, Texas, Washington, Idaho, Nevada, New Mexico, and Wisconsin.

9. *Lucas v. Earl,* 281 U.S. 111 (1930). In that case, decided before *Poe v. Seaborn,* the taxpayer lived in California but attempted to create separate property by contractual agreement. There was a quirk in California law that caused the courts to treat California as not a "true" community property tax regime. That quirk was subsequently fixed.

10. *Lucas,* 281 U.S.

11. Five states and Hawaii (Hawaii didn't become a state until 1959) converted from common-law property states. See Carolyn Jones, "Split Income and Separate Spheres: Tax Law and Gender Roles in the 1940s," *Law and History Review* 6, no. 2 (Fall 1988): 259–310. "Five states and the territory of Hawaii abandoned their common-law marital property systems and adopted community property regimes," 259.

12. "Community Dilemma," *Newsweek,* Oct. 13, 1947, 64–65.

13. Mildred L. Amer, Congressional Research Service Report for Congress, *Women in the United States Congress: 1917–2008,* https://www.everycrsreport.com/files/20080723_RL30261_6a27ad4b40f53b0186024073788e830d33036988.pdf.

14. Jacqueline Jones, *Labor of Love, Labor of Sorrow: Black Women, Work, and the Family, from Slavery to the Present* (New York: Basic Books, 2010).

15. Claudia Goldin, "Female Labor Force Participation: the Origin of Black and White Differences, 1870 and 1880," *Journal of Economic History* 37, no. 1 (March 1977): 87–108.

16. Elizabeth Potamites, "Why Do Black Women Work More? A Comparison of White and Black Married Women's Labor Sup-

ply," http://citeseerx.ist.psu.edu/viewdoc/download?doi=10.1.1.4
73.978&rep=rep1&type=pdf; see also Dorothy A. Brown, "Lessons from Barack and Michelle Obama's Tax Returns," *Tax Notes,* March 10, 2014, 1112n25, https://taxprof.typepad.com
/files/brown-142-tax-notes-1109.pdf.

17. Author's calculations from Sarah Flood, Miriam King, Renae
Rodgers, Steven Ruggles, and J. Robert Warren, Integrated Public
Use Microdata Series, Current Population Survey: Version 6.0
[dataset] (Minneapolis, Minn.: IPUMS, 2018), https://doi
.org/10.18128/D030.V6.0.

18. Goldin, "Female Labor Force Participation," 87–108.

19. Kessler-Harris, *In Pursuit of Equity,* 198.

20. Benjamin Bridgman, Andrew Dugan, Mikhael Lal, Matthew Osborne, and Shaunda Villones, "Accounting for Household Production in the National Accounts, 1965–2010," *Survey of
Current Business* (May 2012): 23–36; Sharon J. Bartley, Priscilla
W. Blanton, and Jennifer L. Gilliard, "Husbands and Wives in
Dual-Earner Marriages: Decision-Making, Gender Role Attitudes, Division of Household Labor, and Equity," *Marriage &
Family Review* 37, no. 4 (Sept. 2005): 69–94.

21. Joyce O. Beckett and Audrey D. Smith, "Work and Family Roles:
Egalitarian Marriage in Black and White Families," *Social Service Review* 55, no. 2 (1981): 321n19: "Charles V. Willie and
Susan L. Grunblett, 'Four "Classic" Studies of Power Relationships in Black Families: A Review and Look to the Future,' *Journal of Social Service Review Marriage and the Family* 40
(November 1978): 691–94; and Katheryn Thomas Dietrich, 'A Reexamination of the Myth of Black Matriarchy,' *Journal of Marriage and Family* 37, no. 2 (May 1975): 367–74."

22. Martin Kroll, "The Civil Rights Act of 1964 and NYC's Minority
Plumbers," *New York Almanack,* Dec. 20, 2015, https://
newyorkalmanack.com/2015/12/the-civil-rights-act-of-1964-and
-nycs-minority-plumbers/.

23. Bernard D. Reams, Jr., *Tax Reform—1969: A Legislative History
of the Tax Reform Act of 1969 (Public Law 91-172) with Related
Amendments* (Buffalo, N.Y.: William S. Hein, 1991), 1996.

24. Reams, 1977.

25. Ida A. Brudnick and Jennifer E. Manning, *African American Members of the United States Congress: 1870–2018,* Congressional Research Service, https://www.senate.gov/CRSpubs/617f17bb -61e9-40bb-b301-50f48fd239fc.pdf.

26. The first black member to serve on the House Ways and Means Committee was Charlie Rangel, a Democrat from New York City, in 1975.

27. This chapter focuses on opposite-sex marriages. It was not until 2013 that same-sex couples were allowed to file joint tax returns, although the IRS did allow couples to amend prior tax returns going back to 2010. Because the Census Bureau data analyzed in this chapter is from 2010, only opposite-sex marriages will be analyzed.

28. Tina Orem, "Married? 6 Times You May Want to File Taxes Separately," *USA Today,* March 20, 2018. An analysis of whether there are race-based differences in the operation of the joint return when it comes to same-sex marriages could be fruitful given Census Bureau survey data that show almost 60 percent of same-sex married couples have two wage earners. The published data, however, are not broken down by race. See Jonathan Vespa, Jamie M. Lewis, and Rose M. Kreider, *America's Families and Living Arrangements: 2012,* U.S. Census Bureau, Aug. 2013, https://www.census.gov/prod/2013pubs/p20-570.pdf.

29. James Gerstenzang, "President Vetoes Bill on 'Marriage Penalty' Tax," *Los Angeles Times,* Aug. 6, 2000.

30. The 25 percent bracket hits singles with incomes between $37,650 and $91,150 and married couples with incomes between $75,300 and $151,900. Notice that the 25 percent bracket starts with married income at twice the level of single income ($75,300 is twice $37,650), but it doesn't end at that level ($151,900 is less than twice $91,150). The marriage penalties begin with income taxed at the 25 percent bracket.

31. The Income Tax Treatment of Married Couples, US Department of Treasury, Office of Tax Analysis, p. 1, November 2015, https:// www.treasury.gov/resource-center/tax-policy/tax-analysis /Documents/Two-Earner-Penalty-and-Marginal-Tax-Rates .pdf.

32. Dorothy A. Brown, "Race, Class, and Gender Essentialism in Tax Literature: The Joint Return," *Washington and Lee Law Review* 54 (1997): 1469–1512.

33. The analysis was performed by Ryan Gibson, an Emory PhD student in sociology, under my direction. The tables were compiled using data from the 2010 Public Use Microdata Sample and are based on a 5 percent sample of the population of same-race heterosexual couples.

34. Households and Families: 2010, U.S. Census Bureau, April 2012, Table 7, 18, https://www.census.gov/prod/cen2010/briefs/c2010br -14.pdf.

35. Goldin, "Female Labor Force Participation," 87–108.

36. "A Week in Los Angeles, CA, on a $1,250,000 Joint Salary," *Money Diaries,* Refinery29, Oct. 5, 2017, https://www.refinery29 .com/en-us/money-diary-los-angeles-executive-director-salary.

37. Thomas Shapiro, Tatjana Meschede, and Sam Osoro, "The Roots of the Widening Racial Wealth Gap: Explaining the Black-White Economic Divide," *Research and Policy Brief* 3 (Feb. 2013), Institute on Assets and Social Policy, Brandeis University, https:// heller.brandeis.edu/iasp/pdfs/racial-wealth-equity/racial-wealth -gap/roots-widening-racial-wealth-gap.pdf. Study showed "getting married . . . significantly increased the wealth holdings for white families by $75,635 but had no statistically significant impact on African-Americans."

38. Robert Rector, "Marriage: America's Greatest Weapon against Child Poverty," The Heritage Foundation, Sept. 5, 2012, https:// www.heritage.org/node/12185/print-display.

39. Angela Onwuachi-Willig, "The Return of the Ring: Welfare Reform's Marriage Cure as the Revival of Post-Bellum Control," *California Law Review* 93 (2005): 1647, 1650.

40. Kyle Pomerleau, Understanding the Marriage Penalty and Marriage Bonus, Tax Foundation, April 2015, 8, https:// taxfoundation.org/understanding-marriage-penalty-and -marriage-bonus/#:~:text=A%20marriage%20penalty%20 or%20bonus,thus%20filing%20their%20taxes%20jointly.&text =Marriage%20penalties%20occur%20when%20two,%2D%20 and%20low%2Dincome%20couples.

41. Anthony C. Infanti, "Decentralizing Family: An Inclusive Proposal for Individual Tax Filing in the United States," *Utah Law Review* (Fall 2010): 605.

42. Reams, 227.

43. Martha Albertson Fineman, *The Neutered Mother, the Sexual Family and Other Twentieth Century Tragedies* (New York: Routledge, 1995), 228–30; Martha Albertson Fineman, "The Sexual Family," in *Feminist and Queer Legal Theory: Intimate Encounters, Uncomfortable Conversations,* ed. M. A. Fineman, J. E. Jackson, and A. P. Romero (Surrey, U.K.: Ashgate, 2009), 45–64; Martha Albertson Fineman, "Why Marriage?," *Virginia Journal of Social Policy & the Law* 9 (2001): 239, 261n60.

44. Francesca Friday, "More Americans Are Single Than Ever Before—and They're Healthier, Too," *Observer*, Jan. 16, 2018, https://observer.com/2018/01/more-americans-are-single-than-ever-before-and-theyre-healthier-too/.

TWO: BLACK HOUSE/WHITE MARKET

1. F. John Devaney, *Tracking the American Dream,* Current Housing Reports, Series H121/94-1 (Washington, D.C.: U.S. Government Printing Office, 1994), 29 (data for 1960).

2. Devaney, 29.

3. Richard Rothstein, *The Color of Law: A Forgotten History of How Our Government Segregated America* (New York: Liveright Publishing Co., 2017).

4. Not to be confused with the National Association of Real Estate Brokers, founded in 1947, whose mission was to provide "fair housing for all"; http://www.nareb.com/.

5. Mechele Dickerson, *Homeownership and America's Financial Underclass* (New York: Cambridge University Press, 2014), 146.

6. Dickerson, 147: "Redlining's racist premises appear to have been derived from a prominent appraiser's 'scientific evidence' that homes in white neighborhoods would automatically depreciate in value if blacks moved into those neighborhoods."

7. Rothstein, *The Color of Law,* 94. According to the report, "the infiltration of Negro owner-occupants has tended to appreciate property values and neighborhood stability."

8. *Shelley v. Kraemer*, 334 U.S. 1 (1948).

9. National Association of Realtors, "You Can't Live Here: The Enduring Impacts of Restrictive Covenants," Feb. 2018, https://www.nar.realtor/sites/default/files/documents/2018-February-Fair-Housing-Story.pdf.

10. Andrew Wiese, *Places of Their Own: African American Suburbanization in the Twentieth Century* (Chicago: University of Chicago Press, 2004), 101.

11. IRC §262.

12. IRC §164. The 2017 Tax Cuts and Jobs Act limited the deduction of state and local income taxes and real property taxes to a maximum combined amount of $10,000. (The limit is the same for singles and married couples.) There is one other rather obscure tax subsidy for homeownership. Homeowners do not get taxed on the fair rental value of their homes, similar to when stay-at-home spouses provide tax-free services to their families. The technical tax term is "imputed income." The theory is if you were not living in your home, you would rent it out and have to include the rent received from your tenant in your income. By living in your own home, you are escaping taxation on that amount. Imputed income is not taxed in the United States, although it is taxed in other countries (Belgium, Finland, Denmark, Germany, and Sweden, to name a few). The most recent estimate from the Obama administration was a projected revenue loss of $96 billion for 2020.

13. Erik Sherman, "Well-Off Whites Get the Biggest Housing Subsidies There Are," *Forbes,* April 1, 2017. See also Adam J. Cole, Geoffrey Gee, and Nicholas Turner, "The Distributional and Revenue Consequences of Reforming the Mortgage Interest Deduction," *National Tax Journal* 64, no. 4 (2011): 977. "Of the 143 million tax returns filed for tax year 2007, 29 percent claimed the [mortgage interest deduction] . . . and among the 50.5 million returns on which taxpayers itemized their deductions, 82 percent claimed the [mortgage interest deduction]."

14. Will Fischer and Chye-Ching Huang, "Mortgage Interest Deduction Is Ripe for Reform," Center on Budget and Policy Priorities, June 25, 2013, http://www.cbpp.org/research/mortgage-interest-deduction-is-ripe-for-reform.

15. Tax Policy Center Briefing Book, "Key Elements of the US Tax System, What Are Itemized Deductions and Who Claims Them?," Urban-Brookings Tax Policy Center, May 2020, https://www.taxpolicycenter.org/sites/default/files/briefing-book/what_are_itemized_deductions_and_who_claims_them_1.pdf.

16. Benjamin H. Harris and Lucie Parker, "The Mortgage Interest Deduction across Zip Codes," Tax Policy Center, Dec. 4, 2014, https://www.brookings.edu/wp-content/uploads/2016/06/mortgage_interest_deductions_harris.pdf.

17. Roger Lowenstein, "Who Needs the Mortgage Interest Deduction?," *New York Times Magazine,* March 5, 2006.

18. Dorothy A. Brown, "Shades of the American Dream," *Washington University Law Review* 87, no. 329 (2009): 336n27 (referring to the legislative history of the 1986 Tax Reform Act).

19. Lou Cannon, "Reagan to Keep Home Mortgage Tax Deduction," *Washington Post,* May 11, 1984.

20. Brown, *Shades of the American Dream*, 333n13. The only category where research suggests the deduction *might* impact the decision to buy is limited to higher-income households in markets where the supply is very sensitive to price increases (elastic supply); see Council of Economic Advisers, *Evaluating the Anticipated Effects of Changes to the Mortgage Interest Deduction,* Nov. 5, 2017, https://www.whitehouse.gov/sites/whitehouse.gov/files/images/Effects of Changes to the Mortgage Interest Deduction FINAL.pdf.

21. Tax Policy Center Briefing Book, "How Did the TCJA Change the Standard Deduction and Itemized Deductions?," Urban-Brookings Tax Policy Center, https://www.taxpolicycenter.org/sites/default/files/briefing-book/how_did_the_tcja_change_the_standard_deduction_and_itemized_deductions_1.pdf.

22. Christine Klein, "A Requiem for the Rollover Rule: Capital Gains, Farmland Loss, and the Law of Unintended Consequences," *Washington and Lee Law Review* 55 (1998): 403–68.

23. Revenue Act of 1951: Hearings Before the Committee on Finance, United States Senate, Eighty-Second Congress, First Session on H.R. 4473, An Act to Provide Revenue, And For Other Purposes Part 1, June 28, 29, July 2 and 3, 1951, and the page is 992.

24. Quintard Taylor, *The Forging of a Black Community: Seattle's Central District from 1870 through the Civil Rights Era* (Seattle: University of Washington Press, 1994).

25. Revenue Act of 1964, Pub. L. No. 88-272, § 206(a), 78 Stat. 19, 38–40. (Section 206(a) created IRC §121.)

26. Pub. L. No. 88-272, § 206(a), 78 Stat. 19, 38–40.

27. Dennis Ventry, "The Accidental Deduction: A History and Critique of the Tax Subsidy for Mortgage Interest," *Law & Contemporary Problems* 73 (Winter 2010): 259n220.

28. H.R. Rep. No. 88-749, at 45 (1964); reprinted in 1964 *United States Code Congressional and Administrative News,* 1313, 1354.

29. Laurie Goodman, Jun Zhu, and Rolf Pendall, "Are Gains in Black Homeownership History?," Urban Institute, Feb. 14, 2017, https://www.urban.org/urban-wire/are-gains-black-homeownership-history.

30. Andrew Gahan, Comment, "The Home-Sale Exclusion: A Proposal Targeted at Eliminating Speculation," *Chapman Law Review* 18 (2014): 267.

31. H.R. Rep. No. 105-148, at 346–49 (1997). Section 1034 was repealed.

32. IRC §165(c).

33. The only loss allowed for personal assets is for certain casualty losses; see IRC §165(c)(3).

34. Janie Boschma and Ronald Brownstein, "The Concentration of Poverty in American Schools," *The Atlantic,* Feb. 29, 2016, https://www.theatlantic.com/education/archive/2016/02/concentration-poverty-american-schools/471414/?utm_source=share&utm_campaign=share.

35. Eric Torres and Richard Weissbourd, "Do Parents Really Want School Integration?," Making Caring Common Project, Harvard Graduate School of Education, Jan. 2020, https://mcc.gse.harvard.edu/reports/do-parents-really-want-school-integration.

36. Brown, "Shades of the American Dream," part IV.D, 354–60; Dorothy A. Brown, "Homeownership in Black and White: The Role of Tax Policy in Increasing Housing Equity," *University of Memphis Law Review* 49 (2018): 205, 214–23.

37. See Gregory D. Squires, "Demobilization of the Individualistic

Bias: Housing Market Discrimination as a Contributor to Labor Market and Economic Inequality," *Annals of the American Academy of Political and Social Science* 609, no. 1 (2007): 200, 204.

38. Brown, "Homeownership in Black and White," 215n64: "'[H]ousing units lose about 16 percent of their value when neighborhood racial composition increases from less than 10 percent black to between 10 percent and 60 percent black. . . . An even larger reduction in housing value is associated with moving from a neighborhood in which less than 10 percent of residents are black to one where at least 60 percent of the neighborhood is black.' David R. Harris, '*"Property Values Drop When Blacks Move In, Because . . .": Racial and Socioeconomic Determinants of Neighborhood Desirability,*' 64 Am. Soc. Rev. 461, 471 (1999). 'Western housing loses no more than 33 percent of its value when located in neighborhoods that are more than 10 percent black. By contrast, reductions in annual costs are as much as 40 percent in the South, 52 percent in the Midwest, and 70 percent in the Northeast for dwellings located in neighborhoods that are more than 10 percent black.' *Id.* at 472. The data Harris used are from the Panel Study of Income Dynamics, a longitudinal survey conducted annually and initiated in 1968. *Id.* at 467. At the time of the study, it included data on 37,500 individuals who resided in one of 4,800 initial sample households (including co-residents or offspring) across the country. *Id.* He looked at the pricing data paid for homes bought and sold. Harris concludes that '[t]hese race effects are highly significant, both statistically and substantively, and are consistent with the observation that "property values drop when black families move in."' *Id.* at 471."

39. Squires, "Demobilization of the Individualistic Bias," 206.

40. Dickerson, *Homeownership and America's Financial Underclass,* 151.

41. Dan Immergluck, Stephanie Earl, and Allison Powell, "Black Homebuying after the Crisis: Appreciation Patterns in Fifteen Large Metropolitan Areas," *City & Community* 18, no. 3 (2019): 983–1002.

42. Breanna Edwards, "'Racial Profiling at Its Finest': White Man

Uses SUV to Block Black Doctor from Entering Gated Community Where She Lives," *The Root,* June 22, 2018, https://www.theroot.com/racial-profiling-at-its-finest-white-man-uses-suv-to-1827057448.

43. https://www.fcsministries.org/what-we-do.

44. Thomas Shapiro, Tatjana Meschede, and Sam Osoro, "The Roots of the Widening Racial Wealth Gap: Explaining the Black-White Economic Divide," *Research and Policy Brief* 3 (Feb. 2013), Institute on Assets and Social Policy, Brandeis University, https://heller.brandeis.edu/iasp/pdfs/racial-wealth-equity/racial-wealth-gap/roots-widening-racial-wealth-gap.pdf.

45. Sandra J. Newman and C. Scott Holupka, "Is Timing Everything? Race, Homeownership and Net Worth in the Tumultuous 2000s," *Real Estate Economics* 44, no. 2 (Summer 2016): 307, 308.

46. Drew Desilver and Kristen Bialik, "Blacks and Hispanics Face Extra Challenges in Getting Home Loans," Pew Research Center, Jan. 10, 2017, https://www.pewresearch.org/fact-tank/2017/01/10/blacks-and-hispanics-face-extra-challenges-in-getting-home-loans/.

47. Robert Siegel, "Black Atlantans Struggle to Stay in the Middle Class," *All Things Considered,* NPR, Dec. 8, 2011, https://www.npr.org/2011/12/08/143378702/black-atlantans-struggle-to-stay-in-the-middle-class: Emily Badger citing NYU sociologist study co-authored by Jacob Faber; see Emily Badger, "This Can't Happen by Accident," *Washington Post Wonkblog,* May 2, 2016, https://www.washingtonpost.com/graphics/business/wonk/housing/atlanta/; Jacob W. Faber, "Racial Dynamics of Subprime Mortgage Lending at the Peak," Housing Policy Debate: Volume 23:2, 328–49 (2013).

48. Algernon Austin, "Subprime Mortgages Are Nearly Double for Hispanics and African Americans," Economic Policy Institute, June 11, 2008, https://www.epi.org/publication/webfeatures_snapshots_20080611/; citing the Joint Center for Political and Economic Studies.

49. Maria Krysan, Mick P. Couper, Reynolds Farley, and Tyrone Forman, "Does Race Matter in Neighborhood Preferences? Results

from a Video Experiment," *American Journal of Sociology* 115, no. 2 (2009): 527, 548.

50. Krysan, 527, 548. The eligibility period requires four years of residence in an impacted neighborhood, and it did not target residents of color who have been displaced by gentrification. See also Pete Harrison, "An Update on Elizabeth Warren's Housing Plan," Data for Progress, March 15, 2019, https://www.dataforprogress .org/blog/2019/3/15/an-update-on-elizabeth-warrens-housing -plan.

51. For renters age sixty-five and over, white net worth is $11,070 compared with homeowner net worth of $384,100. The net worth of minority homeowners is $145,300 compared with renters' net worth of $2,000. See Joint Center for Housing Studies of Harvard University, *Housing America's Older Adults: 2018*, https://www.jchs.harvard.edu/sites/default/files/Harvard_JCHS _Housing_Americas_Older_Adults_2018_1.pdf.

52. Paul Taylor et al., "Wealth Gaps Rise to Record Highs between Whites, Blacks, and Hispanics," Pew Research Center, July 26, 2011, https://www.pewresearch.org/wp-content/uploads /sites/3/2011/07/SDT-Wealth-Report_7-26-11_FINAL.pdf.

53. Making the deduction a refundable credit will be difficult in light of the history of the problems expanding the earned income tax credit (a refundable credit) encountered in the 1990s. See Dorothy A. Brown, "The Tax Treatment of Children: Separate but Unequal," *Emory Law Journal* 54, no. 2 (2005): 797–801.

54. Organization for Economic Cooperation and Development, "PH2.2 Tax Relief for Home Ownership," Dec. 16, 2019, https:// www.oecd.org/els/family/PH2-2-Tax-relief-for-home-ownership .pdf.

55. Council of Economic Advisers, *Evaluating the Anticipated Effects of Changes to the Mortgage Interest Deduction*, Nov. 2017, 7. https://www.whitehouse.gov/sites/whitehouse.gov/files /images/Effects%20of%20Changes%20to%20the%20 Mortgage%20Interest%20Deduction%20FINAL.pdf.

56. Council of Economic Advisers, *Evaluating the Anticipated Effects of Changes to the Mortgage Interest Deduction*, 6.

57. Council of Economic Advisers, *Evaluating the Anticipated Ef-*

fects of Changes to the Mortgage Interest Deduction, 7. The report goes on to acknowledge that there will be differences across areas depending on whether housing supply can respond to reduced demand.

58. Anthony Cilluffo, A. W. Geiger, and Richard Fry, "More U.S. Households Are Renting Than at Any Point in 50 Years," Pew Research Center, July 19, 2017, https://www.pewresearch.org /fact-tank/2017/07/19/more-u-s-households-are-renting-than-at -any-point-in-50-years.

59. Jim Tankersley and Ben Casselman, "As Mortgage-Interest Deduction Vanishes, Housing Market Offers a Shrug," *New York Times,* Aug. 4, 2019.

60. San Antonio Independent School District v. Rodriguez, 411 U.S. 1 (1973).

THREE: THE GREAT *UN*-EQUALIZER

1. Associated Press, "Billionaire Robert F. Smith Pledges to Pay Off Morehouse College Class of 2019's Student Loans," May 19, 2019, https://www.pennlive.com/nation-world/2019/05 /billionaire-robert-f-smith-pledges-to-pay-off-morehouse -college-class-of-2019s-student-loans.html. In October 2020, Smith entered into an agreement with the Justice Department to settle an IRS investigation into alleged tax evasion. As part of the settlement, Smith admitted wrongdoing. The investigation was unrelated to the gift that would pay off the Morehouse students' debt. Jordan Williams, "Billionaire Who Said He Would Pay off Morehouse Student Debt Admits to Tax Fraud," *The Hill,* Oct. 16, 2020, https://thehill.com/policy/finance/521389 -billionaire-who-said-he-would-pay-off-morehouse-student -debt-admits-to-tax.

2. Judith Scott-Clayton and Jing Li, "Black-White Disparity in Student Loan Debt More Than Triples after Graduation," Brookings Institution, Oct. 20, 2016, https://www.brookings.edu/wp -content/uploads/2016/10/es_20161020_scott-clayton_evidence _speaks.pdf.

3. F. R. Addo, J. N. Houle, and D. Simon, "Young, Black, and (Still)

in the Red: Parental Wealth, Race, and Student Loan Debt," *Race and Social Problems* 8, no. 1 (2016): 64–76.

4. Karin Fischer, "Engine of Inequality," *Chronicle of Higher Education*, Jan. 17, 2016.

5. Bethany Romano, "Racial Wealth Gap Continues to Grow between Black and White Families, regardless of College Attainment," Brandeis, July 16, 2018, http://heller.brandeis.edu/news /items/releases/2018/meschede-taylor-college-attainment-racial -wealth-gap.html.

6. Sean F. Reardon, Rachel Baker, and Daniel Klasik, "Race, Income, and Enrollment Patterns in Highly Selective Colleges, 1982–2004," Center for Education Policy Analysis, Stanford University, Aug. 3, 2012, https://cepa.stanford.edu/sites/default/files /race%20income%20%26%20selective%20college%20 enrollment%20august%203%202012.pdf.

7. Department of Education, *Advancing Diversity and Inclusion in Higher Education,* Nov. 2016, https://www2.ed.gov/rschstat /research/pubs/advancing-diversity-inclusion.pdf.

8. Richard D. Kahlenberg, introduction to *Affirmative Action for the Rich: Legacy Preferences in College Admissions* (The Century Foundation, 2010).

9. Congressional Research Service, "Higher Education Tax Benefits: Brief Overview and Budgetary Effects," updated July 20, 2020; https://fas.org/sgp/crs/misc/R41967.pdf.

10. Even though the 2017 Tax Cuts and Jobs Act enacted a very small (1.4 percent) excise tax on the net investment income of endowments held by private colleges and universities, it will impact only about twenty-five of the most selective colleges and universities because they are among the wealthiest and that impact may be slight. See J. Barclay Collins, Mary Burke Baker, Barry J. Hart, William N. Myhre, and Charles H. Purcell, "Just Passed Tax Cuts and Jobs Act Will Significantly Impact Higher Education," K&L Gates, Dec. 20, 2017, http://www.klgates.com/just-passed-tax -cuts-and-jobs-act-will-significantly-impact-higher-education -12-20-2017/.

11. Richard Fry and Anthony Cilluffo, "A Rising Share of Undergraduates Are from Poor Families, Especially at Less

Selective Colleges," Pew Research Center, May 22, 2019, https://www.pewsocialtrends.org/2019/05/22/a-rising-share-of-under graduates-are-from-poor-families-especially-at-less-selective -colleges/.

12. Reardon, Baker, and Klasik, "Race, Income, and Enrollment Patterns in Highly Selective Colleges."

13. Jeremy Ashkenas, Haeyoun Park, and Adam Pearce, "Even with Affirmative Action, Blacks and Hispanics Are More Underrepresented at Top Colleges Than 35 Years Ago," *New York Times,* Aug. 24, 2017.

14. Emma Dyer, "UChicago Poised to Become Most Expensive College Education in the U.S.," *Chicago Maroon,* July 14, 2019.

15. Romano, "Racial Wealth Gap Continues to Grow"; Anthony Abraham Jack, "It's Hard to Be Hungry on Spring Break," *New York Times,* March 17, 2018. For more information about food insecurity and other issues facing college students, see Sara Goldrick-Rab, *Paying the Price: College Costs, Financial Aid, and the Betrayal of the American Dream* (Chicago: University of Chicago Press, 2016).

16. Kelly Phillips Erb, "Would You Lie about Where You Live to Get Your Child into a Better School?," *Forbes,* Nov. 6, 2016.

17. Nicole Breeden, "Students Show What It's Like to Be Black at Harvard: 'I Too Am Harvard,'" *Vibe,* March 5, 2014, https://www.vibe.com/2014/03/students-show-what-its-like-to-be-black -at-harvard-i-too-am-harvard.

18. Emma Whitford, "Smith Finds No Bias in Incident That Roiled Campus," *Inside Higher Ed,* Oct. 30, 2018, https://www.insidehighered.com/news/2018/10/30/investigation-finds-no -policy-violations-when-police-were-called-black-student.

19. Karishma Mehrotra, "Emory Reflects on Black Students' Demands, Racial Climate," *Emory Wheel,* Dec. 13, 2015.

20. Department of Education, *Advancing Diversity and Inclusion in Higher Education.*

21. The Project on Predatory Student Lending, "For-Profit Colleges and Racial Justice: Perpetuating Racial Inequality under the Guise of Higher Education," Law Services Center of Harvard

University, https://predatorystudentlending.org/predatory
-industry/racial-justice/.

22. Ashley A. Smith, "New Nonprofit Owner for EDMC," *Inside Higher Ed,* March 6, 2017, https://www.insidehighered.com /news/2017/03/06/large-profit-chain-edmc-be-bought-dream -center-missionary-group.

23. American Association of Collegiate Registrars and Admissions Officers, "Foundation to Buy Education Management Corp., Convert Campuses into Nonprofits," March 6, 2017, https:// www.chronicle.com/blogs/ticker/foundation-to-buy-education -management-corp-convert-campuses-into-nonprofits/117169.

24. Doctor of Psychology (PsyD) Salary, PayScale, https://www .payscale.com/research/US/Degree=Doctor_of_Psychology _(PsyD)/Salary.

25. Tressie McMillan Cottom, *Lower Ed* (New York: The New Press, 2017), 11.

26. Gabriella Demczuk, "DeVos Repeals Obama-Era Rule Cracking Down on For-Profit Colleges," *New York Times,* June 28, 2019.

27. Stephanie Riegg Cellini, "Gainfully Employed? New Evidence on the Earnings, Employment, and Debt of For-Profit Certificate Students," Brown Center Chalkboard, Brookings Institution, Feb. 9, 2018, https://www.brookings.edu/blog/brown-center-chalk board/2018/02/09/gainfully-employed-new-evidence-on-the -earnings-employment-and-debt-of-for-profit-certificate-students/.

28. Morehouse and Spelman have been accused by some students of not taking sexual assault/harassment concerns seriously enough. See Grace Elletson, "How a 'Defunct' Title IX Office and a Cul-ture of Hypermasculinity Fueled a Sexual-Misconduct Problem at Morehouse College," *Chronicle of Higher Education,* Sept. 6, 2019; Eric Stirgus, "Morehouse Ignored Sexual Harassment Complaint, Alleged Victim Says," *Atlanta Journal-Constitution,* July 18, 2019; Audra Melton, "Two Colleges Bound by History Are Roiled by the #MeToo Moment," *New York Times,* Dec. 2, 2017.

29. Julian Wyllie, "How Are Black Colleges Doing? Better Than You Think, Study Finds," *Chronicle of Higher Education,* April 13, 2018.

30. *New York Times,* The Upshot, https://www.nytimes.com
     /interactive/projects/college-mobility/emory-university. Source:
     Raj Chetty, John Friedman, Emmanuel Saez, Nicholas Turner,
     and Danny Yagan, "Mobility Report Cards: The Role of Colleges
     in Intergenerational Mobility," NBER Working Paper No. 23618,
     July 2017.

31. There's little tax incentive for anyone, black or white, to pay for
     their college education outright; the tax breaks are highly restric-
     tive and offer little relief compared to the cost of college. They
     include two tax credits—the Lifetime Learning Credit (begun in
     1998) and the American Opportunity Tax Credit (enacted in
     2009)—that, instead of being deducted from income, are used to
     offset the taxpayer's tax liability. Both are limited by income, and
     the maximum credit is $2,000 for the Lifetime Learning Credit
     and $2,500 for the American Opportunity Tax Credit. A tax
     credit is better than a deduction: As we saw in chapter 1, while a
     deduction reduces your taxable income, it is only as valuable as
     your marginal (highest) tax rate under the progressive tax rate
     system. The higher the tax rate, the more valuable the deduction.
     A tax credit, on the other hand, is a dollar-for-dollar reduction of
     your taxes due. Tax credits reduce your tax bill—as long as you
     have a tax bill. Nondependent children are eligible for the Ameri-
     can Opportunity Tax Credit and the Lifetime Learning Credit—
     but of course, they can't have a job that pays too well, or they get
     no credit.

32. Romano, "Racial Wealth Gap Continues to Grow"; Tatjana Me-
     schede, Joanna Taylor, Alexis Mann, and Thomas Shapiro,
     " 'Family Achievements?': How a College Degree Accumulates
     Wealth for Whites and Not for Blacks," *Federal Reserve Bank of
     St. Louis Review* 99, no. 1 (First Quarter 2017): 121–37.

33. Addo, Houle, and Simon, "Young, Black, and (Still) in the Red,"
     64–76.

34. Fernanda Santos, "Spontaneity Again Causes Mayor Trouble,"
     New York Times, May 21, 2011; Zak Cheney-Rice, "Pete Butti-
     gieg's Willful Illusion," *New York,* Dec. 3, 2019.

35. Laurel Puchner and Linda Markowitz, "Do Black Families Value
     Education?," *Multicultural Education* 23, no. 1 (Fall 2015): 9–18.

36. Renee Stepler, "Hispanic, Black Parents See College Degree as Key for Children's Success," Pew Research Center, Feb. 24, 2016, http://www.pewresearch.org/fact-tank/2016/02/24/hispanic-black -parents-see-college-degree-as-key-for-childrens-success/.

37. Meschede et al., " 'Family Achievements?' "; citing C. Z. Charles, V. J. Roscigno, and K. C. Torres, "Racial Inequality and College Attendance: The Mediating Role of Parental Investments," *Social Science Research* 36, no. 1 (2007): 329–52.

38. Scott-Clayton and Li, "Black-White Disparity in Student Loan Debt," 4.

39. Ben Miller, "The Continued Student Loan Crisis for Black Bor- rowers," Center for American Progress, Dec. 2, 2019, https:// www.americanprogress.org/issues/education-postsecondary /reports/2019/12/02/477929/continued-student-loan-crisis-black -borrowers/.

40. https://www.npr.org/2019/09/05/754656294/congress-promised -student-borrowers-a-break-then-ed-dept-rejected-99-of-them.

41. https://studentaid.gov/data-center/student/loan-forgiveness/pslf -data.

42. https://studentaid.gov/manage-loans/repayment/plans/income -driven.

43. IRC §102.

44. IRC §2501.

45. Susan T. Hill, *The Traditionally Black Institutions of Higher Ed- ucation 1860–1962,* National Center for Education Statistics, 1985, https://nces.ed.gov/pubs84/84308.pdf; Hilary Herbold, "It Was Never a Level Playing Field: Blacks and the GI Bill," *Journal of Blacks in Higher Education* 6 (1994–95): 104–8; https://www -jstor-org.proxy.library.emory.edu/stable/pdf/2962479.pdf?refreqid =excelsior%3Adabd5745f73b17c410d3fbebdcc2ee3d.

46. IRC §117.

47. "The Pell Grant: Free Money for College," CollegeScholarships .org, http://www.collegescholarships.org/grants/pell.htm; Con- gressional Research Service, *Federal Pell Grant Program of the Higher Education Act: Primer,* Nov. 28, 2018, https://fas.org/sgp /crs/misc/R45418.pdf.

48. "African American Students in Higher Education," Postsecond-

ary National Policy Institute, June 12, 2020, https://pnpi.org
/african-american-students/.

49. Spiros Protopsaltis and Sharon Parrott, "Pell Grants—a Key Tool
for Expanding College Access and Economic Opportunity—
Need Strengthening, Not Cuts," Center on Budget and Policy
Priorities, July 27, 2017, https://www.cbpp.org/research/federal
-budget/pell-grants-a-key-tool-for-expanding-college-access-and
-economic-opportunity.

50. Edward B. Fiske, "Is Access for Disadvantaged in Peril?," *New
York Times,* Oct. 20, 1981.

51. William J. Bennett, "Our Greedy Colleges," *New York Times,*
Feb. 18, 1987.

52. "A Small Percentage of Families Save in 529 Plans," United States
Government Accountability Office, GAO-13-64 at 18-19, https://
www.gao.gov/assets/660/650759.pdf.

53. Fenaba R. Addo, "Parents' Wealth Helps Explain Racial Disparities in Student Loan Debt," The Center for Household Financial
Stability at the Federal Reserve Bank of St. Louis, Issue 19, March
2018, https://www.stlouisfed.org/~/media/publications/in-the
-balance/images/issue_19/itb19_march_2018.pdf.

54. IRC §221.

55. *Education Tax Proposals: Hearings Before the Comm. on Finance,* 105th Cong. 31–33 (1997) (statement of Jennifer Long,
student, State University of New York at Buffalo School of Dental Medicine, on Behalf of American Association of Dental
Schools, Buffalo, New York).

56. IRC §221(b)(1).

57. Lorelle L. Espinosa, Jonathan M. Turk, Morgan Taylor, and Hol-
lie M. Chessman, *Race and Ethnicity in Higher Education: A
Status Report* (Washington, D.C.: American Council on Education, 2019), 171, table 7.7.

58. Rick Seltzer, "Wealthy Students Borrowing More for College over
Last Two Decades, Report Finds," Inside Higher Ed, December
4, 2019, https://www.insidehighered.com/print/news/2019/12/04
/wealthy-students-borrowing-more-college-over-last-two
-decades-report-finds.

59. Andrew Kreighbaum, "How Parent PLUS Worsens the Racial

Wealth Gap," *Inside Higher Ed,* May 15, 2018, https://www
.insidehighered.com/news/2018/05/15/report-finds-parent-plus
-loans-worsen-outcomes-poorest-families-urges-policy-reforms.

60. Protopsaltis and Parrott, "Pell Grants."

61. Wesley Whistle and Tamara Hiler, "The Pell Divide: How Four-Year Institutions Are Failing to Graduate Low- and Moderate-Income Students," Third Way, May 1, 2018, https://thirdway
.imgix.net/downloads/the-pell-divide-how-four-year-institutions
-are-failing-to-graduate-low-and-moderate-income-students/The
-Pell-Divide_180501_131431.pdf.

62. Paul Tough, "What College Admissions Offices Really Want," *New York Times Magazine,* Sept. 10, 2019.

63. National Center for Education Statistics, *Digest of Education Statistics,* 2018 Tables and Figures, Table 333.90: Endowment Funds of the 120 Degree-Granting Postsecondary Institutions with the Largest Endowments, by Rank Order: Fiscal Year 2017, https://nces.ed.gov/programs/digest/d18/tables/dt18_333.90
.asp?current=yes. Even a high-profile recent gift from Mackenzie Scott doesn't put Howard in the top 120. Lauren Lumpkin, "Howard University Announces Largest Single-Donor Gift, from Philanthropist MacKenzie Scott," *Washington Post,* July 28, 2020.

64. David Leonhardt, "America's Great Working Class Colleges," *New York Times,* Jan. 18, 2017.

65. Anthony P. Carnevale, Tamara Jayasundera, and Artem Gulish, *America's Divided Recovery: College Haves and Have-Nots,* Georgetown University, 2016, https://cew.georgetown.edu/wp
-content/uploads/Americas-Divided-Recovery-web.pdf.

66. Reardon, Baker, and Klasik, "Race, Income, and Enrollment Patterns in Highly Selective Colleges."

67. William R. Emmons and Bryan J. Noeth, "Why Didn't Higher Education Protect Hispanic and Black Wealth?," *In the Balance* 12 (Aug. 2015), Federal Reserve Bank of St. Louis, https://www
.stlouisfed.org/~/media/publications/in-the-balance/images
/issue_12/ itb_august_2015.pdf; see also Darrick Hamilton, William Darity, Jr., Anne E. Price, Vishnu Sridharan, and Rebecca Tippett, *Umbrellas Don't Make It Rain: Why Studying and*

Working Hard Isn't Enough for Black Americans, April 2015, https://socialequity.duke.edu/wp-content/uploads/2019/10 /Umbrellas_Dont_Make_It_Rain_Final.pdf.

68. Romano, "Racial Wealth Gap Continues to Grow."

FOUR: THE BEST JOBS

1. Janelle Jones and John Schmitt, "A College Degree Is No Guarantee," Center for Economic and Policy Research, May 2014, 5.

2. S. Michael Gaddis, "Discrimination in the Credential Society: An Audit Study of Race and College Selectivity in the Labor Market," *Social Forces* 93, no. 4 (2015): 1451–79.

3. Marianne Bertrand and Sendhil Mullainathan, "Are Emily and Greg More Employable Than Lakisha and Jamal? A Field Experiment on Labor Market Discrimination," *American Economic Review* 94, no. 4 (2004): 992.

4. Anthony P. Carnevale, Stephen J. Rose, and Ban Cheah, *The College Payoff: Education, Occupations, Lifetime Earnings,* Georgetown University Center on Education and the Workforce, 2011, 12, https://cew.georgetown.edu/cew-reports/the-college -payoff.

5. Dorothy A. Brown, "Pensions, Risk, and Race," *Washington & Lee Law Review* 61 (2004): 1507n18.

6. IRC §162 (for employers); IRC §106 (for employees' exclusion).

7. Larry DeWitt, "The Decision to Exclude Agricultural and Domestic Workers from the 1935 Social Security Act," *Social Security Bulletin* 70, no. 4 (2010): 49–68.

8. Ira Katznelson, *When Affirmative Action Was White: An Untold History of Racial Inequality in Twentieth-Century America* (New York: W. W. Norton, 2005), 59–60.

9. Beth Stevens, "Blurring the Boundaries: How the Federal Government Has Influenced Welfare Benefits in the Private Sector," in *The Politics of Social Policy in the United States,* ed. Margaret Weir, Ann Shola Orloff, and Theda Skocpol (Princeton, N.J.: Princeton University Press, 1988), 126.

10. Stevens, 130, citing the Revenue Act of 1942.

11. There was some conflict among IRS policy as to whether health

insurance was tax-free. Although prior rulings suggested that premiums paid by employers would be considered tax-free to the employee, in 1953 the IRS reversed itself and ruled those amounts would be taxable income. Within a year Congress overturned the IRS ruling and enacted Internal Revenue Code section 106.

12. Stevens, "Blurring the Boundaries," 134, citing the Revenue Act of 1942.

13. Walter W. Kolodrubetz, "Two Decades of Employee-Benefit Plans, 1950–70: A Review," *Social Security Bulletin* 35, no. 4 (1972): 10–22.

14. "Time for a Crackdown," *New York Times,* May 6, 1964.

15. Dorothy A. Brown, "Pensions and Risk Aversion: The Influence of Race, Ethnicity, and Class on Investor Behavior," *Lewis & Clark Law Review* 11, no. 2 (2007): 385–406.

16. "The Professional and Technical Workforce: By the Numbers," Fact Sheet 2019, Department for Professional Employees, AFL-CIO, https://www.dpeaflcio.org/factsheets/the-professional-and -technical-workforce-by-the-numbers.

17. Laura Sullivan, Tatjana Meschede, Thomas Shapiro, Teresa Kroeger, and Fernanda Escobar, *Not Only Unequal Paychecks: Occupational Segregation, Benefits, and the Racial Wealth Gap,* Institute on Assets and Social Policy, Brandeis University, April 2019, https://heller.brandeis.edu/iasp/pdfs/racial-wealth-equity /asset-integration/occupational_segregation_report_40219.pdf.

18. U.S. Bureau of Labor Statistics, *Occupational Outlook Handbook,* "Healthcare Occupations," https://www.bls.gov/ooh /healthcare/home.htm.

19. Sullivan et al., *Not Only Unequal Paychecks.*

20. Working Partnerships USA, *Tech's Invisible Workforce: Silicon Valley Rising,* March 2016, https://www.wpusa.org/files/reports /TechsInvisibleWorkforce.pdf; Sullivan et al., *Not Only Unequal Paychecks.*

21. Kelly Yamanouchi, "Delta to Pay Out $1.6 Billion in Profit Sharing to Workers," *Atlanta Journal-Constitution,* Feb. 14, 2020.

22. Kelly Yamanouchi, "Delta Employees Welcome Valentine's Day Bonus, but Not Everyone Profits," *Atlanta Journal-Constitution,* Feb. 14, 2020.

23. Bertrand and Mullainathan, "Are Emily and Greg More Employable Than Lakisha and Jamal?," 992.
24. Lauren Rivera, *Pedigree: How Elite Students Get Elite Jobs* (Princeton, N.J.: Princeton University Press, 2015); Lauren A. Rivera, "Ivies, Extracurriculars, and Exclusion: Elite Employers' Use of Educational Credentials," *Research in Social Stratification and Mobility* 29, no. 1 (2011): 71–90.
25. Rivera, "Ivies, Extracurriculars, and Exclusion."
26. Rivera, "Ivies, Extracurriculars, and Exclusion."
27. Arin N. Reeves, "Written in Black and White: Exploring Confirmation Bias in Racialized Perceptions of Writing Skills," Nextions, April 2014; https://nextions.com/wp-content/uploads/2017/05/written-in-black-and-white-yellow-paper-series.pdf.
28. Gaddis, "Discrimination in the Credential Society."
29. Craig Copeland, "Employee Based Retirement Plan Participation: Geographic Differences and Trends, 2013," October 2014; https://www.ebri.org/content/employment-based-retirement-plan-participation-geographic-differences-and-trends-2013-5451.
30. Justin Fox, "Government Work Has Been Going Out of Style," Bloomberg Opinion, Sept. 7, 2018, https://www.bloomberg.com/opinion/articles/2018-09-07/jobs-report-government-work-has-been-going-out-of-style.
31. National Center for Education Statistics, "Post-Bachelor's Employment Outcomes by Sex and Race/Ethnicity," in *The Condition of Education 2016,* 24–32, https://nces.ed.gov/pubs2016/2016144.pdf.
32. Ariel Education Initiative and Aon Hewitt, *401(k) Plans in Living Color: A Study of 401(k) Savings Disparities across Racial and Ethnic Groups: The Ariel/Aon Hewitt Study 2012,* https://www.arielinvestments.com/images/stories/PDF/ariel-aonhewitt-2012.pdf.
33. Amy Traub, Laura Sullivan, Tatjana Meschede, and Thomas Shapiro, *The Asset Value of Whiteness: Understanding the Racial Wealth Gap,* Demos, Feb. 6, 2017, 11, https://www.demos.org/sites/default/files/publications/Asset%20Value%20of%20Whiteness_0.pdf.
34. Traub, *The Asset Value of Whiteness.*

35. Tatjana Meschede, Joanna Taylor, Alexis Mann, and Thomas Shapiro, "'Family Achievements?': How a College Degree Accumulates Wealth for Whites and Not for Blacks," *Federal Reserve Bank of St. Louis Review* 99, no. 1 (First Quarter 2017): 121–37; Rourke L. O'Brien, "Depleting Capital? Race, Wealth and Informal Financial Assistance," *Social Forces* 91, no. 2 (2012): 375–96.

36. Darrick Hamilton, William Darity, Jr., Anne E. Price, Vishnu Sridharan, and Rebecca Tippett, *Umbrellas Don't Make It Rain: Why Studying and Working Hard Isn't Enough for Black Americans,* April 2015, https://socialequity.duke.edu/wp-content/uploads/2019/10/Umbrellas_Dont_Make_It_Rain_Final.pdf.

37. Meschede et al., "'Family Achievements?'"

38. The penalty is levied to the extent you make an early withdrawal prior to turning 59½ years of age.

39. Ariel Education Initiative and Aon Hewitt, *401(k) Plans in Living Color.*

40. The Ariel/Aon Hewitt Study 2012, 401(k) Plans in Living Color, 11, https://www.arielinvestments.com/images/stories/PDF/ariel-aonhewitt-2012.pdf.

41. U.S. Bureau of Labor Statistics, "Black Women Made Up 53 Percent of the Black Labor Force in 2018," Feb. 26, 2019, https://www.bls.gov/opub/ted/2019/black-women-made-up-53-percent-of-the-black-labor-force-in-2018.htm.

42. Author's calculation from BLS statistics for workers twenty and older; https://www.bls.gov/cps/cpsaat05.pdf.

43. Dorothy A. Brown, "Shades of the American Dream," *Washington University Law Review* 87, no. 329 (2009): 376n181; Jamie Hopkins, "Why Buying a Home Is Not a Good Investment (It's a Service)," *Forbes,* July 28, 2018.

44. Brown, "Pensions and Risk Aversion"; Dorothy A. Brown, "The 535 Report: A Pathway to Fundamental Tax Reform," *Pepperdine Law Review* 40, no. 5 (2013): 1155–72; Dorothy A. Brown, "Teaching Civil Rights through the Basic Tax Course," *Saint Louis University Law Journal* 54, no. 3 (2010): 809–20.

45. Dorothy A. Brown, "Racial Equality in the Twenty-First Century: What's Tax Policy Got to Do with It?," *University of Arkansas at Little Rock Law Review* 21, no. 4 (1999): 759, 763.

46. Samantha Artiga, Kendal Orgera, and Anthony Damico, "Changes in Health Coverage by Race and Ethnicity since the ACA, 2010–2018," Issue Brief, Kaiser Family Foundation, March 2020, http://files.kff.org/attachment/Issue-Brief-Changes-in -Health-Coverage-by-Race-and-Ethnicity-since-the-ACA-2010 -2018.pdf.

47. National Partnership for Women & Families, "Black Women Experience Pervasive Disparities in Access to Health Insurance," Fact Sheet, April 2019, https://www.nationalpartnership.org/our -work/resources/health-care/black-womens-health-insurance -coverage.pdf.

48. Signe-Mary McKernan, Steven Brown, and Genevieve M. Kenney, "Past-Due Medical Debt a Problem, Especially for Black Americans," Urban Institute, March 26, 2017, https://www.urban.org /urban-wire/past-due-medical-debt-problem-especially-black -americans.

49. Dorothy Roberts, *Killing the Black Body: Race, Reproduction, and the Meaning of Liberty* (New York: Vintage, 1999); Dorothy Roberts, *Fatal Invention: How Science, Politics, and Big Business Re-create Race in the Twenty-First Century* (New York: The New Press, 2011).

50. Steve Cameron and Meredith Cash, "Serena Williams and Alexis Ohanian Have a Combined Net Worth of $189 Million. Here's How They Make and Spend Their Money," Business Insider, July 9, 2019, https://www.businessinsider.com/serena-williams -alexis-ohanian-net-worth-make-spend-millions-2019-5.

51. Rob Haskell, "Serena Williams on Motherhood, Marriage, and Making Her Comeback," *Vogue,* Jan. 10, 2018.

52. Sarah Jones, "There's a Problem with Elizabeth Warren's Maternal Mortality Plan," *New York,* Intelligencer, April 25, 2019, https://nymag.com/intelligencer/2019/04/the-problem-with -elizabeth-warrens-maternal-mortality-plan.html.

FIVE: LEGACY

1. Ernie Suggs, "Wealth Gap between Whites and Blacks Widened after Great Recession," *Atlanta Journal-Constitution,* Jan. 2, 2019.

2. Calculations from the 2016 Survey of Consumer Finances by Dr. Ana Hernández Kent, a policy analyst for the Center for Household Financial Stability at the Federal Reserve Bank of St. Louis.

3. IRC §103.

4. If the taxpayer has a net gain, they may also be subject to an additional tax of 3.8 percent on their net investment income if their adjusted gross income is greater than $200,000 if single and $250,000 if married—yet another marriage-penalty provision because the married income limit is not double the single limit. See Laura Sanders, "WSJ Tax Guide 2019: Taxes on Investment Income," *Wall Street Journal,* Feb. 15, 2019.

5. Tax computation by author: .10 ($9875 - 0) +.12 ($40,125 - 9875) + .22 ($85,525 - 40,125 + .24 ($150,000 - 85,525) = $30,079.50. The taxpayer's marginal tax rate (the rate at which her last dollar of income is taxed) is 24 percent, while her first dollar of taxable income is taxed at 10 percent. Here the taxpayer has no capital gains income, but if she did, the first $40,000 of it would be received tax-free, and the balance would be taxed at a flat rate of 15 percent because her taxable income is less than $441,450 because she is single.

6. Tax computation by author: $14,605.50 + .24 ($100,000 - 85,525) + .15 ($50,000) = $25,579.50.

7. Will Freeland, "Tax Equity and the Growth in Nonpayers," Tax Foundation, July 20, 2012, https://taxfoundation.org/tax-equity-and-growth-nonpayers/.

8. "F.F. Brewster, 86, a Financier, Dead: Son of Standard Oil Official Was Philanthropist in New Haven and Yachtsman," *New York Times,* Sept. 15, 1958, 32.

9. "More Standard Oil Men in New Haven," *New York Times,* June 8, 1907.

10. Online calculator used is at https://www.dollartimes.com/inflation/inflation.php?.

11. Walsh v. Brewster, 255 U.S. 536 (1921).

12. Don't feel too bad for Frederick; the IRS conceded that they had miscalculated the amount of his gain. That resulted in a reduced 1916 tax bill from $17,756 to *only* $12,823. In 2020 dollars that is $319,920.16—a savings of almost $100,000.

13. "Historical Highest Marginal Income Tax Rates: 1913 to 2020," Tax Policy Center, Feb. 4, 2020, https://www.taxpolicycenter.org /statistics/historical-highest-marginal-income-tax-rates.

14. Roy G. Blakey, "The Revenue Act of 1921," *American Economic Review* 12 (March 1922): 82.

15. Gerald Auten, "Capital Gains Taxation," in *Encyclopedia of Taxation & Tax Policy,* 2nd ed., ed. Joseph Cordes, Robert Ebel, and Jane Gravelle (Washington, D.C.: Urban Institute Press, 2005), 58–61; https://www.urban.org/sites/default/files /publication/71031/1000519-Capital-Gains-Taxation.PDF.

16. Leonard E. Burman, "Capital Gains Cuts Won't Cure the Covid-19 Economy," Tax Vox: Business Taxes, Tax Policy Center, May 11, 2020, https://www.taxpolicycenter.org/taxvox/capital-gains -cuts-wont-cure-covid-19-economy.

17. Marjorie E. Kornhauser, "The Origins of Capital Gains Taxa-tion: What's Law Got to Do with It?," *Southwestern Law Jour-nal* 39, no. 4 (1985): 869–928.

18. Dorothy A. Brown, "The 535 Report: A Pathway to Fundamental Tax Reform," *Pepperdine Law Review* 40, no. 5 (2013): 1167.

19. Sherman D. Hanna, Cong Wang, and Yoonkyung Yuh, "Racial/ Ethnic Differences in High Return Investment Ownership: A De-composition Analysis," *Journal of Financial Counseling and Planning* 21, no. 2 (2010): 46.

20. Dorothy A. Brown, "Teaching Civil Rights through the Basic Tax Course," *Saint Louis University Law Journal* 54, no. 3 (2010): 819 fn 74; N. S. Chiteji and Darrick Hamilton, "Family Connec-tions and the Black-White Wealth Gap among Middle-Class Families," *Review of Black Political Economy* 30, no. 1 (2002): 9, 16: "Among middle-class families, the proportion of white fami-lies that own stock is more than twice as high as the proportion of similarly situated black families—about 35 percent compared to 13 percent."

21. Sharmila Choudhury, "Racial and Ethnic Differences in Wealth and Asset Choices," *Social Security Bulletin* 64, no. 4 (2001/2002): 9.

22. Evanston, Illinois, today has a different racial composition: 58.6 percent white, 16.6 percent black, and 11.5 percent Latinx; see https://datausa.io/profile/geo/evanston-il/.

23. Stefano Natella, Tatjana Meschede, and Laura Sullivan, "Wealth Patterns among the Top 5% of African-Americans," Credit Suisse Research and Institute on Assets and Social Policy, Nov. 2014, https://research-doc.credit-suisse.com /docView?sourceid=em&document_id=x603305&serialid=EPbp ZVC9yQSzQAcQybZ8trdJT5i1wtDSIYihG%2b07VaQ%3d.

24. Dorothy A. Brown, "Pensions, Risk, and Race," *Washington & Lee Law Review* 61 (2004): 1501, 1536–38.

25. Paulette Thomas, "Investing Survey Shows Race Plays a Part," *Wall Street Journal,* June 6, 2001, C21.

26. Alan R. Elliott, "What Investing in Stocks Tells Us about the Racial Wealth Gap," *Investor's Business Daily,* March 9, 2019.

27. Dan Mangan, "Wall Street an Elusive Dream for Black Americans," NBC News, Aug. 28, 2013, https://www.nbcnews.com /businessmain/wall-street-elusive-dream-black-americans -8C11022224.

28. Tristan Mabry, "Black Investors Lack Trust in Brokers, Shy Away from Investing in Stocks," *Wall Street Journal,* May 14, 1999, A2.

29. Christy Ford Chapin, " 'Going Behind with That Fifteen Cent Policy': Black-Owned Insurance Companies and the State," *Journal of Policy History* 24, no. 4 (2012): 645.

30. IRC §101(a)(2). There are exceptions depending on who the sale is to and the type of transaction that resulted in the sale. (While life insurance proceeds paid to beneficiaries are generally received tax-free, if an individual sells the policy to get cash—as one might if faced with a healthcare crisis, a family member in need, or a job loss—they generally will have to pay taxes on the income.)

31. Daniel Fernandes, John G. Lynch, and Richard G. Netemeyer, "Financial Literacy, Financial Education, and Downstream Financial Behaviors," *Management Science* 60, no. 8 (Aug. 2014): 1872.

32. Choudhury, "Racial and Ethnic Differences in Wealth and Asset Choices"; Daniel J. Benjamin, James J. Choi, and A. Joshua Strickland, "Social Identity and Preferences," *American Economic Review* 100, no. 4 (2010): 1913–28.

33. William A. Klein, "An Enigma in the Federal Income Tax: The Meaning of the Word 'Gift,'" *Minnesota Law Review* 48 (1963–64): 215, 224.

34. Tatjana Meschede, Joanna Taylor, Alexis Mann, and Thomas Shapiro, "'Family Achievements?': How a College Degree Accumulates Wealth for Whites and Not for Blacks," *Federal Reserve Bank of St. Louis Review* 99, no. 1 (First Quarter 2017): 121–37.

35. Hannah Thomas, Tatjana Meschede, Alexis Mann, Janet Boguslaw, and Thomas Shapiro, "The Web of Wealth: Resiliency and Opportunity or Driver of Inequality?," Institute on Assets and Social Policy, Brandeis University, July 2014, https://heller .brandeis.edu/iasp/pdfs/racial-wealth-equity/leveraging-mobility /web-of-wealth.pdf.

36. Thomas et al., "The Web of Wealth."

37. Thomas et al., "The Web of Wealth."

38. Rourke L. O'Brien, "Depleting Capital? Race, Wealth and Informal Financial Assistance," *Social Forces* 91, no. 2 (2012): 388.

39. Chiteji and Hamilton, "Family Connections and the Black-White Wealth Gap among Middle-Class Families," 24.

40. This hypothetical assumes the property is also a capital asset in the hands of the children. If not, then they would pay taxes at the progressive rate.

41. Edward Rodrigue and Richard V. Reeves, "Five Bleak Facts on Black Opportunity," Brookings Institution, Jan. 15, 2015, https:// www.brookings.edu/blog/social-mobility-memos/2015/01/15/five -bleak-facts-on-black-opportunity/.

42. Darrick Hamilton and Michael Linden, "Hidden Rules of Race Are Embedded in the New Tax Law," Roosevelt Institute, May 2018, https://rooseveltinstitute.org/wp-content/uploads/2018/05 /Hidden-Rules-of-Race-and-Trump-Tax-Law.pdf.

43. Elise Viebeck, "Booker Wants a 'Baby Bond' for Every U.S. Child. Would It Work?," *Washington Post,* Aug. 19, 2019.

44. William Darity, Jr., Darrick Hamilton, Mark Paul, Alan Aja, Anne Price, Antonio Moore, and Caterina Chiopris, *What We Get Wrong about Closing the Racial Wealth Gap,* Samuel DuBois Cook Center on Social Equity, Duke University, April 2018,

https://socialequity.duke.edu/wp-content/uploads/2019/10/what
-we-get-wrong.pdf.

45. Omnibus Budget Reconciliation Act of 1990, Pub. L. No. 101-
    508, 104 Stat. 1388 (1990).

46. John W. Lee III, "Class Warfare 1988–2005 over Top Individual
    Income Tax Rates: Teeter-Totter from Soak-the-Rich to Robin-
    Hood-in-Reverse," *Hastings Business Law Journal* 2, no. 1
    (2006): 47, 54.

47. Lee, 56, citing 139 Cong. Rec. S76992-3 (daily ed. June 23, 1993)
    (statement of Sen. Bradley [emphasis supplied]).

48. Ann Choi, Keith Herbert, Olivia Winslow, and project editor
    Arthur Browne, "Long Island Divided," *Newsday,* Nov. 17,
    2019.

49. Cedric Herring and Loren Henderson, "Wealth Inequality in
    Black and White: Cultural and Structural Sources of the Racial
    Wealth Gap," *Race and Social Problems* 8 (2016): 14.

SIX: WHAT'S NEXT?

1. L. G. Sherrod, "Back Talk: 40 Acres and a Mule," *Essence,* April
   1993. Sherrod cited the People's Institute for Economics as the
   source of the $43,209.

2. "Schemes, Scams and Cons: The IRS Strikes Back," Hearing Before the Committee on Finance United States Senate One Hundred Seventh Congress Second Session April 11, 2002, at 84.

3. Ernie Suggs, "Officials: 'Black Tax' Scam Preys on the Elderly,"
   Atlanta Journal-Constitution, April 8, 2001.

4. Associated Press, "2 Jailed in Slavery Tax Refund Case," *Los Angeles Times,* Oct. 4, 2003.

5. Allison Aubrey, "IRS Punishes Reparations Filers," *All Things
   Considered,* NPR, Oct. 24, 2003, https://www.npr.org/templates
   /story/story.php?storyId=1478085.

6. Jeremy Bearer-Friend, "Should the IRS Know Your Race? The
   Challenge of Colorblind Tax Data," *Tax Law Review* 73, no. 1
   (2019): 65.

7. Benjamin H. Harris and Lucie Parker, "The Mortgage Interest
   Deduction across Zip Codes," Tax Policy Center, Dec. 4, 2014,

https://www.brookings.edu/wp-content/uploads/2016/06/mortgage_interest_deductions_harris.pdf.

8. Marissa J. Lang, "'Where's My Go-Go Music?' Residents Say Turn Up the Funk after a Complaint Silenced a D.C. Intersection," *Washington Post,* April 9, 2019.

9. Bob Oakes and Walter Wuthmann, "Where Parents Have More Choice, Schools Appear to Become More Segregated," WBUR, Jan. 31, 2020, https://www.wbur.org/edify/2020/01/29/parent-choice-school-segregation.

10. Mark Travers, "The Racial Wealth Gap Is Not Improving, but We Think It Is," *Psychology Today,* Oct. 7, 2019.

11. 163 U.S. 537 (1896).

12. 347 U.S. 483 (1954).

13. Dorothy A. Brown, "Tax Law: Implicit Bias and the Earned Income Tax Credit," in *Implicit Racial Bias across the Law,* ed. Justin D. Levinson and Robert J. Smith (New York: Cambridge University Press, 2012), 164–78.

14. William A. Darity, Jr., and A. Kirsten Mullen, *From Here to Equality: Reparations for Black Americans in the Twenty-First Century* (Chapel Hill, N.C.: University of North Carolina Press, 2020), 261.

15. *United States v. Armstrong,* 517 U.S. 456, 469 (1996); Erwin Chemerinsky, *Constitutional Law: Principles and Policies,* 5th ed. (New York: Wolters Kluwer, 2015), 744.

16. Personnel Administrator of *Massachusetts v. Feeney,* 422 U.S. 256, 279 (1979).

17. *Washington v. Davis,* 426 U.S. 229, 248 (1976).

18. 118 U.S. 356 (1886).

19. 411 U.S. 1 (1973).

20. Dayana Yochim, "What's Your Net Worth, and How Do You Compare to Others?" MarketWatch, Jan. 29, 2019, https://www.marketwatch.com/story/whats-your-net-worth-and-how-do-you-compare-to-others-2018-09-24.

21. Giovanni Russonello, "Why Most Americans Support the Protests," *New York Times,* June 5, 2020.

INDEX

Dorothy A. Brown is an Asa Griggs Candler Professor at Emory University School of Law. A graduate of Fordham University and Georgetown Law, she received her LLM in taxation from New York University. A nationally recognized scholar in the areas of race, class, and tax policy, she has published dozens of articles, essays, and book chapters on the topic. She has appeared on CNN, MSNBC, PBS, and NPR, and her opinion pieces have been published in CNN Opinion, *Forbes, The New York Times,* and *The Washington Post.* Born and raised in the South Bronx in New York City, Brown currently resides in Atlanta, Georgia.

Twitter: @DorothyABrown